East European *phrase book*

How best to use this phrase book

This phrase book is designed to provide you with the essential key phrases you'll need for travelling in and around Eastern Europe.

- **Colour margins** will help you locate quickly the language that you require.

- Each language is divided into essential **topic sections**. The following content table will help you find your way around:

Basic expressions	Shops, stores & services
Hotel-Accommodation	incl. bank, post office, telephone
Eating out	Time, date and Numbers
Travelling around	Emergency
Sightseeing	Guide to pronunciation

- Each expression appears with a transliteration next to it. Simply read this imitated pronunciation as if it were English, stressing the syllables printed in bold type. For further help, consult the **Guide to pronunciation** at the back of each language section.

- In the **Eating out** section, a selection of popular traditional dishes are listed alphabetically, followed by brief explanations, to help you decipher dishes appearing on a menu.

- Throughout the book, this symbol ☞ suggests phrases your listener can use to answer you, simply by pointing to the appropriate answer.

Note: Where languages vary slightly according to gender, parentheses ( ) indicate the version to be spoken *by* a female speaker; brackets [ ] indicate the form to be spoken *to* a female listener.

Contacting the Editors
Every effort has been made to provide accurate information in this publication, but changes are inevitable. The publisher cannot be responsible for any resulting loss, inconvenience or injury. We would appreciate it if readers would call our attention to any errors or outdated information by contacting Berlitz Publishing, 95 Progress Street, Union, NJ 07083, USA. Fax: 1-908-206-1103

Reprinted 2002 Printed in Singapore

Hotel–Accommodation *Hotel–Sistemim*

I've a reservation.	**Kam një rezervim.**	kahm n^{y}er rehzehr**veem**
Do you have any vacancies?	**Keni ndonjë vend bosh?**	**keh**nee **ndoh**n^{y}er vehnd bohsh
I'd like a … room.	**Dua një dhomë …**	dooah n^{y}er **dhoh**mer
single/double	**teke/çift**	**teh**keh/cheeft
with twin beds	**me dy krevate teke**	meh du^y kreh**vah**teh **teh**keh
with a double bed	**me një krevat dopjo**	meh n^{y}er kreh**vaht** **doh**pyo
with a bath/shower	**me vaskë/dush**	meh **vah**sker/doosh
We'll be staying …	**Ne do të qëndrojmë …**	neh doh ter ch^{y}ern**droy**mer
overnight only	**vetëm një natë**	**veh**term n^{y}er **nah**ter
a few days	**disa ditë**	**dee**sah **dee**ter
a week	**një javë**	n^{y}er **yah**ver

Decision *Vendim*

May I see the room?	**A mund t'a shoh dhomën?**	ah moond tah shoh **dhoh**mern
That's fine. I'll take it.	**Shumë e mirë. Do t'a marr.**	shoom eh meer. doh tah mahrr
No. I don't like it.	**Jo. Nuk më pëlqen.**	yoh. nook mer **perl**ch^{y}ehn
It's too …	**Është tepër …**	**ersh**ter **teh**per
dark/small	**e errët/e vogël**	eh **eh**rrert/eh **voh**gerl
noisy	**me zhurmë**	meh **zhoor**mer
Do you have anything …?	**A keni ndonjë …?**	ah **keh**nee **ndoh**n^{y}er
bigger	**më të madhe**	mer ter **mah**dheh
cheaper	**më të lirë**	mer ter **lee**rer
quieter	**më të qetë**	mer ter **ch^{y}eh**ter
May I please have my bill?	**A mund të më jepni faturën?**	ah moond ter mer **yehp**nee fah**too**rern
It's been a very enjoyable stay.	**Ishte një qëndrim shumë i këndshëm**	**eesh**teh n^{y}er **ch^{y}ern**dreem shoom ee **kern**dsherm

DAYS OF THE WEEK, see page 15

Eating out *Në restorant*

I'd like to reserve a table for 4.	**Dua të rezervoj një tavolinë për katër vetë.**	dooah ter rehzehr**voy** n^{y}er tahvoh**leen** per **kah**ter **veh**ter
We'll come at 8.	**Do të vimë në orën tetë.**	doh ter **vee**mer ner **oh**rern **teh**ter
I'd like breakfast/lunch/ dinner.	**Dua të ha mëngjes/drekë/ darkë.**	dooah ter hah mern**j^{y}es/dreh**ker/ **dahr**ker
What do you recommend?	**Çfare më rekomandoni?**	**chfah**rer mer rehkohmahn**doh**nee
Do you have vegetarian dishes?	**A keni gjellë vegjetariane?**	ah **keh**nee **j^{y}eh**ler vehj^{y}ehtah**reeah**neh

Breakfast *Mëngjes*

I'd like an/some …	**Dua një …**	dooah n^{y}er
bread/butter	**bukë/gjalpë**	**boo**ker/**jyahl**per
cheese	**djathë**	**dya**ther
egg	**vezë**	**veh**zer
ham	**proshutë**	proh**shoo**ter
jam	**reçel**	reh**chehl**
rolls/sugar	**panine/sheger**	pah**nee**neh/**sheh**^{y}ehr

Starters *Pjatë e parë*

byrek me djathë	**bu**^{y}rehk meh **dya**ther	cheese pie
djathë i fërguar	**dya**ther ee fer**gooahr**	fried cheese
fërgesë me mëlçi	fer**gehs** meh merl**chee**	liver ferges
supë barishte	**soo**per bah**reesh**teh	vegetable soup
supë magjericë	**soo**per mahj^{y}eh**reets**	chicken giblets soup
tarator	tahrah**tohr**	yoghurt salad
ullij të mbushur	oo**lleey** ter **mboo**shoor	stuffed olives

baked/boiled	**e pjekur/e zjerë**	eh **pye**koor/eh zyer
fried/grilled	**e skuqur/e skarës**	eh **skooch**^{y}oor/eh **skah**rers
roast	**e pjekur**	eh **pye**koor
underdone (rare)	**e pabërë**	eh pah**ber**rer
medium	**e mesme**	eh **mehs**meh
well-done	**e pjekur tamam**	eh **pye**koor **tah**mahm

NUMBERS, see page 16

Meat *Mish*

I'd like some …	**Dua …**	dooah
beef	**mish lope**	meesh **loh**peh
lamb	**mish qengji**	meesh **ch'ehn**j^{y}ee
pork/veal	**mish derri/viçi**	meesh **deh**rree/**vee**chee
chicken/duck	**pula/rika**	**poo**lah/**ree**kah
çomlek me qepë	chohm**lehk** meh **ch^{y}eh**per	veal with onion
japrakë me mish	ya**prahk** meh meesh	vine leaf stuffed with meat and rice
qofte	**ch^{y}ohf**teh	meatballs
tasqebap	tahsch^{y}eh**bahb**	kebab
tavë Elbasani	**tah**ver ehlbah**sah**nee	lamb and yoghurt casserole

Fish and seafood *Peshk dhe prodhime deti*

fileto peshku	fee**leh**toh **pehsh**koo	fish fillet
karkaleca të zier	kahrkah**leh**tsah ter **zee**ehr	boiled prawns
koce e zgarës	**koh**tseh eh **zgah**rer	grilled place
ngjalë e skuqur	**nj^{y}ah**ler eh **skoo**ch^{y}oor	fried eels
peshk i pjekur	pehshk ee **pye**koor	roast fish
tavë me peshk	**tah**ver meh pehshk	fish casserole

Vegetables *Perime*

beans	**fasule**	fah**soo**leh
cabbage	**lakër**	**lah**ker
leeks	**presh**	prehsh
mushroom	**këpurdhë**	ker**poor**dher
onion	**qepë**	**ch^{y}eh**per
potatoes	**patate**	pah**tah**teh
tomato	**domate**	doh**mah**teh
lakër e mbushur	**lah**ker eh **mboo**shoor	stuffed cabbage
patëllxhane të mbushura	pahterll**jah**neh ter **mboo**shoorah	stuffed aubergines

spinaq me vezë e qumësht	spee**nach^{y}** meh **vehz** eh **ch^{y}oo**mersht	spinach with eggs and milk

Fruit & dessert *Fruta dhe ëmbëlsira*

apple	**mollë**	**moh**ller
banana	**banane**	bah**nah**neh
lemon	**limon**	lee**mohn**
orange	**portokall**	pohrtoh**kahll**
plum	**kumbull**	**koom**booll
strawberries	**luleshtrydhe**	looleh**shtry**dheh
akullore	ahkoo**lloh**reh	ice-cream
sheqerpare	shehch^{y}ehr**pah**reh	syrup cake
shëndetlie	shern**deht**lye	honey cake
sultiash	sool**teeahsh**	milk rice

Drinks *Pije*

beer	**birrë**	**bee**rrer
(hot) chocolate	**kakao**	kah**kahoh**
coffee	**kafe**	kah**feh**
with/without milk	**me/pa qumësht**	meh/pah **ch^{y}oo**mersht
fruit juice	**lëng frutash**	lerng **froo**tahsh
mineral water	**ujë mineral**	ooy meeneh**rahl**
tea	**çaj**	chay
wine	**verë**	**veh**rer
red	**e kuqe**	eh **kooch^{y}**eh
white	**e bardhë**	eh **bahr**dher

Complaints and paying *Ankime dhe pagesa*

This is too …	**Kjo është tepër…**	kyoh **ersh**ter **teh**per
bitter/sweet	**e hidhur/e ëmbël**	eh **hee**dhoor/eh **erm**berl
That's not what I ordered.	**Unë nuk porosita këtë.**	oon nook pohroh**see**tah **ker**ter
I'd like to pay.	**Dua të paguaj.**	dooah ter pah**gooay**
I think you made a mistake in the bill.	**Mendoj se keni bërë një gabim në faturë.**	mehn**doy** seh **keh**nee **ber**rer n^{y}er **gah**bem ner fah**too**rer
We enjoyed it, thank you.	**U kënaqëm, faleminderit.**	oo ker**nah**ch^{y}erm fahlehmeen**deh**reet

NUMBERS, see page 16

Travelling around *Në udhëtim*

Plane *Avion*

Is there a flight to Shkoder?	**A ka avion për në Shkodër?**	ah kah ah**veeon** per ner **shkoh**der
What time do I check in?	**Kur duhet të paraqitem?**	koor **doo**heht ter pahrah**ch^{y}ee**tehm
I'd like to … my reservation.	**Dua të … rezervimin.**	dooah ter rehzehr**vee**meen
cancel/change	**anulloj/ndryshoj**	ah**noo**lloy/**ndru^{y}**shoy
confirm	**konfirmoj**	kohnfeer**moy**

Train *Tren*

I want a ticket to Durrës.	**Dua një biletë për në Durrës.**	dooah n^{y}er bee**leh**ter per ner **door**^{y}ers
single (one-way)	**vajtje**	**vay**tye
return (roundtrip)	**vajtje-ardhje**	**vay**tye **ahrdh**yeh
first class	**klasi i parë**	**klah**see ee **pah**rer
second class	**klasi i dytë**	**klah**see ee **du^{y}**ter
How long does the journey (trip) take?	**Sa zgjat udhëtimi?**	sah zj^{y}aht oodher**tee**mee
When is the … train to Vlora?	**Kur ka tren … për në Vlorë?**	koor kah trehn … per ner vlohr
first/next	**i pari/tjetri**	ee **pah**ree/**tyet**ree
last	**i fundit**	ee **foon**deet
Is this the right train to Durres?	**A është ky treni për në Durrës?**	ah **ersh**ter ku^{y} **treh**nee per ner

Bus *Autobuz*

What bus do I take to the centre/downtown?	**Çfarë autobuzi duhet të marr për në qendër?**	chfahr autoh**boo**zee **doo**heht ter mahrr per ner **ch^{y}en**der
How much is the fare to …?	**Sa bën bileta për në …?**	sah bern be**leh**tah per ner **ch^{y}ehn**der
Will you tell me when to get off?	**A mund të më thoni kur duhet të zbres?**	ah moond ter mer **thoh**nee koor **doo**heht ter zbrehs

TELLING THE TIME, see page 15

Taxi *Taksi*

How much is it to …	**Sa bën deri në …**	sah bern **deh**ree ner
Take me to this address.	**Më ço në këtë adresë.**	mer choh ner **ker**ter ahd**reh**ser
Please stop here.	**Të lutem më ndalo këtu.**	ter **loo**tehm mer **ndah**loh **ker**too

Car hire (rental) *Makinë me qera*

I'd like to hire (rent) a car.	**Dua të marr një makinë me qera.**	dooah ter mahrr n^{y}er mah**kee**ner meh **ch^{y}eh**rah
I'd like it for a day/week.	**E dua për një ditë/për një javë.**	eh dooah per n^{y}er **dee**ter/per n^{y}er **yah**ver
Where's the nearest filling station?	**Ku është stacioni më i afërt i karburantit?**	koo **ersh**ter stah**tseeoh**nee mer ee **a**fert ee kahrboo**rahn**teet
Full tank, please.	**Serbatorin plot, të lutem.**	sehrbah**toh**reen ploht ter **loo**tehm
Give me … litres of petrol (gasoline).	**Mund të më jepni ... litra benzinë**	moond ter mer **yep**nee **lee**trah behn**zeen**
How do I get to …?	**Si mund të shkoj në?**	see moond ter shkoy ner
I've had a breakdown at …	**Pata një avari në …**	**pah**tah n^{y}er ah**vah**ree ner
Can you send a mechanic?	**A mund të më dërgoni një mekanik?**	ah moond ter mer der**goh**nee n^{y}er mehkah**neek**
Can you mend this puncture (fix this flat)?	**A mund t'i vini një pullë kësaj gomës.**	ah moond tee **vee**nee n^{y}er **poo**ller **ker**say **goh**mers

☞ You're on the wrong road.	**Keni ngatërruar rrugën.** ☜
Go straight ahead.	**Ec drejt.**
It's down there on the …	**Është pak më poshtë në të …**
left/right	**në të majtë/në të djathtë**
opposite/behind …	**përballë/prapa …**
next to/after …	**ngjitur/pas …**
north/south/east/west	**veri/jug/lindje/perëndim**

NUMBERS, see page 16

Sightseeing *Shëtitje*

Where's the tourist office?	**Ku është zyra turistike?**	koo **ersh**ter **zu**^{y}rah tooreess**tee**keh
Is there an English-speaking guide?	**A ka ndonjë guid anglisht-folës?**	ah kah **ndoh**n^{y}er gooeed ahng**leesht-fohl**ers
Where is/are the …?	**Ku është/janë …?**	koo **ersh**ter/yahn
beach	**plazhi**	**plah**zhee
castle	**kështjella**	kersh**tye**llah
cathedral	**katedralja**	kahteh**drahl**ya
city centre/downtown	**qendra e qytetit**	**ch^{y}en**drah eh ch^{y}u^{y}**teh**teet
harbour	**porti**	**pohr**tee
market	**pazari**	pah**zah**ree
museum	**muzeumi**	moozeh**oo**mee
zoo	**kopështi zoologjik**	**koh**pershtee zoohloh**j^{y}eek**
When does it open/close?	**Kur hapet/mbyllet?**	koor **hah**peht/**mbu**^{y}leht
How much is the entrance fee?	**Sa është bileta e hyrjes?**	sah **ersh**ter bee**leh**tah eh **hu**^{y}**r**yes

Entertainment *Argëtim*

What's playing at the theatre?	**Çfarë shfaqje ka sot në teater?**	chfahr **shfahch**^{y}ye kah soht ner **teh**ahter
How much are the seats?	**Sa kushtojnë biletat?**	sah koosh**toyn** be**leh**taht
Would you like to go out with me tonight?	**A doni të vini me mua sonte**	ah **doh**nee ter **vee**nee meh mooah **sohn**teh
Is there a discotheque in town?	**A ka ndonjë diskotekë në qytet?**	ah kah **ndoh**n^{y}yer **dees**kohtehker ner **ch^{y}y**teht
Would you like to dance?	**A doni të vallzoni?**	ah **doh**nee ter vahll**zoh**nee
Thank you. It's been a wonderful evening.	**Faleminderit. Ishte nje mbremje e mrekullueshme.**	fahlehmeen**deh**reet. **eesh**teh n^{y}er **mbrerm**ye eh mrehkoo**llooesh**meh

Shops, stores and services *Dyqanet dhe shërbimet*

Where's the nearest …?	**Ku është … më i afërt?**	koo **ersh**ter … mer ee **ah**fert
bakery	**dyqani i bukës**	du^{y}**ch^{y}ah**nee ee **boo**kehs
bookshop/store	**libraria**	leebrah**reeah**
butcher's	**dyqani i mishit**	du^{y}**ch^{y}ah**nee ee **mee**sheet
chemist's/drugstore	**farmacia**	fahrmah**tseeah**
dentist	**dentisti**	dehn**tees**tee
department store	**mapo**	**mah**poh
grocery	**ushqimorja**	ooshch^{y}ee**mohr**yah
newsagent	**dyqan gazetash**	du^{y}**ch^{y}ahn** gah**zeh**tahsh
post office	**posta**	**pohs**tah
souvenir shop	**dyqani i dhuratave**	du^{y}**ch^{y}ah**nee ee dhoo**rah**tahveh
supermarket	**supertregu**	soopehr**treh**goo

General expressions *Shprehje të përgjithëshme*

Where's the main shopping area?	**Ku janë dyqanet?**	koo yahn du^{y}**ch^{y}ah**neht
Do you have any …?	**A keni …?**	ah **keh**nee
Do you have anything …?	**A keni ndonjë gjë …?**	ah **keh**nee **ndoh**n^{y}er j^{y}er
cheaper	**më të lirë**	mer ter leer
better	**më të mirë**	mer ter meer
larger	**më të madhe**	mer ter **mah**dheh
smaller	**më të vogël**	mer ter **voh**gerl
Can I try it on?	**A mund t'a provoj?**	ah moond tah proh**voy**
How much is this?	**Sa kushton kjo?**	sah koosh**tohn** kyoh
Please write it down.	**Të lutem m'a shkruaj.**	ter **loo**tehm mah shkrooay
No, I don't like it.	**Jo, nuk më pëlqen.**	yoh nook mer perl**ch^{y}ehn**
I'll take it.	**Do ta marr.**	doh tah mahrr
Do you accept credit cards?	**A pranoni karta krediti?**	ah prah**noh**nee **kahr**tah kreh**dee**tee

NUMBERS, see page 16

black	**e zezë**	eh **zeh**zer	orange	**portokalli**	pohrtoh**kahllee**
blue	**blu**	bloo	red	**e kuqe**	eh **kooch**^{y}eh
brown	**kafe**	kah**feh**	yellow	**e verdhë**	eh **vehr**dher
green	**jeshile**	yeh**shee**leh	white	**e bardhë**	eh **bahr**dher

I want to buy …	**Dua te blej …**	dooah ter bley
aspirin	**aspirinë**	ahspee**reen**
batteries	**bateri**	bahteh**ree**
newspaper	**gazetë**	gah**zeh**ter
English	**angleze**	ahng**leh**zeh
American	**amerikane**	ahmehree**kah**neh
shampoo	**shampo**	**shahm**poh
sun-tan cream	**krem plazhi**	krehm **plah**zhee
soap	**sapun**	sah**poon**
toothpaste	**pastë dhëmbësh**	**pah**ster **dherm**bersh
a half-kilo of apples	**gjysmë kile mollë**	**j**^{y}**ys**mer **kee**leh **moh**ller
a litre of milk	**një litër qumësht**	n^{y}er **lee**ter **ch**^{y}**oo**mersht
I'd like … film for this camera.	**Do të doja … një film për këtë aparat.**	doh ter **doh**yah … n^{y}er feelm per **ker**ter ahpah**raht**
black and white	**bardhë e zi**	bahrdh eh zee
colour	**me ngjyra**	meh **nj**^{y}**y**rah

Souvenirs *Dhurata*

bucele druri	bootsehl **droo**ree	wooden flask
çantë leshi	chahnt **leh**shee	decorated woollen bag
çorape leshi	choh**rah**peh **leh**shee	woollen slipper-socks
kuti druri me motive	koo**tee droo**ree meh moh**tee**veh	decorated wooden jewellery box
llullë druri	**lloo**ller **droo**ree	wooden pipe
pjatë druri	**pyah**ter **droo**ree	decorated wooden plate

At the bank *Në bankë*

Where's the nearest bank	**Ku është banka më e afërteh.**	koo **ersh**ter **bahn**kah mer **ah**fot
I want to change some dollars/pounds into lek.	**Dua të shkëmbej disa dollarë/ stërlina në lekë.**	dooah ter shkerm**bey** **dee**sah doh**llahr/** ster**lee**nah ner lehk
What's the exchange rate?	**Sa është kursi i shkëmbimit?**	sah ersht **koor**see ee shkerm**bee**meet

At the post office *Në postë*

I want to send this by …	**Dua të dërgoj këtë me …**	dooah ter der**goy** **ker**ter meh
airmail/express	**postë ajrore/ ekspres**	pohst ay**roh**reh/ ehks**prehs**
I want … 20-lek stamps.	**Dua … pulla poste njëzet lekëshe.**	dooah … **poo**llah **poh**steh **n^{y}er**zeht **lehk**sheh
What's the postage for a letter/postcard to the United States?	**Sa bën të nisësh një letër/kartolinë për në Amerikë.**	sah bern ter **nee**sersh n^{y}er **leh**ter/kahrtoh**leen** per ner ahmeh**reek**
Is there any mail for me? My name is …	**Ka ndonjë letër për mua? Më quajnë …**	kah **ndoh**n^{y}er **leh**ter per mooah. mer ch^{y}ooayn

Telephoning *Në telefon*

Where's the nearest public phone.	**Ku është telefoni më i afërt.**	koo ersht tehleh**foh**nee mer ee **a**fert
May I use your phone?	**A mund të flas pak në telefon?**	ah moond ter flahs pahk ner tehleh**fohn**
Hello. This is … speaking.	**Alo. Jam ….**	ah**loh.** yahm
I want to speak to …	**Dua të flas me ….**	dooah ter flahs meh
When will he/she be back?	**Kur do të kthehet ai/ajo?**	koor doh ter ktheh**heht** ah**ee**/a**yoh**
Will you tell him/her that I called?	**A mund t'i thoni që e mora në telefon?**	ah moond tee **thoh**nee ch^{y}er eh **moh**rah ner tehleh**fohn**

NUMBERS, see page 16

Time and date *Koha dhe data*

It's …	**Është …**	ersht
five past one	**një e pesë**	n^{y}er eh **peh**ser
quarter past three	**tre e njëcerek**	treh eh n^{y}ercheh**rehk**
twenty past five	**pesë e njëzet**	**peh**ser eh n^{y}er**zeht**
half-past seven	**shtatë e gjysëm**	**shtah**ter eh **j^{y}y**serm
twenty-five to nine	**nëntë pa njëzet e pesë**	**nern**ter pah **n^{y}er**zeht eh **peh**ser
ten to ten	**dhjetë pa dhjetë**	**dhye**ter pah dhyet
noon/midnight	**mesditë/mesnatë**	mehs**deet**/mes**naht**
in the morning	**në mëngjes**	ner mern**j^{y}es**
during the day	**gjatë ditës**	j^{y}aht **dee**ters
at night	**natën**	**nah**tern
yesterday/today	**dje/sot**	dyeh/soht
tomorrow	**nesër**	**neh**ser
spring/summer	**pranverë/verë**	prahn**vehr**/vehr
autumn/winter	**vjeshtë/dimër**	vyesht/**de**mer

Sunday	**e dielë**	eh dyel
Monday	**e henë**	eh **her**ner
Tuesday	**e martë**	eh **mahr**ter
Wednesday	**e mërkurë**	eh mer**koor**
Thursday	**e enjte**	eh **ehn^{y}**teh
Friday	**e premte**	eh **prehm**teh
Saturday	**e shtunë**	eh shtoon
January	**janar**	**yah**nahr
February	**shkurt**	shkoort
March	**mars**	mahrs
April	**prill**	preell
May	**maj**	may
June	**qershor**	ch^{y}ehr**shohr**
July	**korrik**	koh**rreek**
August	**gusht**	goosht
September	**shtator**	shtah**tohr**
October	**tetor**	teh**tohr**
November	**nëntor**	nern**tohr**
December	**dhjetor**	dhye**tohr**

Numbers *Numrat*

0	**zero**	**zeh**roh	11	**njëmbëdhjetë**	n^{y}ermber**dhyet**
1	**një**	n^{y}er	12	**dymbëdhjetë**	du^{y}mber**dhyeh**ter
2	**dy**	du^{y}	13	**trembëdhjetë**	trehmber**dhyeh**ter
3	**tre**	treh	14	**katërmbëdhjetë**	**kah**termber**dhyeh**ter
4	**katër**	**kah**ter	15	**pesëmbëdhjetë**	**peh**sermber**dhyeh**ter
5	**pesë**	**peh**ser	16	**gjashtëmbëdhjetë**	**j^{y}ahsh**termber**dhyeh**ter
6	**gjashtë**	j^{y}asht	17	**shtatëmbëdhjetë**	**shtah**termber**dhyeh**ter
7	**shtatë**	shtaht	18	**tetëmbëdhjetë**	**teh**termber**dhyeh**ter
8	**tetë**	teht	19	**nëntëmbëdhjetë**	**nern**termber**dhyeh**ter
9	**nëntë**	nernt	20	**njëzetë**	n^{y}er**zeht**
10	**dhjetë**	dhyet	21	**njëzetë një**	n^{y}er**zeht** n^{y}er

30	**tridhjetë**	**tree**dhyeht
40	**dyzetë**	**du^{y}**zeht
50	**pesëdhjetë**	**peh**serdhyeht
60	**gjashtëdhjetë**	**j^{y}ahsh**terdhyeht
70	**shtatëdhjetë**	**shtah**terdhyeht
80	**tetëdhjetë**	**teh**terdhyeht
90	**nëntëdhjetë**	**nern**terdhyeht
100/1,000	**njëqind/njëmijë**	n^{y}er**ch^{y}eend/n^{y}er**meey
first	**i pari**	ee **pah**ree
second	**i dyti**	ee **du^{y}**tee
once/twice	**një herë/dy herë**	n^{y}er **heh**rer/dy **heh**rer
a half	**gjysmë**	**j^{y}y**smer

Emergency *Urgjenca*

Call the police	**Thirrni policinë**	**theer**nee pohlee**tseen**
Get a doctor	**Thirrni doktorin**	**theer**nee dohk**toh**reen
HELP	**NDIHMË**	**ndeeh**mer
I'm ill	**Jam sëmurë**	yahm ser**moor**
I'm lost	**Kam humbur**	kahm **hoom**boor
Leave me alone	**Më lini të qetë**	mer **lee**nee ter **ch^{y}eh**ter
STOP THIEF	**Kapeni hajdutin**	**kah**pehnee hay**doo**teen
My … has been stolen.	**Më kanë vjedhur …**	mer kahn **vye**dhoor
I've lost my …	**Kam humbur …**	kahm **hoom**boor
handbag	**çantën e dorës**	**chahn**tern eh **doh**rers
passport	**pasaportën**	pahsah**pohr**tern
luggage	**bagazhin**	bah**gah**zheen

TELEPHONING, see page 14

Albanian

Basic expressions *Shprehje baze*

Yes/No.	**Po/Jo.**	poh/yoh
Please.	**Të lutem.**	ter **loot**ehm
Thank you.	**Faleminderit.**	fahlehmeen**deh**reet
I beg your pardon?	**Më falni?**	mer **fahl**nee

Introductions *Prezantime*

Good morning.	**Mirëmëngjes.**	meermern**j^{y}ehs**
Good afternoon.	**Mirëdita.**	meer**dee**tah
Good night.	**Natën e mirë.**	**nah**tern eh meer
Good-bye.	**Mirupafshim.**	meeroo**pahf**sheem
My name is …	**Unë quhem …**	oon **ch^{y}oo**hehm
What's your name?	**Si ju quajnë?**	see yoo **ch^{y}oo**ayn
How are you?	**Si jeni?**	see **yeh**nee
Fine thanks. And you?	**Mirë faleminderit. Po ju?**	meer fahlehmeen**deh**reet poh yoo
Where do you come from?	**Nga vini?**	ngah **vee**nee
I'm from …	**Unë jam nga …**	oon yahm ngah
Australia	**Australia**	austrah**leeah**
Britain	**Britania**	breetah**neeah**
Canada	**Kanadaja**	kahnah**dah**yah
USA	**Amerika/USA**	ahmeh**ree**kah /**ooh**sah
I'm with my …	**Jam me …**	yahm meh
wife	**gruan time**	**groo**ahn **tee**meh
husband	**burrin tim**	**boo**rreen teem
family	**familjen time**	fah**mee**lyehn **tee**meh
boyfriend	**të dashurin tim**	ter **dah**shooreen teem
girlfriend	**të dashurën time**	ter **dah**shoorern **tee**meh
I'm on my own.	**Jam vetëm.**	yahm **veh**term
I'm on holiday (vacation).	**Jam me pushime.**	yahm meh poo**shee**meh

GUIDE TO PRONUNCIATION, see page 17/EMERGENCIES, see page 16

Questions *Pyetje*

When?/How?	**Kur?/Si?**	koor/see
What?/Why?	**Çfarë?/Pse?**	chfahr/pseh
Who?/Which?	**Kush?/Cili?**	koosh/**tsee**lee
Where is/are …?	**Ku është/janë …?**	koo **ersh**ter/yahn
Where can I get/find …?	**Ku mund të marr/gjej …?**	koo moond ter mahrr/j^{y}ey
How far?	**Sa larg?**	sah lahrg
How long?	**Për sa kohë?**	per sah koh
How much?	**Sa?**	sah
Can you help me?	**Mund të më ndihmoni?**	moond ter mer ndeeh**moh**nee
I understand.	**E kuptoj.**	eh koop**toy**
I don't understand.	**Nuk kuptoj.**	nook koop**toy**
Can you translate this for me?	**Mund të ma përktheni këtë ?**	moond ter mah perk**thehn**ee **ker**ter
May I?	**Mund të …**	moond ter
Can I have …?	**Mund të marr..?**	moond ter mahrr
Do you speak English?	**Flisni anglisht?**	**flees**nee ahng**leesht**
I don't speak (much) Albanian.	**Nuk flas (shumë) shqip.**	nook flahs (shoom) shch^{y}eep

A few useful words *Disa fjalë të përdorshme*

better	**më i mirë**	mer ee meer
worse	**më i keq**	mer ee kehch^{y}
big/small	**i madh/i vogël**	ee mahdh/ee **voh**gerl
cheap	**i lirë**	ee leer
expensive	**i kushtueshëm**	ee koosh**too**ehsherm
early/late	**shpejt/vonë**	shpeyt/**voh**ner
good/bad	**i mirë/i keq**	ee **mee**rer/ee kehch^{y}
hot/cold	**i nxehtë/i ftohtë**	ee **ndseh**ter/ee **ftoh**ter
near/far	**afër/larg**	**ah**fer /lahrg
right/wrong	**në rregull/gabim**	ner **rreh**gool/**gah**beem
vacant/occupied	**i lirë /i zënë**	ee **lee**rer/ee **zer**ner

Guide to Albanian pronunciation

Consonants

Letter	Approximate pronunciation	Symbol	Example	
c	like **ts** in cats	ts	**cili**	**tsee**lee
ç	like **ch** in **ch**in	ch	**çfarë**	**chfah**rer
dh	like **th** in **th**is	dh	**dhomë**	**dhoh**mer
th	like **th** in **th**ick	th	**thirrni**	**theer**nee
q	similar to **ch** in **ch**air	ch^y	**quhem**	$\mathbf{ch^yoo}$hehm
gj	similar to **j** in **j**am	j^y	**gjej**	j^yey
g	like **g** in **g**irl	g	**gëzohem**	**ger**zohehm
j	like **y** in **y**es	y	**jam**	yahm
l	like **l** in **l**ake	l	**letër**	**leh**ter
ll	like **ll** in bi**ll**	ll	**mollë**	**mohl**ler
nj	like **n** in o**n**ion	n^y	**një**	n^yer
rr	like a rolled Scottish **r**	rr	**burrë**	**boo**rrer
s	like **s** in **s**oup	s	**supë**	**soo**per
sh	like **s** in **s**ure	sh	**shoh**	shoh
x	like **ds** in be**ds**	dz	**nxehtë**	**ndzeh**ter
xh	like **j** in **j**am	xh	**xhan**	xhahn
zh	like **s** in mea**s**ure	zh	**zhvesh**	zhvehsh
b, d, f, h, k, m, n, p, r, t, v, z		are pronounced as in English		

Vowels

a	like **a** in bath	ah	**marr**	mahr
e	like **e** in let	eh	**del**	dehl
ë	like **er** in moth**er**, but without pronouncing the **r**	er	**punë**	**poo**ner
i	like **ee** in m**ee**t	ee	**mirë**	**meer**ë
o	like **a** in b**a**ll	oh	**po**	poh
u	like **oo** in b**oo**t	oo	**ju**	yoo
y	between **u** and **i**	u^y	**dy**	du^y

Note:

ë is the most frequent vowel in Albanian. When it occurs at the end of the words it is usually dropped, making the vowel in the preceeding syllable longer, e.g. **mirë** is pronounced meer.

Bulgarian

Basic expressions *Основни изрази*

Yes/No.	**Да/Не.**	dah/neh
Please.	**Извинете.**	eezvee**neh**teh
Thank you.	**Благодаря.**	blahgodah**ryah**
I beg your pardon?	**Моля?**	**mo**lyah

Introductions *Запознанства*

Good morning.	**Добро утро.**	dob**ro oot**ro
Good afternoon.	**Добър ден.**	**do**bir dehn
Good night.	**Лека нощ.**	**leh**kah nosht
Good-bye.	**Довиждане.**	do**veezh**dahneh
My name is …	**Казвам се...**	**kahz**vahm seh
What's your name?	**Как се казвате?**	kahk seh **kahz**vahteh
How are you?	**Как сте?**	kahk steh
Fine thanks. And you?	**Благодаря, добре. А Вие?**	blahgodah**ryah** dob**reh**. ah **vee**eh
Where do you come from?	**От къде сте?**	otki**deh** steh
I'm from …	**Аз съм от..**	ahz sim ot
Australia	**Австралия**	ahv**strah**leeyah
Britain	**Великобритания**	vehleekobree**tah**neeyah
Canada	**Канада**	kah**nah**dah
USA	**Съединените щати**	siehdee**neh**neeteh **shtah**tee
I'm with my …	**Тук съм със...**	took sim sis
wife	**жена ми**	zheh**nah** mee
husband	**мъжа ми**	mi**zhah** mee
family	**семейството ми**	seh**mehy**stvoto mee
boyfriend	**приятеля ми**	pree**yah**tehlyah mee
girlfriend	**приятелката ми**	pree**yah**tehlkatah mee
I'm on my own.	**Тук съм сам (сама).**	took sim sahm (sah**mah**)
I'm on holiday/ vacation.	**Тук съм на почивка.**	took sim nah po**cheev**kah

Questions *Въпроси*

When?/How?	**Кога?/Как?**	ko**gah**/kahk
What?/Why?	**Какво?/Защо?**	kahk**vo**/zah**shto**
Who?/Which?	**Кой?/Кое?**	koy/ko**eh**
Where is/are …?	**Къде е/са …?**	ki**deh** eh/sah
Where can I find/get …?	**Къде мога да открия/намеря …?**	ki**deh mo**gah dah ot**kree**yah/nah**meh**ryah
How far?	**Колко далече?**	**kol**ko dah**leh**cheh
How long?	**Колко дълго?**	**kol**ko **dil**go
How much?	**Колко струва?**	**kol**ko **stroo**vah
Can I have …?	**Може ли да ми дадете...?**	**mo**zheh lee dah mee dah**deh**teh
Can you help me?	**Може ли да ми помогнете?**	**mo**zheh lee dah mee po**mog**nehteh
I understand.	**Разбирам.**	rahz**bee**rahm
I don't understand.	**Не разбирам.**	neh rahz**bee**rahm
Can you translate this for me?	**Може ли да ми преведете това?**	**moh**zheh lee dah mee prehveh**deh**teh tovah
Do you speak English?	**Говорите ли английски?**	govo**reeteh** lee ahngl**eeyskee**
I don't speak (much) Bulgarian.	**Аз не говоря (много) български.**	Ahz neh go**voryah** (mnogo) **bil**gahrskee

A few useful words *Няколко Полезни Думи*

better/worse	**по-добро/по-лошо**	**po** dob**ro**/**po lo**sho
big/small	**голямо/малко**	go**lyah**mo/**mahl**ko
cheap/expensive	**евтино/скъпо**	**ehv**teeno/**ski**po
early/late	**рано/късно**	**rah**no/**kis**no
good/bad	**добро/лошо**	dob**ro**/**lo**sho
hot/cold	**горещо/студено**	go**reh**shto/stoo**deh**no
near/far	**близо/далече**	**blee**zo/dah**leh**cheh
old/new	**стар/млад**	stahr/mlahd
right	**правилно**	**prah**veelno
wrong	**неправилно**	neh**prah**veelno
vacant/occupied	**свободно/заето**	svo**bod**no/zah**eh**to

Hotel—Accommodation *Настаняване в хотел*

I've a reservation.	**Имам резервация.**	**ee**mahm rehzehr**vah**tseeyah
Do you have any vacancies?	**Имате ли свободни стаи?**	**ee**mahteh lee svo**bod**nee **stah**ee
I'd like a … room.	**Искам … стая.**	**ees**kahm … **stah**yah
single	**самостоятелна**	sahmosto**yah**tehlnah
double	**за двама**	zah **dvah**mah
with twin beds	**с две легла**	s dveh lehg**lah**
with a double bed	**с двойно легло**	s **dvoy**no lehg**lo**
with a bath/shower	**с вана/с душ**	s **vah**na/s doosh
We'll be staying …	**Ще останем …**	shteh os**tah**nehm
overnight only	**само тази вечер**	**sah**mo **tah**zee **veh**chehr
a few days	**няколко дни**	**nyah**kolko dnee
a week (at least)	**седмица (поне)**	**sehd**meetsah (po**neh**)
Is there a campsite near here?	**Наблизо има ли къмпинг?**	nah**blee**zo **ee**mah lee **kahm**peeng

Decision *Решение*

May I see the room?	**Може ли да видя стаята?**	**mo**zheh lee dah **vee**dyah **stah**yahtah
That's fine. I'll take it.	**Харесва ми. Ще я наема.**	khah**rehs**vah mee. shteh yah nah**eh**mah
No. I don't like it.	**Не. Не ми харесва.**	neh. neh mee **kharehs**vah
It's too …	**Тук е твърде...**	took eh **twir**deh
dark/small	**тъмно/тясно**	**tim**no/**tyahs**no
noisy	**шумно**	**shoom**no
Do you have anything …?	**Имате ли нещо...?**	**ee**mahteh lee **neh**shto
better	**по-добро**	**po** do**bro**
bigger	**по-просторно**	**po** pro**stor**no
cheaper/quieter	**по-евтино/по-тихо**	**po ehv**teeno/**po tee**kho
May I please have my bill?	**Извинете, може ли сметката?**	eezvee**neh**teh **mo**zheh lee **smeht**kahtah
It's been a very enjoyable stay.	**Много приятно беше тук.**	**mno**go pree**yah**tno **beh**sheh took

DAYS OF THE WEEK, see page 30

Eating out *На ресторант*

I'd like to reserve a table for 4.	**Искам да резервирам маса за четирима.**	**ees**kahm dah rehzehr**vee**rahm **mah**sah zah chehtee**reemah**
We'll come at 8.	**Ще дойдем в осем.**	shteh **doy**dehm v **o**sehm
I'd like …	**Искам да …**	**ees**kahm dah
breakfast	**закуся**	zah**koo**syah
lunch	**обядвам**	ob**yahd**vahm
dinner	**вечерям**	veh**cheh**ryahm
What do you recommend?	**Какво бихте препоръчали?**	kahk**vo beekh**teh prepo**ri**chahlee
Do you have vegetarian dishes?	**Имате ли вегетариански ястия?**	**ee**mahteh lee vehgehtahree**ahn**skee **yahs**teeyah

Breakfast *Сакус*

I'd like (an/some) ...	**Искам …**	**ees**kahm
bread/butter	**хляб/масло**	khlyab/**mah**slo
cheese	**сирене**	**see**rehneh
egg	**яйце**	yahy**tse**
ham	**шунка**	**shoon**kah
jam	**конфитюр**	konfee**tyoor**
rolls	**кифли**	**keef**lee

Starters *Закуски*

луканка	loo**kahn**kah	piquant flat sausage
лютеница	**lyoo**tehneetsah	red peppers and tomato paste sauce
сирене по шопски	**see**rehneh po **shop**skee	white cheese baked in earthenware
тарама салата	tahrah**mah** sah**lah**tah	taramasalata
таратор	tahrah**tor**	cold cucumber and yoghurt soup
шкембе чорба	shkehm**beh** chor**bah**	thick tripe broth
шопска салата	**shop**skah sah**lah**tah	tomato, cucumber and white cheese salad

NUMBERS, see page 31

baked/boiled	**на фурна/варено**	nah **foor**nah/vah**reh**no
fried/grilled	**пържено/на скара**	**pir**zhehno/nah **skah**rah
roast	**печено**	**peh**chehno
stewed	**задушено**	zahdoo**sheh**no
underdone (rare)	**леко запечено**	**leh**ko zah**peh**chehno
medium	**средно опечено**	**srehd**no o**peh**chehno
well-done	**добре опечено**	dob**reh** o**peh**chehno

Meat *Meco*

I'd like some …	**Искам малко...**	**ee**skahm **mahl**ko
beef	**говеждо**	go**vehzh**do
lamb	**агнешко**	**ahg**nehshko
pork/veal	**свинско/телешко**	**sveen**sko/**teh**lehshko
chicken/duck	**пиле/патица**	**pee**leh/**pah**teetsah
кебап	keh**bahp**	meat in a rich sauce
кюфте	kyoof**teh**	meat ball
мусака	moosah**kah**	mousaka
пържола	pir**zho**lah	grilled pork steak
сарми	sahr**mee**	stuffed vine leaves
свинско със зеле	**sveen**sko sis **zeh**leh	pork and sauerkraut

Fish and seafood *Риба и ястия от морски продукти*

бяла риба пане	**byah**lah **ree**bah pah**neh**	pike-perch in batter
миди с ориз	**mee**dee s **o**reez	mussels with rice
пушен паламуд	**poo**shehn pahlah**mood**	smoked tuna
пържена цаца	**pir**zhehnah **tsah**tsah	fried sprat
рибена чорба	**ree**behnah chor**bah**	fish broth

Vegetables *Зеленчуци*

beans	**боб**	bob
cabbage	**зеле**	**zeh**leh
gherkin	**краставички**	**krahs**tahveechkee
leek	**праз**	prahz
mushroom	**гъби**	**gi**bee
onion	**лук**	look
potatoes	**картофи**	kahr**to**fee
tomato	**домати**	do**mah**tee

баница	bah**nee**tsah	cheese pastry
вегетариански гювеч	vehgehtahree**ahn**skee gyoo**vehch**	stewed vegetables
пълнени пиперки с ориз	**pil**nehnee pee**pehr**kee s o**reez**	peppers stuffed with rice

Fruit & dessert *Плодове и десерт*

apple	**ябълка**	**yah**bilkah
lemon	**лимон**	lee**mon**
orange	**портокал**	porto**kahl**
plum	**слива**	**slee**vah
strawberries	**ягоди**	**yah**godee
катми	kaht**mee**	jam or cheese pancakes
сладолед	slahdo**lehd**	ice-cream
торта	**tor**tah	gateau

Drinks *Напитки*

beer	**бира**	**bee**rah
(hot) chocolate	**(мляко с) какао**	(**mlyah**ko s) kahk**aho**
coffee	**кафе**	kah**feh**
black	**без мляко**	behz **mlyah**ko
with milk	**с мляко**	s **mlyah**ko
fruit juice	**плодов сок**	**plo**dov sok
mineral water	**минерална вода**	meeneh**rahl**nah vo**dah**
tea	**чай**	chahy
vodka	**водка**	**vod**kah
wine	**вино**	**vee**no
red/white	**червено/бяло**	chehr**veh**no/**byah**lo

Complaints and paying *Оплаквания и плащане*

That's not what I ordered.	**Не това поръчах.**	neh to**vah** po**ri**chahk
I'd like to pay.	**Искам да платя.**	**ees**kahm dah plah**tyah**
I think you made a mistake in the bill.	**Имате грешка в сметката.**	**ee**mahteh **grehs**kah v **smeht**kahtah
Is service included?	**Обслужването включено ли е?**	obs**loo**zheevahnehto **vklyoo**chehno lee eh
We enjoyed it, thank you.	**Хареса ни, благодарим Ви.**	khah**reh**sah nee blahgodah**reem** vee

Travelling around *Пътуване*

Plane *Самолет*

Is there a flight to Sofia?	**Има ли полет до София?**	**ee**mah lee **po**leht do **so**feeyah
What time do I check in?	**Кога трябва да се регистрирам?**	kog**ah tryahb**vah dah seh rehgee**stree**rahm
I'd like to … my reservation.	**Искам да ... моята резервация.**	**ees**kahm dah... **mo**yahtah rehzehr**vaht**seeyah
cancel	**отменя**	otmeh**nyah**
change	**променя**	promeh**nyah**
confirm	**потвърдя**	potvir**dyah**

Train *Влак*

I want a ticket to Plovdiv.	**Искам един билет до Пловдив.**	**ees**kahm eh**deen** bee**leht** do **plov**deev
single (one-way)	**отиване**	o**tee**vahneh
return (roundtrip)	**отиване и връщане**	o**tee**vahneh ee **vri**shtahneh
first/second class	**първа/втора класа**	**pir**vah/**vto**rah **klah**sah
How long does the journey (trip) take?	**Колко дълго се пътува?**	**kol**ko **dil**go seh pi**too**vah
When is the … train to Burgas?	**Кога е ... влака до Бургас?**	kog**ah** eh ... vlahka do boor**gahs**
first	**първият**	**pir**veeyaht
next	**следващият**	**slehd**vahshteeyaht
last	**последният**	po**slehd**neeyaht
Is this the right train to Varna?	**Това ли е влакът за Варна?**	to**vah** lee eh **vlah**kit zah **vahr**nah

Bus *Автобус*

What bus do I take to the centre/downtown?	**Кой автобус отива до центъра?**	koy ahvto**boos** o**tee**vah do **tsehn**tirah
How much is the fare to ...?	**Колко струва билетът до ...?**	**kol**ko **stroo**vah bee**leh**tit do
Will you tell me when to get off?	**Извинете, кога трябва да сляза?**	eezvee**neh**teh ko**gah tryahb**vah dah **slyah**zah

TELLING THE TIME, see page 30

Taxi *Такси*

How much is it to …?	**Колко ще струва до ...?**	**kol**ko shteh **stroo**vah do
Take me to this address.	**Откарайте ме на този адрес.**	ot**kah**rahyteh meh nah **to**zee ahd**rehs**
Please stop here.	**Моля, спрете тук.**	**mo**lyah **spreh**teh took

Car hire (rental) *Лека кола под наем*

I'd like to hire (rent) a car.	**Искам да наема лека кола.**	**ees**kahm dah nah**eh**mah **leh**kah ko**lah**
I'd like it for a day/week.	**Трябва ми за един ден/ една седмица.**	**tryahb**vah mee zah eh**deen** dehn/ ehd**nah sehd**meetsah
Where's the nearest filling station?	**Къде е най-близката бензиностанция?**	ki**deh** eh nahy-**bleez**kahtah behn**zeen**ostahntseeyah
Full tank, please.	**Напълнете резервоара, моля.**	nahpil**neh**teh rehzehrvo**ah**rah **mo**lyah
Give me … litres of petrol (gasoline).	**Дайте ми ... литра бензин.**	**dahy**teh mee ... **leet**rah behn**zeen**
How do I get to …?	**Как мога да стигна до?**	kahkh **mo**gah dah **steeg**nah do
I've had a breakdown at …	**Колата се повреди при ...**	ko**lah**tah seh pov**reh**dee pree
Can you send a mechanic?	**Може ли да пратите монтьор?**	**mo**zheh lee dah **prah**teeteh mon**tyor**
Can you mend this puncture (fix this flat)?	**Може ли да залепите тази гума?**	**mo**zheh lee dah zahleh**pee**teh **tah**zee **goo**mah

☞ You're on the wrong road.	**На погрешен път сте.** ☜
Go straight ahead.	**Продължете направо.**
It's down there on the …	**Ето там ....**
left/right	**отляво/отдясно**
next to/after …	**до/след ...**
north/south/east/west	**север/юг/изток/запад**

NUMBERS, see page 31

Sightseeing *Разглеждане на забележителности*

Where's the tourist office?	**Къде е туристическото бюро?**	ki**deh** eh tooreés**tee**chehskoto byoo**ro**
Is there an English-speaking guide?	**Има ли екскурсовод с английски?**	**ee**mah lee ehkskoorzo**vod** s ahn**gleey**skee
Where is/are the ...?	**Къде е/са ...?**	ki**deh** eh/sah
beach	**плаж**	plahzh
castle	**крепостта**	krehpos**tah**
cathedral	**храмът**	**khrah**mit
city centre	**градският център**	**grahd**skeeyaht **tsehn**tir
harbour	**пристанището**	prees**tah**neeshtehto
market	**пазарят**	pah**zah**ryat
museum	**музеят**	moo**zeh**yaht
shops	**магазините**	mahgah**zee**neeteh
zoo	**зоопаркът**	**zo**opahrkit
When does it open/close?	**Кога отварят/затварят?**	ko**gah** ot**vah**ryaht/ zaht**vah**ryaht
How much is the entrance fee?	**Каква е входната такса?**	kahk**vah** eh **vkhod**nahtah **tahk**sah

Entertainment *Развлечение*

What's playing at the ... Theatre?	**Коя пиеса представят в театър ...?**	ko**yah** pee-e**sah** prehd**stah**vyaht v teh**ah**tir
How much are the seats?	**Колко струват билетите?**	**kol**ko **stroo**vaht bee**leh**teeteh
Would you like to go out with me tonight?	**Искате ли да излезем заедно довечера?**	**ees**kahteh lee dah eez**leh**zehm **zah**ehdno do**veh**chehrah
Is there a discotheque in town?	**В града има ли дискотека?**	v grah**dah ee**mah lee deesko**teh**kah
Would you like to dance?	**Искате ли да танцуваме?**	**ees**kahteh lee dah tahn**tsoo**vahmeh
Thank you. It's been a wonderful evening.	**Благодаря. Прекарах чудесна вечер.**	blahgodah**ryah**. preh**kah**rakh choo**dehs**nah **veh**chehr

EMERGENCIES, see page 31

Shops, stores and services *Магазини и услуги*

Where's the nearest ...?	**Къде наблизо ...?**	ki**deh** nah**blee**zo
baker's	**хлебарница**	khleh**bahr**neetsah
bookshop	**книжарница**	knee**zhar**neetsah
chemist's/pharmacy	**аптека**	ahp**teh**kah
dentist	**зъболекар**	zibo**leh**kahr
department store	**универсален магазин**	ooneevehr**sah**lehn mahgah**zeen**
grocery	**бакалия**	bahkah**lee**yah
hairdresser	**фризьорски салон**	free**zyor**skee sah**lon**
post office	**поща**	**po**shtah
supermarket	**супермаркет**	**soo**pehrmahrkeht

General expressions *Общи изрази*

Where's the main shopping area?	**Къде е тъговският център?**	ki**deh** eh tir**gov**skeeyaht **tsehn**tir
Do you have any ...?	**Имате ли ...?**	**ee**mahteh lee
Do you have anything ...?	**Имате ли нещо ...?**	**ee**mahteh lee **neh**shto
cheaper/better	**по-евтино/по-добро**	**po-eh**vteeno/**po**-dob**ro**
larger/smaller	**по-голямо/по-малко**	**po**-go**lyah**mo/**po-mahl**ko
Can I try it on?	**Може ли да го пробвам?**	**mo**zheh lee dah go **prob**vahm
How much is this?	**Колко струва това?**	**kol**ko **stroo**vah to**vah**
Please write it down.	**Моля, напишете го.**	**mo**lyah nahpee**sheh**teh go
No, I don't like it.	**Не, не ми харесва.**	neh neh mee khah**rehs**vah
I'll take it.	**Ще го взема.**	shteh go **vzeh**mah
Do you accept credit cards?	**Приемате ли кредитни карти?**	pree**eh**mahteh lee **kreh**deetnee **kahr**tee

black	**черно**	**chehr**no	orange	**оранжево**	o**rahn**zhehvo
blue	**синьо**	**see**nyo	red	**червено**	chehr**veh**no
brown	**кафяво**	kah**fyah**vo	yellow	**жълто**	**zhil**to
green	**зелено**	zeh**leh**no	white	**бяло**	**byah**lo

NUMBERS, see page 31

I want to buy …	**Искам да купя …**	**ees**kahm dah **koo**pyah
aspirin	**аспирин**	ahspee**reen**
batteries	**батерии**	bah**teh**ree-ee
newspaper	**вестник**	**vehst**neek
English	**английски**	ahn**gleey**skee
American	**американски**	ahmehree**kahn**skee
shampoo	**шампоан**	shahmpo**ahn**
sun-tan cream	**плажен крем**	**plah**zhehn krehm
soap	**сапун**	sah**poon**
toothpaste	**паста за зъби**	**pahs**tah zah **zi**bee
a half-kilo of apples	**половин кило ябълки**	polo**veen** kee**lo** **yah**bilkee
a litre of milk	**един литър мляко**	eh**deen** **lee**tir **mlyah**ko
I'd like … film for this camera.	**Искам ... филм за този фотоапарат.**	**ees**kahm ... feelm zah **to**zee **fo**toahpahraht
black and white	**черно-бял**	**chehr**no byahl
colour	**цветен**	**tsveh**tehn
I'd like a hair-cut.	**Искам подстригване.**	**ees**kahm pod**streeg**vahneh

Souvenirs *Сувенири*

българска бродерия	**bil**gahrskah bro**deh**reeyah	Bulgarian embroidery
дърворезба	dirvorehz**bah**	woodcarving
кована мед	ko**vahn**ah med	copperware
керамика и глинени съдове	keh**rah**meekah ee **glee**nehnee **si**doveh	ceramics and earthenware

At the bank *В банката*

Where's the nearest bank/currency exchange office?	**Къде наблизо има банка/ валутното бюро?**	**kideh** nah**blee**zo **ee**mah **bahn**kah/ va**loot**noto byoo**ro**
I want to change some dollars/pounds into lev.	**Искам да обмена долари/ лири в левове.**	**ees**kahm dah obmeh**nyah** **do**lahree/ **lee**ree v **leh**voveh
What's the exchange rate?	**Какъв е обменният курс?**	kah**kiv** eh ob**mehn**neeyaht koors

NUMBERS, see page 31

At the post office *В пощата*

I want to send this by …	**Искам да пратя това ...**	**ees**kahm dah **prah**tyah to**vah**
airmail	**с въздшна поща**	s viz**doosh**nah **po**shtah
express	**екпрес**	ehks**prehs**
I want … -lev stamps.	**Искам марки за ... лева.**	**ees**kahm **mahr**kee zah ... **leh**vah
What's the postage for a letter/postcard to England?	**Каква е таксата за писмо/ пощенска картичка до Англия?**	kahk**vah** eh **tahk**sahtah zah pees**mo/ po**shtehnskah **kahr**teechkah do **ahn**gleeyah
Is there any mail for me? My name is …	**Има ли поща за мен? Казвам се ...**	**ee**mah lee **po**shtah zah mehn. **kahz**vahm seh

Telephoning *Телефониране*

Where's the nearest public phone?	**Къде наблизо има телефонна кабина?**	ki**deh** nah**blee**zo **ee**mah tehleh**fon**nah kah**bee**nah
May I use your phone?	**Може ли да ползвам телефона Ви?**	**mo**zheh lee dah **pol**zvahm tehleh**fo**nah vee
Can I have a 1-lev coin for the public phone?	**Имате ли монета от един лев за уличен телефон?**	**ee**mahteh lee mo**neh**tah ot ehd**no** lehv zah ooleechehn tehleh**fon**
Hello. This is … speaking.	**Ало. Обажда се ...**	**ah**lo. o**bah**zhdah seh
I want to speak to …	**Искам да говоря с ...**	**ees**kahm dah go**vo**ryah s
When will he/ she be back?	**Кога ще се върне?**	ko**gah** shteh seh **vir**neh
Will you tell him/ her that I called?	**Моля, предайте му/й, че съм се обаждал(а)?**	**mo**lyah preh**dahy**teh moo/ee cheh seh sim o**bahzh**dahl(ah)

Sunday	**неделя**	neh**deh**lyah
Monday	**понеделник**	poneh**dehl**neek
Tuesday	**вторник**	**vtor**neek
Wednesday	**сряда**	**sryah**dah
Thursday	**четвъртък**	cheht**vir**tik
Friday	**петък**	**peh**tik
Saturday	**събота**	**si**botah
January	**януари**	yahnoo**ah**ree
February	**февруари**	fehvroo**ah**ree
March	**март**	mahrt
April	**април**	ahp**reel**
May	**май**	mahy
June	**юни**	**yoo**nee
July	**юли**	**yoo**lee
August	**август**	**ahv**goost
September	**септември**	sehp**tehm**vree
October	**октомври**	ok**tom**vree
November	**ноември**	no**ehm**vree
December	**декември**	deh**kehm**vree

Time and date *Час и дата*

It's …	**Сега е ...**	seh**gah** eh
five past one	**един и пет**	eh**deen** ee peht
quarter past three	**три и четвърт**	tree ee **cheht**virt
twenty past five	**пет и двадесет**	peht ee **dvahdeh**seht
half-past seven	**седем и половина**	**seh**dehm ee polo**vee**nah
twenty-five to nine	**девет без двадесет и пет**	**deh**veht behz **dvahdeh**seht ee peht
ten to ten	**десет без десет**	**deh**seht behz **deh**seht
noon/midnight	**обяд/полунощ**	o**byahd**/poloo**nosht**
in the morning	**сутринта**	sootreen**tah**
during the day	**през деня**	prehz deh**nyah**
at night	**през нощта**	prehz nosh**tah**
yesterday/today	**вчера/днес**	**vcheh**rah/dnehs
tomorrow	**утре**	**oot**reh
spring/summer	**пролет/лято**	**pro**leht/**lyah**to
autumn/winter	**есен/зима**	**eh**sehn/**zee**mah

Numbers *Цифри*

0	**нула**	**noo**lah	11	**единадесет**	ehdee**nahdeh**seht
1	**едно**	ehd**no**	12	**дванадесет**	dvah**nahdeh**seht
2	**две**	dveh	13	**тринадесет**	tree**nahdeh**seht
3	**три**	tree	14	**четиринадесет**	chehteeree**nahdeh**seht
4	**четири**	**cheh**teeree	15	**петнадесет**	peh**nahdeh**seht
5	**пет**	peht	16	**шестнадесет**	shehst**nahdeh**seht
6	**шест**	shehst	17	**седемнадесет**	sehdehm**nahdeh**seht
7	**седем**	**seh**dehm	18	**оемнадесет**	osehm**nahdeh**seht
8	**осем**	osehm	19	**деветнадесет**	dehveht**nahdeh**seht
9	**девет**	**deh**veht	20	**двадесет**	**dvahdeh**seht
10	**десет**	**deh**seht	21	**двадесет едно**	**dvahdeh**seht ehd**no**

30	**тридесет**	**treedeh**seht
40	**четиридесет**	chehtee**reedeh**seht
50	**петдесет**	pehtdeh**seht**
60	**шестдесет**	shehstdeh**seht**
70	**седемдесет**	sehdehmdeh**seht**
80	**осемдесет**	osehmdeh**seht**
90	**деветдесет**	dehvehtde**seht**
100/1,000	**сто/хиляда**	sto/khee**lyah**dah
first/second	**първи/втори**	**pir**vee/**vto**ree
once/twice	**веднъж/два пъти**	vehd**nizh**/dvah **pi**tee
a half	**половина**	pol**vee**nah

Emergency *Произшествия*

Call the police	**Обадете се в полицията**	obah**deh**teh seh v po**lee**tseeyahtah
HELP	**ПОМОЩ**	**po**mosht
I'm ill	**Болен (Болна) съм**	**bo**lehn (**bol**nah) sim
I'm lost	**Изгубих се**	eez**goo**beekh seh
Leave me alone	**Остави ме на мира**	ostah**vee** meh nah **mee**rah
My … has been stolen.	**Откраднаха ми ...**	ot**krahd**nahkhah mee
I've lost my …	**Изчезна ми ...**	eez**chehz**nah
handbag	**ръчната чанта**	**rich**nahtah **chahn**tah
luggage/passport	**багажът/паспортът**	bah**gah**zhit/pahs**por**tit
Where can I find a doctor who speaks English?	**Къде да намеря лекар, който говори английски?**	**kideh** dah nah**meh**ryah **leh**kahr **koy**to gov**o**ree ahn**glee**yskee

Guide to Bulgarian pronunciation

Consonants

Letter	Approximate pronounciation	Symbol	Example	
б	like **b** in **b**ed	b	**бял**	byahl
в	like **v** in **v**oice	v	**вар**	vahr
г	like **g** in **g**ood	g	**гол**	gol
д	like **d** in **d**ot	d	**дебел**	**deh**behl
ж	like **s** in measure	zh	**жена**	zheh**nah**
з	like **z** in **z**ero	z	**зима**	zee**mah**
й	like **y** in **y**oghourt	y	**йод**	yod
к	like **k** in **k**it	k	**килим**	**kee**leem
л	like **l** in **l**ook	l	**лом**	lom
м	like **m** in **m**an	m	**мене**	meh**neh**
н	like **n** in **n**ight	n	**нар**	nahr
п	like **p** in **p**et	p	**пипам**	**pee**pahm
р	like **r** in **r**od	r	**ренде**	rehn**deh**
с	like **s** in **s**ip	s	**сопа**	**so**pah
т	like **t** in **t**op	t	**там**	tahm
ф	like **f** in **f**ond	f	**фосфор**	**fos**for
х	like **h** in **h**ot	kh	**хала**	**khah**lah
ц	like **ts** in bi**ts**	ts	**цаца**	**tsa**tsah
ч	like **ch** in **ch**air	ch	**чудо**	**choo**do
ш	like **sh** in **sh**ut	sh	**шега**	sheh**gah**
щ	represents two consonants like -**shed** in ma**shed**	sht	**щур**	shtoor

Vowels

а	like **a** in **a**rm (but shorter)	ah	**апарат**	ahpah**raht**
е	like **e** in **e**nd	eh	**ето**	**eh**to
и	like **i** in l**i**t	ee	**или**	**ee**lee
о	like **o** in **o**n	o	**отбор**	ot**bor**
у	like **oo** in m**oo**d (but shorter)	oo	**ухо**	**oo**kho
ъ	like **i** in b**i**rd	i	**ъгъл**	**i**gil
ь	like **y** in **y**et, but very short	y	**актьор**	akt[y]**or**
ю	like **u** in English d**u**ty	yoo	**юг**	yook
я	like **ya** in **ya**rd	yah	**деня**	deh**nyah**

TELEPHONE, see page 29

Croatian

Basic expressions *Osnovni izrazi*

Yes/No.	**Da/Ne.**	dah/neh
Please.	**Molim.**	**mo**leem
Thank you.	**Hvala vam.**	**hvah**lah vahm
I beg your pardon?	**Molim?**	**mo**leem

Introductions *Upoznavanje*

Good morning.	**Dobro jutro.**	**do**bro **yoo**tro
Good afternoon.	**Dobar dan.**	**do**bahr dahn
Good night.	**Laku noć.**	**lah**koo noch
Hello/Hi.	**Zdravo/Bog.**	**zdrah**vo/bog
Good-bye.	**Doviđenja.**	dovee**jehn**^{y}ah
My name is …	**Ime mi je …**	**ee**meh mee yeh
Pleased to meet you.	**Drago mi je.**	**drah**go mee yeh
What's your name?	**Kako se zovete?**	**kah**ko seh **zo**vehteh
How are you?	**Kako ste?**	**kah**ko steh
Fine thanks. And you?	**Dobro, hvala. A vi?**	**do**bro **hvah**lah. ah vee
Where do you come from?	**Odakle ste?**	**odah**kleh steh
I'm from …	**Ja sam iz …**	yah sahm eez
Australia	**Australije**	ahoo**strah**leeyeh
Britain	**Velike Britanije**	**veh**leekeh bree**tah**neeyeh
Canada	**Kanade**	kah**nah**deh
USA	**Sjedinjenih Američkih Država**	**syeh**deen^{y}ehneeh ah**meh**reecheeh **drzhah**vah
I'm with my …	**Ja sam sa …**	yah sahm sah
wife/husband	**svojom/svojim suprugom**	**svo**yom/**svo**yeem **soo**proogom
family	**svojom porodicom**	**svo**yom **po**rodeetsom
boyfriend	**svojim dečkom**	**svo**yeem **deh**chom
girlfriend	**svojom djevojkom**	**svo**yom **dyeh**voykom
I'm on my own.	**Sam(a) sam.**	sahm(ah) sahm
I'm on holiday.	**Ja sam na praznicima.**	yah sahm nah **prah**zneetseemah

GUIDE TO PRONUNCIATION, see page 48/EMERGENCIES, see page 47

Questions *Pitanja*

Where is/are …?	**Gdje je/su …?**	gdyeh yeh/su
When?/How?	**Kada?/Kako?**	**kah**dah/**kah**ko
What?/Why?	**Što?/Zašto?**	shto/**zah**shto
Who?/Which?	**Tko?/Koji?**	tko/**ko**yee
Where can I get/find …?	**Gdje mogu dobiti/naći …?**	gdyeh **mo**goo **do**beetee/**nah**chee
How far?	**Koliko je daleko odavde?**	**ko**leeko yeh dah**leh**ko **o**dahvdeh
How much?	**Koliko?**	**ko**leeko
May I?	**Mogu li?/Da li mogu?**	**mo**goo lee/dah lee **mo**goo
Can I have …?	**Da li mogu dobiti ...?**	dah lee **mo**goo **do**beetee
Can you help me?	**Možete li mi pomoći?**	**mo**zhehteh lee mee po**mo**chee
What does this mean?	**Što ovo znači?**	shto **o**vo **znah**chee
I understand.	**Razumijem.**	rah**zoomee**yehm
I don't understand.	**Ne razumijem.**	neh rah**zoomee**yehm
Can you translate this for me?	**Možete li mi ovo prevesti?**	**mo**zhehteh lee mee **o**vo prehv**eh**stee
Do you speak English?	**Govorite li Engleski?**	**go**voreeteh lee ehn**gleh**skee
I don't speak much Croatian.	**Ja malo govorim hrvatski jezik.**	yah **mah**lo **go**voreem **hrvaht**skee **yeh**zeek

A few useful words *Nekoliko korisnih riječi*

beautiful/ugly	**lijep/ružan**	**lee**yehp/**roo**zhahn
better/worse	**bolje/lošije**	**bol**^{y}eh/**lo**sheeyeh
big/small	**veliki/mali**	**veh**leekee/**mah**lee
cheap/expensive	**jeftin/skup**	**yeh**fteen/skoop
early/late	**rano/kasno**	**rah**no/**kah**sno
good/bad	**dobar/loš**	**do**bahr/losh
hot/cold	**vruć/hladan**	vrooch/**hlah**dahn
near/far	**blizu/daleko**	**blee**zoo/dah**leh**ko
old/new	**stari/novi**	**stah**ree/**no**vee
right/wrong	**točno/pogrešno**	**to**chno/**po**grehshno
vacant/occupied	**slobodan/zauzet**	**slo**bodahn/**zah**oozeht

Hotel–Accommodation *Hotelski smeštaj*

I've a reservation.	**Imam rezervaciju.**	**ee**mahm rehzehr**vah**tseeyoo
Do you have any vacancies?	**Imate li slobodnih soba?**	**ee**mahteh lee **slo**bodneeh **so**bah
I'd like a … room.	**Želio (Željela) bih … sobu.**	**zheh**leeo (**zhehl**^{y}ehlah) beeh … **so**boo
single	**jednokrevetnu sobu**	yehdno**kreh**vehtnoo **so**boo
double	**dvokrevetnu sobu**	dvo**kreh**vehtnoo **so**boo
with twin beds	**sa dva kreveta**	sah dvah **kreh**vehtah
with a double bed	**sa bračnim krevetom**	sah **brah**chneem **kreh**vehtom
with a bath/shower	**sa kadom/tušem**	sah **kah**dom/**too**shem
We'll be staying …	**Mi ćemo ostati ...**	mee **cheh**mo **o**stahtee
overnight only	**samo preko noći**	**sah**mo **preh**ko **no**chee
a few days	**nekoliko dana**	**neh**koleeko **dah**nah
a week	**tjedan dana**	**tyeh**dahn **dah**nah

Decision *Odluka*

May I see the room?	**Mogu li pogledati sobu?**	**mo**goo lee **po**glehdahtee **so**boo
That's fine. I'll take it.	**U redu je. Uzet ću je.**	oo **reh**doo yeh. **oo**zeht choo yeh
No. I don't like it.	**Ne. Ne sviđa mi se.**	neh. neh **svee**jah mee seh
It's too …	**Previše je …**	**preh**veesheh yeh
noisy/small	**bučna/malena**	**boo**chnah/**mah**lehnah
Do you have anything …?	**Imate li nešto …?**	**ee**mahteh lee **neh**shto
better/bigger	**bolje/veće**	**bol**^{y}eh/**veh**cheh
cheaper/quieter	**jeftinije/tiše**	yehf**teenee**yeh/**tee**sheh
May I please have my bill?	**Da li bih mogao (mogla) dobiti račun?**	dah lee beeh **mo**gaho (**mo**glah) **do**beetee **rah**choon
It's been a very enjoyable stay.	**Bio nam je jako ugodan boravak ovdje.**	**bee**o nahm yeh **yah**ko **oo**godahn **bo**rahvahk ovdyeh

Eating out *Objedi u ugostiteljskim kućama*

I'd like to reserve a table for 4.	**Htio (Htjela) bih rezervirati stol za četvero.**	**htee**o (**htyeh**lah) beeh rehzehr**vee**rahtee stol zah **cheh**tvehro
We'll come at 8.	**Doći ćemo u osam sati.**	**do**chee **cheh**mo oo **o**sahm **sah**tee
I'd like breakfast/ lunch/dinner.	**Želio (Žel'ela) bih doručak/ ručak/večeru.**	**zheh**leeo (**zheh**l[y]ehlah) beeh **do**roochahk/ **roo**chahk/veh**cheh**roo
What do you recommend?	**Što nam preporučujete?**	shto nahm prehpo**roo**chooyehteh
Do you have vegetarian dishes?	**Imate li vegetarijanska jela?**	**ee**mahteh lee vehgehtah**reeyahn**skah **yeh**lah

Breakfast *Doručak*

I'd like some …	**Želio (Željela) bih …**	**zhe**leeo (**zheh**l[y]ehlah) beeh
bread/butter	**kruh/maslac**	krooh/**mah**slats
cheese	**sir**	seer
egg	**jaje**	**yah**yeh
ham	**šunka**	**shoo**nkah
jam/rolls	**džem/kifle**	dzhehm/**kee**fleh

Starters *Laki obroci/Predjela*

burek sa sirom	**boo**rehk sah **see**rohm	filo pastry with cheese
dalmatinski sir	dahlmah**teen**skee seer	Dalmation cheese
domaća šunka	**do**mahchah **shoo**nkah	county ham
domaći pršut	**do**mahchee prshoot	Dalmation ham
šampinjoni sa kiselim vrhnjem	shahmpeen[y]onee sah **kee**sehleem vrhn[y]ehm	mushrooms with sour cream

baked/boiled	**pečen/kuhan**	**peh**chehn/**koo**hahn
fried/grilled	**pržen/na roštilju**	przhehn/nah rosh**tee**l[y]oo
roast/stewed	**pečen/pirjan**	**peh**chehn/**peer**yahn
underdone (rare)	**nedopečeno**	**neh**dopeh**cheh**no
medium	**srednje pečeno**	**sreh**dn[y]eh peh**cheh**no
well-done	**dobro pečeno**	**do**bro peh**cheh**no

NUMBERS, see page 46

Meat *Meso*

I'd like some …	**Žehlio (Žel'ela) bih …**	**zhe**leeo (**zhehl**^{y}ehlah) beeh
beef	**govedinu**	go**veh**deenoo
chicken/duck	**piletinu/patku**	pee**leh**teenoo/**pa**htkoo
lamb	**janjetinu**	yah**n**^{y}**eh**teenoo
pork	**svinjetinu**	svee**n**^{y}**eh**teenoo
veal	**teletinu**	teh**leh**teenoo
ćevapčići	cheh**vahp**cheechee	rolled pieces of grilled minced meat
pljeskavica sa lukom	**pl**^{y}**eh**skahveetsah sa **look**om	hamburger steak with raw onion
punjene paprike	**poon**^{y}ehneh pah**pree**keh	stuffed peppers
ražnjići	rahzh**n**^{y}**ee**chee	kebabs
sarma	**sahr**mah	stuffed cabbage leaves
zagrebački odrezak	**zah**grehbahchkee od**reh**zahk	Zagreb schnitzel

Fish and seafood *Riba i morski plodovi*

carp	**šaran**	**shah**rahn
caviar	**ikra**	**ee**krah
cod	**bakalar**	bah**kah**lahr
crab/lobster	**rakovi/jastog**	**rah**kovee/**yah**stog
scampi/squid	**škampi/lignje**	**shkah**mpee/**lee**gn^{y}eh

Vegetables *Povrće*

beans/cabbage	**grah/kupus**	grahe/**koo**poos
cauliflower	**cvjetača**	**tsvyeh**tahchah
gherkin	**krastavčići**	krah**stahv**cheechee
mushroom	**šampinjoni**	shahmpee**n**^{y}**o**nee
onion	**luk**	look
peas	**mahune**	**mah**hooneh
potatoes	**krumpir**	**kroom**peer
tomato	**rajčica**	rahy**chee**tsah
omlet sa sirom	**o**mleht sah **see**rom	cheese omelet
omlet sa šampinjonima	**o**mleht sah shahmpee**n**^{y}**o**neemah	mushroom omelet

Fruit and dessert *Voće i slatko poslije jela*

apple/banana	**jabuka/banana**	**yah**bookah/bah**nah**nah
lemon/orange	**limun/naranča**	**lee**moon/**nah**rahnchah
plum/strawberries	**šljiva/jagode**	**shl^{y}ee**vah/**yah**godeh
makovnjača	mah**ko**vn^{y}yahchah	roll with poppy seeds
sladoled	**slah**dolehd	ice-cream
torta	**tor**tah	gateau
voćna torta sa šlagom	**vo**chnah **tor**tah sah **shlah**gom	fruit cake with whipped cream

Drinks *Pića*

beer	**pivo**	**pee**vo
(hot) chocolate	**topla čokolada**	**to**plah choko**lah**dah
coffee	**kava**	**kah**vah
black/with milk	**crna/s mlijekom**	tsrnah/s mlee**yeh**kom
fruit juice	**voćni sok**	**vo**chnee sok
mineral water	**mineralna voda**	**mee**nehrahlnah **vo**dah
tea	**čaj**	chahy
vodka	**votka**	**vo**tkah
wine	**vino**	**vee**no
red/white	**crno/bijelo**	tsrno/**beeyeh**lo

Complaints and paying *Žalbe i plaćanje*

This is too …	**Ovo je previše ...**	**o**vo yeh **preh**veesheh
bitter/salty	**gorko/slano**	**gor**ko/**slah**no
That's not what I ordered.	**Ja nisam ovo naručio (naručila).**	yah **nee**sahm **o**vo nah**roo**cheeo (nah**roo**cheelah)
I'd like to pay.	**Htio (Htjela) bih platiti.**	**htee**o (**htyeh**lah) beeh **plah**teetee
Can I pay with this credit card?	**Mogu li platiti ovom kreditnom karticom?**	**mo**goo lee **plah**teetee **o**vom kreh**dee**tnom kahr**tee**tsom
Is service included?	**Da li je uključena napojnica?**	dah lee yeh oo**kl^{y}oo**chehnah nah**poy**neetsah
We enjoyed it, thank you.	**Bilo je jako ukusno, hvala vam.**	**bee**lo yeh **yah**ko oo**koo**sno vahm

NUMBERS, see page 46

Travelling around *Prilikom putovanja*

Plane *Avion*

Is there a flight to Zagreb?	**Ima li let za Zagreb?**	**ee**mah lee leht zah **zah**grehb
What time do I check in?	**Kada trebam predati prtljagu?**	**kah**dah **treh**bahm **preh**dahtee prtl^y**ah**goo
I'd like to … my reservation.	**Htio bih … svoju rezervaciju.**	**htee**o beeh… **svo**yoo rehzehr**vah**tseeyoo
cancel	**poništiti**	po**neesh**teetee
change	**promijeniti**	promee**yeh**neetee
confirm	**potvrditi**	po**tvr**deetee

Train *Vlak*

I want a ticket to Rijeka.	**Htio bih kartu za Rijeku.**	**htee**o beeh **kahr**too zah ree**yeh**koo
single (one-way)	**u jednom smjeru**	oo **yeh**dnom smee**yeh**roo
return (roundtrip)	**povratna karta**	**po**vrahtnah **kah**rtah pooto**vahn**^{y}eh
first/second class	**prva/druga klasa**	**pr**vah/**drgoo**gah **klah**sah
How long does the journey (trip) take?	**Koliko dugo traje putovanje?**	**ko**leeko **doo**go **trah**yeh pooto**vahn**^{y}eh
When is the … train to Osijek?	**Kada je … vlak za Osijek?**	**kah**dah yeh … vlahk zah **o**seeyehk
first/next	**prvi/slijedeći**	**pr**vee/slee**yehdeh**chee
last	**zadnji**	**zah**dn^{y}ee
Is this the right train to Split?	**Je li ovo vlak za Split?**	yeh lee **o**vo vlahk zah spleet

Bus–Tram (streetcar) *Autobus–Tramvaj*

What bus do I take to the centre/downtown?	**Koji autobus vozi do centra?**	**ko**yee ah-oo**to**boos vozee do **tsehn**trah
How much is the fare to …?	**Koliko je karta do ...?**	**ko**leeko yeh **kahr**tah do
Will you tell me when to get off?	**Hoćete li mi reći kada trebam sići?**	ho**cheh**teh lee mee **reh**chee **kah**dah **treh**bahm **see**chee

TELLING THE TIME, see page 45

Taxi *Taksi*

How much is it to …?	**Koliko košta taksi do ...?**	**ko**leeko **ko**shtah **tah**ksee do
Take me to this address.	**Odvezite me na ovu adresu.**	od**veh**zeeteh meh nah **o**voo ah**dreh**soo
Please stop here.	**Molim stanite ovdje.**	**mo**leem **stah**neeteh **o**vdyeh

Car hire *Unajmljivanje automobila*

I'd like to hire (rent) a car.	**Htio (htjela) bih unajmiti automobil.**	**htee**o (**htyeh**lah) beeh oo**nahy**meetee aooto**mo**beel
I'd like it for a day/week.	**Htio (htjela) bih unajmiti na jedan dan/ tjedan.**	**htee**o (**htyeh**lah) beeh oo**nahy**meetee nah **yeh**dahn dahn/ **tyeh**dahn
Where's the nearest filling station?	**Gdje je najbliža benzinska crpka?**	gdyeh yeh nahy**blee**zhah behn**zeen**skah **tsr**pkah
Full tank, please.	**Pun rezervoar, molim.**	poon rehzehr**vo**ahr **mo**leem
Give me … litres of petrol (gasoline).	**Dajte mi ... litara benzina.**	**dahy**teh mee **lee**tahrah behn**zee**nah
How do I get to …?	**Kako mogu doći do ...?**	**kah**ko **mo**goo **do**chee do
I've had a breakdown at …	**Auto mi je stalo kod …**	**ahoo**to mee yeh **stah**lo kod
Can you send a mechanic?	**Možete li poslati auto-mehaničara?**	**mo**zhehteh lee **po**slahtee **ahoo**to-meh**hah**neechahrah

☞ You're on the wrong road.	**Vi ste na krivom putu.**
Go straight ahead.	**Idi (Idite) pravo.**
It's down there on the left/right	**To je dolje na … lijevo/desno**
opposite/behind …	**preko puta/iza …**
next to/after …	**do/poslije ...**
north/south/east/west	**sjever/jug/istok/zapad**

TELLING THE TIME, see page 45/DAYS OF THE WEEK, see page 46

Sightseeing *Razgledanije mjesta*

Where's the tourist office?	**Gdje je turistička agencija?**	gdyeh yeh too**rees**teechkah ah**gehn**tseeyah
Is there an English-speaking guide?	**Ima li vodič koji govori engleski?**	**ee**mah lee **vo**deech **ko**yee **go**voree ehn**gleh**skee
Where is/are the …?	**Gdje je/su ...?**	gdyeh yeh/soo
beach	**plaža**	**plah**zhah
castle	**zamak/dvorac**	**zah**mahk/**dvo**rahts
cathedral	**katedrala**	kahteh**drah**lah
city centre/downtown	**centar grada**	**tsen**tahr **grah**dah
exhibition	**izložba**	**eez**lozhbah
harbour	**luka**	**loo**kah
market	**tržnica**	**trzhnee**tsah
museum	**muzej**	**moo**zehy
shops	**prodavaonice**	prodahvah**o**neetseh
zoo	**zoološki vrt**	zo**o**loshkee vrt
When does it open/close?	**Kada se otvara/zatvara?**	**kah**dah seh **o**tvahrah/**zah**tvahrah
How much is the entrance fee?	**Koliko košta ulaznica?**	**ko**leeko **ko**shtah **oo**lahz**nee**tsah

Entertainment *Zabava i izlasci*

What's playing at the … Theatre?	**Što igra u ... kazalištu?**	shto **ee**grah oo … **kah**zah**lee**shtoo
How much are the seats?	**Koliko košta ulaznica/karta?**	**ko**leeko **ko**shtah **oo**lahz**nee**tsah/**kahr**tah
Would you like to go out with me tonight?	**Da li bi htio [htjela] izaći sa mnom večeras?**	dah lee bee **htee**o [**htyeh**lah] ee**zah**chee sah mnom veh**cheh**rahs
Would you like to dance?	**Da li bi htio [htjela] plesati sa mnom?**	dah lee bee **htee**o [**htyeh**lah] **pleh**sahtee sah mnom
Thank you. It's been a wonderful evening.	**Hvala ti. Bilo je jako ugodno veče.**	**hvah**lah tee. **bee**lo jeh **yah**ko oo**god**no **veh**cheh

Shops, stores and services *Prodavaonice i usluge*

Where's the nearest …?	**Gdje je najbliža ...?**	gdyeh yeh nahy**blee**zhah
baker's	**pekara**	peh**kah**rah
bookshop	**knjižara**	kn^{y}ee**zhah**rah
butcher's	**mesnica**	**mehs**neetsah
chemist's	**ljekarna/ apoteka**	l^{y}eh**kahr**nah/ ahpo**teh**kah
dentist	**zubar**	**zoo**bahr
department store	**robna kuća**	**rob**nah **koo**chah
hairdresser	**frizer**	**free**zehr
newsagent	**prodavaonica novina**	prodahvah**o**neetsah **no**veenah
post office	**pošta**	**po**shtah
souvenir shop	**prodavaonica suvenira**	prodahvah**o**neetsah soovehn**ee**rah
supermarket	**robna kuća**	**rob**nah **koo**chah

General expressions *Opći izrazi*

Where's the main shopping area?	**Gdje je glavni centar za kupovinu?**	gdyeh yeh **glahv**nee **tsehn**tahr zah koo**po**veenoo
Do you have any …?	**Imate li …?**	**ee**mahteh lee
Can you show me this/that?	**Možete li mi pokazati ovo/ono?**	**mo**zhehteh lee mee po**kah**zahtee **o**vo/**o**no
Do you have anything …?	**Imate li šta …?**	**ee**mah teh lee shtah
cheaper/better	**jeftinije/bolje**	yehf**teenee**yeh/**bo**l^{y}eh
larger/smaller	**veće/manje**	**veh**cheh/**mah**n^{y}eh
Can I try it on?	**Mogu li probati?**	**mo**goo lee **pro**bahtee
Where's the fitting room?	**Gdje mogu probati?**	gdyeh **mo**goo **pro**bahtee
Can you order it for me?	**Možete li to naručiti za mene?**	**mo**zhehteh lee to nah**roo**cheetee zah **meh**neh
How long will it take?	**Koliko dugo će to trajati?**	**ko**leeko **doo**go cheh to **trah**yahtee

NUMBERS, see page 46

How much is this?	**Koliko to košta?**	**ko**leeko to **ko**shtah
Please write it down.	**Molim, napišite mi to.**	**mo**leem nah**pee**sheeteh mee to
No, I don't like it.	**Ne, ne sviđa mi se to.**	neh neh svee**jah** mee seh to
I'll take it.	**Ipak ću uzeti.**	**ee**pahk choo oo**zeh**tee
Do you accept credit cards?	**Da li se može platiti kreditnom karticom?**	dah lee seh **mo**zheh **plah**teetee kreh**deet**nom kahr**tee**tsom

black	**crn**	tsrn	orange	**narančast**	nah**rahn**chahst
blue	**plav**	plahv	red	**crven**	tsrvehn
brown	**smeđi**	**smeh**jee	yellow	**žut**	zhoot
green	**zelen**	**zeh**lehn	white	**bijel**	**bee**yehl

I want to buy …	**Želim kupiti ...**	**zheh**leem **koo**peetee
aspirin	**aspirin**	ahs**pee**reen
batteries	**baterije**	bah**teh**reeyeh
film	**film**	feelm
newspaper	**novine**	**no**veeneh
English	**engleske**	ehn**gleh**skeh
American	**američke**	ah**meh**reecheh
shampoo	**šampon**	**shah**mpon
sun-tan cream	**kremu za sunčanje**	**kreh**moo zah **soon**chan^y^eh
soap	**sapun**	**sah**poon
toothpaste	**pastu za zube**	**pah**stoo zah **zoo**beh
a half-kilo of apples	**pola kilograma jabuka**	**po**lah **keelo**grahmah **yah**bookah
a litre of milk	**litru mlijeka**	**lee**troo mlee**yeh**kah
I'd like … film for this camera.	**Htio (Htjela) bih ... film za ovaj foto-aparat.**	**htee**o (**htyeh**lah) beeh…feelm zah **o**vahy **fo**to-ah**pah**raht
black and white	**crno-bijeli**	tsrno-bee**yeh**lee
colour	**u boji**	oo **bo**yee
I'd like a hair-cut.	**Htio (Htjela) bih se ošišati.**	**htee**o (**htyeh**lah) beeh seh o**shee**shahtee

CROATIAN

Hrvatski

Souvenirs *Suveniri*

lutke u narodnim nošnjama	**loot**keh oo **nahr**odneem **no**shn^{y}ahmah	dolls in national costumes
narodni vez	**nahr**odnee vehz	traditional embroidery
ručno rađeni ćilimi	**rooch**no **rah**jehnee **chee**leemee	hand-made carpets
slike naivne umjetnosti	**slee**keh **nah**eevneh oo**myeht**nostee	native paintings on glass
školjke/koralji	**shkol**^{y}keh/ko**rahl**^{y}ee	seashells/corals

At the bank *U banci*

Where's the nearest bank/currency exchange office?	**Gdje je najbliža banka/ mjenjačnica?**	gdyeh yeh nahy**blee**zhah **bahn**kah/ myeh**n^{y}ah**chneetsah
I want to change some dollars/pounds into kunas.	**Želim promijeniti dolare/funte u kune.**	**zheh**leem promee**yeh**neetee **do**lahreh/**foon**teh oo **koo**neh
What's the exchange rate?	**Kakav je tečaj?**	**kah**kahv yeh **teh**chahy

At the post office *U pošti*

I want to send this by …	**Htio (Htjela) bih ovo poslati …**	**htee**o (**htyeh**lah) beeh **o**vo **pos**lahtee
airmail	**avionskim putem**	ah**veeon**skeem **poo**tehm
express	**hitno**	**heet**no
I want … 10-kuna stamps.	**Želim ... marki od 10 kuna.**	**zheh**leem … **mahr**kee od **deh**seht **koo**nah
What's the postage for a letter to the United States?	**Koliko košta marka za pismo za Sjedinjene Američke Države?**	**ko**leeko **kosh**tah **mahr**kah zah **pees**mo zah syeh**deen**^{y}eneh ah**meh**reechkeh **drzhah**veh
Is there any mail for me? My name is …	**Ima li pošte za mene? Moje ime je ...**	**ee**mah lee **posh**teh zah **meh**neh. **mo**yeh **ee**meh yeh

NUMBERS, see page 46

Telephoning *Telefoniranje*

Where's the nearest public phone?	**Gdje se nalazi najbliža telefonska govornica?**	gdyeh seh **nah**lahzee nahy**blee**zhah tehleh**fon**skah govor**nee**tsah
Do you have some change for the phone?	**Imate li sitnog novca za telefon?**	**ee**mah teh lee **seet**nog **nov**tsah zah teh**leh**fon
May I use your phone?	**Mogu li se poslužiti vašim telefonom?**	**mo**goo lee seh pos**loo**zheetee **vah**sheem tehleh**fo**nom
Hello. This is … speaking.	**Zdravo. Ovdje je …**	**zdrah**vo. **o**vdyeh yeh
I want to speak to …	**Želim razgovarati sa …:**	**zheh**leem rahzgo**vah**rahtee sah
When will he/she be back?	**Kada će se on/ona vratiti?**	**kah**dah cheh seh on/**o**nah **vrah**teetee
Will you tell him/her that I called?	**Hoćete li mu/joj reći da sam ja zvao?**	ho**cheh**teh lee moo/yoy **reh**chee dah sahm yah **zvah**o

Time and date *Vrijeme i datum*

It's …	**Sada je ...**	**sah**dah yeh
five past one	**jedan sat i pet minuta**	**yeh**dahn saht ee peht mee**noo**tah
quarter past three	**tri i četvrt**	tree ee chehtvrt
twenty past five	**pet i dvadeset minuta**	peht ee **dvah**dehseht mee**noo**tah
half-past seven	**pola osam**	**po**lah **o**sahm
twenty-five to nine	**dvadeset i pet minuta do devet**	**dvah**dehset ee peht mee**noo**tah do **deh**veht
ten to ten	**deset minuta do deset sati**	**deh**seht mee**noo**tah do **deh**seht **sah**tee
noon/midnight	**podne/ponoć**	**pod**neh/**po**noch
in the morning	**ujutro**	**oo**yootro
during the day	**tokom dana**	**to**kom **dah**nah
in the evening	**navečer**	**nah**vehehehr
at night	**noću**	**no**choo

yesterday	**jučer**	**yoo**chehr
today	**danas**	**dah**nahs
tomorrow	**sutra**	**soot**rah
spring/summer	**proljeće/ljeto**	**pro**l^{y}ehcheh/**l^{y}eh**to
autumn/winter	**jesen/zima**	**yeh**sehn/**zee**mah

Sunday	**nedjelja**	neh**dyeh**l^{y}ah
Monday	**ponedjeljak**	poneh**dyeh**l^{y}ahk
Tuesday	**utorak**	oo**to**rahk
Wednesday	**srijeda**	sree**yeh**dah
Thursday	**četvrtak**	**chehtvr**tahk
Friday	**petak**	**peh**tahk
Saturday	**subota**	soo**bo**tah
January	**siječanj**	see**yeh**chahn^{y}
February	**veljača**	**veh**l^{y}ahchah
March	**ožujak**	o**zhoo**yahk
April	**travanj**	**trah**vahn^{y}
May	**svibanj**	**svee**bahn^{y}
June	**lipanj**	**lee**pahn^{y}
July	**srpanj**	srpahn^{y}
August	**kolovoz**	**ko**lovoz
September	**rujan**	**roo**yahn
October	**listopad**	**lee**stopahd
November	**studeni**	**stoo**dehnee
December	**prosinac**	**pro**seenahts

Numbers *Brojevi*

0	**nula**	**noo**lah	11	**jedanaest**	yeh**dah**nahehst
1	**jedan**	**yeh**dahn	12	**dvanaest**	**dvah**nahehst
2	**dva**	dvah	13	**trinaest**	**tree**nahehst
3	**tri**	tree	14	**četrnaest**	**chehtr**nahehst
4	**četiri**	**cheh**teeree	15	**petnaest**	**peht**nahehst
5	**pet**	peht	16	**šestnaest**	**sheht**nahehst
6	**šest**	shehst	17	**sedamnaest**	seh**dahm**nahehst
7	**sedam**	**seh**dahm	18	**osamnaest**	o**sahm**nahehst
8	**osam**	**o**sahm	19	**devetnaest**	deh**veht**nahehst
9	**devet**	**deh**veht	20	**dvadeset**	**dvah**dehseht
10	**deset**	**deh**seht	21	**dvadeset jedan**	**dvah**dehseht **yeh**dahn

30	**trideset**	**tree**dehseht
40	**četrdeset**	chehtr**deh**seht
50	**pedeset**	peh**deh**seht
60	**šezdeset**	shehz**deh**seht
70	**sedamdeset**	sehdahm**deh**seht
80	**osamdeset**	osahm**deh**seht
90	**devedeset**	dehveh**deh**seht
100/1,000	**sto/tisuća**	sto/**tee**soochah
first/second	**prvi/drugi**	prvee/**droo**gee
once/twice	**jednom/dvaput**	**yehd**nom/**dvah**poot
a half	**pol/polovina**	**pol**/polo**vee**nah

Emergency *Za slučaj nužde*

Call the police!	**Zovite policiju!**	**zo**veeteh po**lee**tseeyoo
Get a doctor.	**Zovite doktora.**	**zo**veeteh **dok**torah
Go away.	**Bježi/Idi odavde.**	**byeh**zhee/**ee**dee o**dahv**deh
HELP!	**U POMOĆ!**	oo **po**moch
I'm ill.	**Bolestan (Bolesna) sam.**	**bo**lehstahn (**bo**lehsnah) sahm
I'm lost.	**Izgubio (Izgubila) sam se.**	eez**goo**beeo (eez**goo**beelah) sahm seh
LOOK OUT!	**PAZITE!**	**pah**zeeteh
STOP THIEF!	**Zaustavite lopova!**	zahoos**tah**veeteh **lo**povah
My … has been stolen.	**Moj … je ukraden.**	moy … yeh oo**krah**dehn
I've lost my …	**Izgubio sam moju ...**	eez**goo**beeo sahm **mo**yoo
handbag	**torbu**	**tor**boo
passport	**putovnicu**	poo**tov**neetsoo
luggage	**prtljagu**	**prtl^{y}ah**goo
Where can I find a doctor who speaks English?	**Gdje mogu naći doktora koji govori engleski?**	gdyeh **mo**goo **nah**chee **dok**torah **ko**yee **go**voree ehn**gleh**skee

TELEPHONING, see page 45

Guide to Croation pronunciation

Croatian is a variant of Serbo-Croat spoken in Croatia. It is similar to Serbian, but differs in a number of respects; some vocabulary, aspects of pronunciation and the alphabet – Serbian is written in the Cyrillic script.
Shown below is the way Croatian sounds are pronounced. The basic pronunciation rule is that every letter is pronounced as it is written and individual letters are pronounced in the same way irrespective of their position in a word. There are no diphtongs and there are no silent letters in the Croatian language.

Consonants

Letter	Approximate pronunciation	Symbol	Example	
c	like **ts** in **tse**-**tse**	ts	cesta	**tseh**stah
č	like **ch** in **ch**urch	ch	čeka	**cheh**ka
ć	like **ch** in **ch**eap	ch	ćup	choop
	(a little further forward in the mouth than **č**; called a soft **č**)			
dž	like **j** in **J**une	j	džep	jehph
đ	like **j** in **j**eep (a soft dž)	j	đak	jahkh
g	like **g** in **g**o	g	gdje	gdyeh
h	like **h** in **h**ouse	h	hvala	hvahlah
j	like **y** in **y**oke	y	ja	yah
lj	like **l** in fai**l**ure	ly	ljubav	lyoobahv
nj	like **ni** in o**ni**on	nj	njegov	**n^{y}eh**gov
r	trilled (like a Scottish **r**)	r	rijeka	ree**yeh**kah
s	like **s** in **s**ister	s	sestra	**seh**strah
š	like **sh** in **sh**ip	sh	što	shto
z	like **z** in **z**ip	z	zvijezda	zveeyehzdah
ž	like **s** in plea**s**ure	zh	želim	zhehleem
b, d, f, k, l, m, n, p, t, v	as in English			

Vowels

a	like **a** in f**a**ther	ah	sat	saht
e	like **e** in g**e**t	eh	svijet	**svee**yeht
i	like **i** in **i**t	ee	iz	eez
o	like **o** in h**o**t	o	ovdje	ovdyeh
u	like **oo** in b**oo**m	oo	put	poot

Czech

Basic expressions *Všeobecné výrazy*

Yes/No.	**Ano/Ne.**	**a**no/ne
Please.	**Prosím.**	**pro**seem
Thank you.	**Děkuji.**	**d^{y}e**kooyi
I beg your pardon?	**Promiňte.**	**pro**min^{y}te

Introductions *Představování*

Good morning.	**Dobré ráno.**	**do**breh **rah**no
Good afternoon.	**Dobré odpoledne.**	**do**breh **ot**poledne
Good night.	**Dobrou noc.**	**do**broh nots
Good-bye.	**Nashledanou.**	**nas**-khledanoh
My name is ...	**Jmenuji se ...**	**y**menooyi se
What's your name?	**Jak se jmenujete?**	yak se **y**menooyete
How are you?	**Jak se máte?**	yak se **mah**te
Very well, thanks.	**Děkuji dobře.**	**d^{y}e**kooyi **do**brzhe.
And you?	**A Vy?**	a vi
Where do you come from?	**Odkud jste?**	**ot**koot yste
I'm from ...	**Já jsem ...**	yah **y**sem
Australia	**ze Austrálie**	ze **aoo**strahliye
Britain	**z Británie**	z **bri**tahniye
Canada	**z Kanadě**	z **ka**nadi
USA	**ze Spojených Států**	ze **spo**yeneekh **stah**to͞o
I'm with my ...	**Já jsem s ...**	yah **y**sem s
wife	**mou ženou**	moh **zhe**noh
husband	**mým manželem**	meem **man**zhelem
family	**mou rodinou**	moh **ro**d^{y}inoh
boyfriend	**mým mládencem**	meem **mlah**dentsem
girlfriend	**mou dívkou**	moh **d^{y}eef**koh
I'm here on a business trip/ vacation.	**Já jsem tady služebně/ na dovolené.**	yah **y**sem **ta**di **sloo**zhebn^{y}e/ **na**dovoleneh

GUIDE TO PRONUNCIATION, see page 63/EMERGENCIES, see page 62

Questions *Otázky*

When?/How?	**Kdy?/Jak?**	gdi/yak
What?/Why?	**Co?/Proč?**	tso/proch
Who?/Which?	**Kdo?/Který?**	gdo/**kte**ree
Where is/are ...?	**Kde je/jsou ...?**	gde ye/**y**soh
Where can I find/ get ...?	**Kde bych našel(a)/ dostal(a) ...?**	gde bikh **na**shel(a)/ **do**stal(a)
How far?	**Jak daleko?**	yak **da**leko
How long?	**Jak dlouho?**	yak **dloh**-ho
How much/many?	**Kolik?**	**ko**lik
Can I have ...?	**Mohl(a) bych dostat ...?**	**mo**-h^{u}l (**mo**-hla) bikh **do**stat
Can you help me?	**Mohl[a] byste mi pomoci?**	**mo**-h^{u}l [**mo**-hla] **bi**ste mi **po**motsi
I understand.	**Rozumím.**	**ro**zoomeem
I don't understand.	**Nerozumím.**	**ne**rozoomeem
Can you translate this for me?	**Mohl[a] byste to pro mne přeložit?**	**mo**-h^{u}l [**mo**-hla] **bi**ste to pro mne **przhe**lozhit
Do you speak English?	**Mluvíte anglicky?**	**mloo**veete **an**glitski
I don't speak (much) Czech.	**Já nemluvím (moc) český.**	yah **ne**mlooveem (mots) **cheh**skee

A few more useful words *Další užitečnáslova*

better/worse	**lepší/horší**	**lep**shee/**hor**shee
big/small	**velké/malé**	**vel**keh/**ma**leh
cheap/expensive	**laciné/drahé**	**lat**sineh/**dra**-heh
early/late	**brzo/pozdě**	**b^{u}r**zo/**poz**d^{y}e
good/bad	**dobré/špatné**	**do**breh/**shpat**neh
hot/cold	**horké/studené**	**hor**keh/**stu**deneh
near/far	**daleko/blízko**	**da**leko/**blee**sko
right/wrong	**správné/špatné**	**sprah**vneh/**shpat**neh
vacant/occupied	**volné/obsazené**	**vol**neh/**op**sazeneh

Hotel—Accommodation *Hotel*

I have a reservation.	**Mám reservaci.**	mahm **re**zervatsi
Do you have any vacancies?	**Máte volný pokoj?**	**mah**te **vol**nee **po**koy
I'd like a ...	**Chtěl(a) bych ...**	kht^{y}el(a) bikh
single room	**jednolůžkový pokoj**	**yed**nolo͞oshkovee **po**koy
double room	**dvoulůžkový pokoj**	**dvoh**lo͞oshkovee **po**koy
with twin beds	**se dvěma postelemi**	**se**dvyema **pos**telemi
with a double bed	**se dvojitou postelí**	**se**dvo-yitoh **pos**telee
with a bath	**s koupelnou**	**skoh**pelnoh
with a shower	**se sprchou**	**se**sp^{u}rkhoh
We'll be staying ...	**Zůstaneme ...**	**zo͞o**staneme
overnight only	**na jednu noc**	**na**yednoo nots
a few days	**několik dnů**	**n^{y}**ekolik dno͞o
a week	**týden**	**tee**den
Is there a camp site near here?	**Je tu blízko kemping?**	ye too **blee**sko **kem**ping

Decision *Rozhodnutí*

May I see the room?	**Mohl(a) bych se podívat na ten pokoj?**	**mo**-h^{u}l (**mo**-hla) bikh se **pod**^{y}eevat na ten **po**koy
That's fine. I'll take it.	**To je v pořadku. Já si ho vezmu.**	to ye **fpor**zhahtkoo. yah si ho **vez**moo
No. I don't like it.	**Mně se nelíbí.**	mn^{y}e se **ne**leebee
It's too ...	**Je moc ...**	ye mots
dark/small	**tmavý/malý**	**tma**vee/**ma**lee
noisy	**hlučný**	**hluch**nee
Do you have anything ... ?	**Máte něco ...?**	**mah**te **n^{y}et**so
better/bigger	**lepšího/většího**	**lep**shee-ho/**vjet**shee-ho
cheaper	**levnějšího**	**lat**sin^{y}ejshee-ho
quieter	**tiššiho**	**t^{y}ish**shee-ho
May I have my bill, please?	**Prosím účet.**	**pro**seem **o͞o**chet
It's been a very enjoyable stay.	**Moc se nám tady líbilo.**	mots se nahm **ta**di **lee**bilo

NUMBERS, see page 62

Eating out *Restaurace*

I'd like to reserve a table for 4.	**Chci si zamluvit stůl pro 4.**	kh-tsi si **zam**loovit stōōl pro **chtir**zhi
We'll come at 8.	**Přijdeme v 8 hodin.**	**przhi**ydeme f osm **hod**^{y}in
I'd like breakfast/lunch/dinner.	**Prosil(a) bych snídani/oběd/večeři.**	**pro**sil(a) bikh **sn**^{y}**ee**dan^{y}i/**o**byet/**ve**cherzh^{y}i
What would you recommend?	**Co doporučujete?**	tso **do**poroochooyete
Do you have any vegetarian dishes?	**Máte bezmasá jídla?**	**mah**te **bez**masah **yee**dla

Breakfast *Snídaně*

I'd like ...	**Chtěl(a) bych ...**	kht^{y}el(a) bikh
bread/butter	**chleba/máslo**	**khle**ba/**mah**slo
eggs	**vejce**	**vey**tse
ham and eggs	**šunku s vajíčkem**	**shoon**koo **sva**-yeechkem
jam/rolls	**džem/rohlíky**	dzhem/**ro**-hleeki

Starters (Appetizers) *Předkrmy*

chut'ovky	**choot**^{y}ovki	savouries
nakládané houby	**na**klahdaneh **hoh**bi	pickled mushrooms
obložené chlebvíčky	**o**blozheneh **khleb**veekh-ki	open sandwich
pražská šunka	**prazh**skah **shoon**kah	Prague ham

Meat *Maso*

I'd like some ...	**Chtěl(a) bych ...**	kht^{y}el(a) bikh
beef/lamb	**hovězí/jehněčí**	**ho**vyezee/**ye**-hn^{y}echee
pork/veal	**vepřové/telecí**	**ve**przhoveh/**te**letsee
chicken/duck	**kuřé/kachní**	**koo**rzheh/**ka**khnee
čevapčiči	**che**vapchichi	meatballs
roštěnky na pivě	**rosht**^{y}enki **na**piv^{y}e	beef stewed in beer
smažene karbanátky	**sma**zhene **kar**banahtki	fried burgers
zajíc na smetaně	**za**-yeets **na**smetan^{y}e	hare in cream sauce
živáňská	**zhi**vahn^{y}skah	Slovak grilled skewer

NUMBERS, see page 62

baked/boiled	**pečené/vařené**	**pe**cheneh/**var**zheneh
fried	**smažené**	**sma**zheneh
grilled	**grilované**	**gri**lovaneh
roast	**pečeně**	**pe**cheneh
stewed	**dušené**	**doo**sheneh
underdone (rare)	**lehce udělané**	**lekh**tse **ood**^{y}elaneh
medium	**středně udělané**	**strzhed**n^{y}e **ood**^{y}elaneh
well-done	**dobře udělané**	**do**brzhe **ood**^{y}elaneh

Vegetables & salads *Zelenina a saláty*

beans	**fazole**	**fa**zole
cabbage	**zelí**	**ze**lee
carrots	**mrkev**	**m^{u}r**kef
lettuce	**salát**	**sa**laht
mushrooms	**houby**	**hoh**bi
onions	**cibule**	**tsi**bool-e
potatoes	**brambory**	**bram**bori
tomatoes	**rajskájablíčka**	**ra**-yskah **ya**bleechka
bramborák	**bram**borahk	spicy potato pancake
hlávkový salát	**hlahv**kovee **sa**laht	green salad
knedlíky	**kned**leeki	dumplings
plněné papriky	**p^{u}l**neneh **pa**priki	stuffed peppers
škubánky s mákem	**shkoo**bahnki **smah**kem	potato dumplings

Fruit & dessert *Ovoce a moučníky*

apple	**jablko**	**yab**^{u}lko
cherries	**třešně**	**trzhesh**n^{y}e
lemon	**citrón**	**tsi**trōn
orange	**pomeranč**	**po**meranch
peach	**broskev**	**bro**skef

pear	**hruška**	**hroosh**ka
plums	**švestky**	**shvest**ki
strawberries	**jahody**	**ya**-hodi
dort	dort	rich cream cake
třešňová bublanina	**trzhesh**novah **boo**blanina	sponge biscuits and cherries
meruňkové knedlíky	**me**roon^{y}koveh **kned**leeki	apricot dumplings
zmrzlina	**zm^{u}r**zlina	ice cream

Drinks *Napoje*

beer	**pivo**	**pi**vo
(hot) chocolate	**(horkou) čokoládu**	(**hor**koh) **cho**kolahdoo
coffee	**kávu**	**kah**voo
black/with milk	**černou/s mlékem**	**cher**noh/**smleh**kem
fruit juice	**ovocná šťáva**	**o**votsnah **sht^{y}ah**va
milk	**mléko**	**mleh**ko
mineral water	**minerálka**	**mi**nerahlka
plum brandy	**slivovice**	**sli**vovitse
sugar	**cukr**	**tsook**^{u}r
tea	**čaj**	cha-y
wine	**víno**	**vee**no
red/white	**červené/bílé**	**cher**venee/**bee**lee

Complaints—Bill (check) *Stížnosti—Účet*

This is too ...	**Tohle je moc ...**	**to**-hle ye mots
bitter/sweet	**hořké/sladké**	**horzh**keh/**slat**keh
That's not what I ordered.	**To jsem si neobjednal(a).**	to **y**sem si **ne**obyednal(a)
I'd like to pay.	**Prosím účet.**	**pro**seem **o͞o**chet
I think there's a mistake in this bill.	**V tom účtu je asi chyba.**	ftom **o͞och**too ye asi **khi**ba
Is everything included?	**Je v tom všechno?**	ye ftom **fshekh**no
We enjoyed it, thank you.	**Moc nám to chutnalo, děkujeme.**	mots nahm to **khoot**nalo **d^{y}**ekooyeme

Travelling around *Cestování*

Plane *Letadlo*

Is there a flight to Prague?	**Je možné letět do Prahy?**	ye **mozh**neh **let**^{y}et **do**pra-hi
What time should I check in?	**Kdy se musíme odbavit?**	gdi se **moo**seeme **od**bavit
I'd like to ... my reservation.	**Chtěl(a) bych ... mou reservaci.**	kht^{y}el(a) bikh ... moh **re**zervatsi
cancel	**zrušit**	**zroo**shit
change/confirm	**změnit/potvrdit**	**zmn^{y}**en^{y}it/**pot**v^{u}rd^{y}it

Train *Vlak*

I'd like a ticket to Cheb.	**Chtěl(a) bych jízdenku do Chebu.**	kht^{y}el(a) bikh **yeez**denkoo **do**kheboo
single (one-way)	**jedním směrem**	**yed**n^{y}eem **smn^{y}**erem
return (round trip)	**zpáteční**	**spah**techn^{y}ee
first/ second class	**první/ druhou třídu**	**p^{u}rv**n^{y}ee/ **droo**-hoh **trzhee**doo
How long does the journey (trip) take?	**Jak dlouho ta cesta trva?**	yak **dloh**-ho ta **tses**ta **t^{u}r**vah
When is the ... train to Pilsen?	**Kdy jede ... vlak do Plzňe?**	gdi **ye**de ... vlak **dop^{u}**lzn^{y}e
first/last	**první/poslední**	**p^{u}rv**n^{y}ee/**pos**ledn^{y}ee
next	**příští**	**przhee**sht^{y}ee
Is this the right train to Břeclav?	**Je tohle vlak do Břeclavi?**	ye to-hle vlak **do**brzhetslavi

Bus—Tram (streetcar) *Autobus—Tramvaj*

Which bus goes to the town centre/ downtown?	**Která autobus jede do centra?**	**kte**rah **aoo**toboos **ye**de **dot**sentra
Will you tell me when to get off?	**Řekněte mi kdy mám vystoupit?**	**rzhek**nete mi gdy mahm **vi**stohpit

Taxi *Taxi*

How much is the fare to ...?	**Kolik to stojí do ...**	**ko**lik to **sto**yee do

TELLING THE TIME, see page 61/NUMBERS, see pae 61

Take me to this address.	**Zavezte mne na tuto adresu.**	**za**veste mne **na**tooto **a**dresoo
Please stop here.	**Zastavte tady prosím.**	**za**stafte **ta**di **pro**seem
Could you wait for me?	**Mohl byste na mne počkat?**	**mo**-h^{u}l **bi**ste **na**mne **poch**kat

Car hire (rental) *Půjčovna auto*

I'd like to hire (rent) a car.	**Rád(a) bych si pronajmul auto.**	rahd(a) bikh si **pro**na-ymool **aoo**to
I'd like it for a day/a week.	**Chci ho na jeden den/na týden.**	khtsi ho na **ye**den den/**na**teeden
Where's the nearest filling station?	**Kde je nejbližší benzinová pumpa?**	gde ye **ney**blishee **ben**zeenovah **poom**pa
Fill it up, please.	**Prosím, plnou nádrž.**	**pro**seem **p^{u}l**noh **nah**d^{u}rsh
Give me ... litres of petrol (gasoline).	**Dejte mi ... litrů benzinu.**	**dey**te mi ... **li**tro͞o **ben**zeenoo
How do I get to ...?	**Jak se dostanu do ...?**	yak se **do**stanoo do
I've had a break-down at ...	**Mně se porouchalo auto ve ...**	mn^{y}e se **por**oh-khalo **aoo**to ve
Can you send a mechanic?	**Můžete mi poslat mechanika?**	**mo͞o**zhete mi **po**slat **me**khanika
Can you mend this puncture (fix this flat)?	**Můžete spravit tuhle píchlou duši?**	**mo͞o**zhete **spra**vit **too**-hle **peekhl**oh **doo**shi

☞ You're on the wrong road.	**Vy jste na špatné silnici.** ☜
Go straight ahead.	**Jeďte/běžte rovně.**
It's down there on the left/right.	**To je tam dole po levé/pravé straně.**
opposite/behind ...	**naproti/za …**
next to/after ...	**vedle/po …**
to the north/south/ east/west	**na sever/na jih/ na západ/na východ**

EMERGENCIES, see page 62

Sightseeing *Prohlížené pa mátek*

Where's the tourist office?	**Kde jsou turistické informace?**	gde **y**soh **too**ristitskeh **in**formatse
Is there an English-speaking guide?	**Je tam anglicky mluvící průvodce?**	ye tam **an**glitski **mloo**veetsee **pro͞o**vot-tse
Where is/are the ... ?	**Kde je/jsou ... ?**	gde ye/ysoh
botanical gardens	**botanická zahrada**	**bo**tanitskah **za**-hrada
castle	**zámek/hrad**	**zah**mek/hrat
church	**kostel**	**kos**tel
city centre/downtown	**městské centrum**	**mn^{y}est**skeh **tsen**troom
market	**trh**	t^{u}rkh
museum	**muzeum**	**moo**zeoom
shopping area	**obchodní čtvrt**	**op**khodn^{y}ee chtv^{u}rt^{y}
square	**náměstí**	**nah**mn^{y}est^{y}ee
tower	**věž**	vyesh
What are the opening hours?	**Jakáje otevírací doba?**	**ya**kah ye **ot**eveeratsee **do**ba
When does it close?	**V kolik se zavírá?**	**fko**lik se **za**veerah
How much is the entrance fee?	**Kolik stojí vstup?**	**ko**lik **sto**yee fstoop

Relaxing *Zábava*

What's playing at the ... Theatre?	**Co dávají dnes v ... divadle?**	tso **dah**va-yee dnes f ... **d^{y}iv**adle
Are there tickets for Tuesday?	**Máte lístek na představení v úterý?**	**mah**te **lee**stek na **przhet**-staven^{y}ee f **o͞o**teree
Would you like to go out with me tonight?	**Mohl(a) bych se večer sejít?**	**mo**-h^{u}l (**mo**-hla) bikh se **ve**cher **se**yeet
Is there a discotheque in town?	**Je někde ve městě diskotéka?**	ye **n^{y}**egde **ve**mn^{y}est^{y}e **dis**kotehka
Would you like to dance?	**Chtěl[a] byste si zatančit?**	kht^{y}el[a] **bi**ste si **za**tanchit
Thank you, it's been a wonderful evening.	**Děkuji za krásný večer.**	**d^{y}e**kooye za krahsnee vecher

DAYS OF THE WEEK, see page 61/NUMBERS, see page 62

Shops, stores and services *Obchody a služby*

Where's the nearest ...?	**Kde je nejbližší ...?**	gde ye **ney**blishee
bakery	**pekařství**	**pe**karzhstvee
bookshop/store	**knihkupectví**	**knikh**-koopets-tvee
chemist's/drugstore	**lékárna**	**leh**kahrna
dentist	**zubař**	**zoo**barzh
department store	**obchodní dům**	**op**khodn^{y}ee do͞om
grocery	**potraviny**	**po**travini
market	**trh**	t^{u}rkh
newsstand	**novinový stánek**	**no**vinovee stahnek
post office	**pošta**	**posh**ta
souvenir shop	**souvenýry**	**soo**veneeri
supermarket	**samoobsluha**	**samo**-opsloo-ha
toilets	**toalety**	**to**aleti

General expressions *Všeobecné dotazy*

Where's the main shopping area?	**Kde je hlavní obchodní centrum?**	gde ye **hlav**n^{y}ee **op**khodn^{y}ee **tsen**troom
Do you have any ...?	**Máte nějaké...?**	**mah**te **n^{y}e**yakeh
Don't you have anything ...?	**Nemáte něco ...?**	**ne**mahte **n^{y}e**tso
cheaper	**lacinějšího**	**la**tsin^{y}eyshee-ho
better	**lepšího**	**lep**shee-ho
larger	**většího**	**vye**tshee-ho
smaller	**menšího**	**men**shee-ho
Can I try it on?	**Můžu si to zkusit?**	**mo͞o**zhoo si to **skoo**sit
How much is this?	**Kolik to stojí?**	**ko**lik to **sto**yee
Please write it down.	**Mohl[a] byste to napsat?**	**mo**-h^{u}l [**mo**hla] **bi**ste to **nap**sat
I don't want to spend more than ... koruna.	**Nechci platit víc než ... korun.**	**ne**kh-tsi **plat**^{y}it veets nesh ... **ko**roon
No, I don't like it.	**Ne děkuji, mně se to nelíbí.**	ne **d^{y}e**kooyi mn^{y}e se to **ne**leebee
I'll take it.	**Já si to vezmu.**	yah si to **vez**moo
Do you accept credit cards?	**Je možné platit úvěrovou kartou?**	ye **mozh**neh **plat**^{y}it **o͞o**vyerovoh **kar**toh

NUMBERS, see page 62

black	**černý**	**cher**nee	red	**červený**	**cher**venee
blue	**modrý**	**mod**ree	white	**bílý**	**bee**lee
brown	**hnědý**	**hn^{y}e**dee	yellow	**žlutý**	**zhloo**tee
green	**zelený**	**ze**lenee	light ...	**světlý**	**svyet**lee
orange	**oranžový**	**o**ranzhovee	dark ...	**tmavý**	**tma**vee

I want to buy a/an/ some ...	**Já chci koupit ...**	yah khtsi **koh**pit
aspirin	**acylpirin**	**a**tsilpireen
batteries	**baterii**	**ba**teriyi
bottle opener	**otvírač na láhve**	**ot**veerach na **lah**ve
bread	**chleba**	**khle**ba
newspaper	**noviny**	**no**vini
American/English	**americké/anglické**	**a**meritskeh/**an**glitskeh
postcard	**pohlednici**	**po**-hledn^{y}itsi
shampoo	**šampón**	**sham**pōn
soap	**mýdlo**	**mee**dlo
sun-tan cream	**krém na opalování**	krehm **na**opalovahn^{y}ee
toothpaste	**zubní pastu**	**zoob**n^{y}ee **pa**stoo
half a kilo of tomatoes	**půl kila rajských jablek**	po͞ol **ki**la **ra**-yskeekh **ya**blek
a litre of milk	**litr mléka**	**lit**^{u}r **mleh**ka
I'd like a film for this camera.	**Chtěl(a) bych film pro tento aparát.**	kht^{y}el(a) bikh film pro **ten**to **a**paraht
black and white	**černo-bílý**	**cher**nobeelee
colour	**barevný**	**ba**revnee
I'd like a haircut, please.	**Chci se nechat ostříhat.**	khtsi se **ne**khat **ost**^{u}rzhee-hat

Souvenirs *Suvenýry*

kniha o umění	**kni**-ha o **oo**mn^{y}en^{y}ee	art book
krajka	**kra**-yka	lace
křišťalové sklo	**k^{y}rzhi**sht^{y}alovee sklo	crystal
ruční práce	**rooch**nee **prah**che	handicrafts
sklo	sklo	glassware
výšivka	**vee**shivka	embroidery

At the bank *V bance*

Where's the nearest bank/currency exchange office?	**Kde je nejbližší banka/směnárna?**	gde ye **ney**blishee **ban**ka/**smn**^{y}**e**nahrna
I want to change some dollars/pounds.	**Chci si vyměnit nějaké dolary/ libry.**	kh-tsi si **vi**mn^{y}en^{y}it n^{y}eyakeh **do**lari/**li**bri
I want to cash a traveller's cheque.	**Chci si vyměnit cestovní šek.**	kh-tsi si **vi**mn^{y}en^{y}et **tse**stovn^{y}ee shek
What's the exchange rate?	**Jaký je dnes kurs?**	**ya**kee ye dnes koors

At the post office *Na poště*

I'd like to send this (by) ...	**Chci tohle poslat ...**	kh-tsi **to**-hle **po**slat
airmail	**leteckou poštou**	**le**tetskoh **posh**toh
express	**expresem**	**eks**presem
A ...-koruna stamp, please.	**... korunovou známku, prosím.**	**ko**roonovoh **znahm**koo **pro**seem
What's the postage for a postcard to Los Angeles?	**Kolik stojí pohled do Los Angeles?**	**ko**lik **sto**yee **po**-hled do los **en**zhelis
Is there any post (mail) for me?	**Je tu pro mne nějaká pošta?**	ye too pro mne n^{y}eyakah **posh**ta.
My name is ...	**Jmenuji se ...**	**y**menooyi se

Telephoning *Používání telefonu*

Where's the nearest telephone booth?	**Kde je tady nejbližší telefonní budka?**	gde ye **ta**di **ne**-yblishee **te**lefon^{y}ee **boot**ka
May I use your phone?	**Můžu si od Vás zatelefonovat?**	**mōō**zhoo si od vahs **za**telefonovat
Hello. This is ...	**Haló. Tady je ...**	**ha**lō. **ta**di ye
I'd like to speak to ...	**Mohl(a) bych mluvit s ...**	**mo**-h^{u}l (**mo**-hla) bikh **mloo**vit s
When will he/she be back?	**Kdy se vrátí?**	gdi se **vraht**^{y}ee
Will you tell him/her I called?	**Mohl byste mu/jí říct, že jsem telefonoval?**	**mo**-h^{u}l **bi**ste moo/yee rzheets-t zhe **y**sem **te**lefonoval

Time and date *Datum a Čas*

It's ...	**Teď je ...**	tet^{y} ye
five past one	**jedna a pět minut**	**yed**na a pyet **mi**noot
a quarter past three	**čtvrt na čtyři**	chtv^{u}rt na **chti**rzhi
twenty past four	**za deset minut půl páté**	za **de**set **mi**noot pool **pah**teh
half-past six	**půl sedmé**	pool **sed**meh
twenty-five to seven	**za deset minut tři čtvrtě na sedm**	za **de**set **mi**noot trzhi **chtv^{u}r**t^{y}e na **se**doom
a quarter to nine	**tři čtvrtě na devět**	trzhi **chtv^{u}r**t^{y}e na **de**vyet
in the morning	**ráno**	**rah**no
afternoon/evening	**odpoledne/večer**	**ot**poledne/**ve**cher
yesterday/today	**včera/dnes**	**vche**ra/dnes
tomorrow	**zítra**	**zee**tra
spring/summer	**jaro/léto**	**ya**ro/**leh**to
autumn/winter	**podzim/zima**	**pod**zim/**zi**ma

Sunday	**neděle**	**ne**d^{y}ele
Monday	**pondělí**	**pon**d^{y}elee
Tuesday	**úterý**	**oo**teree
Wednesday	**středa**	**strzhe**da
Thursday	**čtvrtek**	**chtv^{u}r**tek
Friday	**pátek**	**pah**tek
Saturday	**sobota**	**so**bota
January	**Leden**	**le**den
February	**Únor**	**oo**nor
March	**Březen**	**brzhe**zen
April	**Duben**	**doo**ben
May	**Květen**	**kvye**ten
June	**Červen**	**cher**ven
July	**Červenec**	**cher**venets
August	**Srpen**	**s^{u}r**pen
September	**Září**	**zah**rzhee
October	**Říjen**	**rzhee**yen
November	**Listopad**	**li**stopat
December	**Prosinec**	**pro**sinets

Numbers *Čísla*

0	**nula**	**noo**la	11	**jedenáct**	**ye**denahtst
1	**jedna**	**yed**na	12	**dvanáct**	**dva**nahtst
2	**dvě**	dvye	13	**třináct**	**trzhi**nahtst
3	**tři**	trzhi	14	**čtrnáct**	**cht^{u}r**nahtst
4	**čtyři**	**chti**rzhi	15	**patnáct**	**pat**nahtst
5	**pět**	pyet	16	**šestnáct**	**shest**nahtst
6	**šest**	shest	17	**sedmnáct**	**se**doomnahtst
7	**sedm**	**se**doom	18	**osmnáct**	**o**soomnahtst
8	**osm**	**o**soom	19	**devatenáct**	**de**vatenahtst
9	**devět**	**de**vyet	20	**dvacet**	**dvat**set
10	**deset**	**de**set	21	**dvacet jedna**	**dvat**set **yed**na

30	**třicet**	**trzhi**tset
40	**čtyřicet**	**chti**rzhitset
50	**padesát**	**pa**desaht
60	**šedesát**	**she**desaht
70	**sedmdesát**	**se**doomdesaht
80	**osmdesát**	**o**soomdesaht
90	**devadesát**	**de**vadesaht
100/1000	**sto/tisíc**	sto/**t^{y}i**seets
first/second	**první/druhý**	**p^{u}r**vn^{y}ee/**droo**-hee
once/twice	**jednou/dvakrát**	**yed**noh/**dva**kraht
a half	**půl**	p$\overline{oo}$l

Emergency *Pohotovost*

Call the police	**Zavolejte policii**	**za**voleyte **po**litsiyi
Get a doctor	**Zavolejte lékaře**	**za**voleyte **leh**karzhe
HELP	**POMOC**	**po**mots
I'm ill	**Jsem nemocný (nemocna)**	ysem **ne**motsn^{y}ee (**ne**motsna)
I'm lost	**Zabloudil(a) jsem**	**za**bloh-dil(a) **y**sem
STOP THIEF	**CHYŤTE ZLODĚJE**	**khit^{y}**te **zlo**d^{y}eye
My ... has been stolen.	**Někdo mi ukradl ...**	**n^{y}**egdo mi **oo**krad^{u}l
I've lost my ...	**Ztratil(a) jsem ...**	**strat^{y}**il(a) ysem
handbag/passport	**kabelku/pas**	**ka**belkoo/pas
wallet	**peněženku**	**pe**n^{y}ezhenkoo

TELEPHONING, see page 60

Guide to Czech pronunciation

Czech is one of the most phonetic of all European languages, and you should have little trouble pronouncing Czech once you've got accustomed to its diacritical marks: the **čárka** (´), the **kroužek** (˚) and the **háček** (ˇ).

Consonants

Letter	Approximate pronunciation	Symbol	Example	
c	like **ts** in cats	ts	**cesta**	**tse**sta
č	like **ch** in **ch**urch	ch	**klíč**	kleech
d'	like **d** in **d**uty; for American speakers close to **j** in **j**am	d^y	**Láď'a**	**lah**d^{y}a
g	like **g** in **g**ood	g	**galerie**	**ga**leriye
h	like **h** in **h**alf	h	**hlava**	**hla**va
ch	like **ch** in Scottish lo**ch**	kh	**chtít**	kht^{y}eet
j	like **y** in **y**es	y	**jídlo**	**yee**dlo
ň	like **nn** in an**nu**al or **ny** in ca**ny**on	n^y	**píseň**	**pee**sen^y
r	rolled (like a Scottish **r**)	r	**ruka**	**roo**ka
ř	a sound unique to Czech; like a rolled **r** but flatten the tip of the tongue to make a short forceful buzz like **ž** (below)	rzh	**tři** **Dvořák**	trzhi **dvo**rzhahk
s	like **s** in **s**et	s	**čas**	chas
š	like **sh** in **sh**ort	sh	**šest**	shest
t'	like **t** in **t**une; for American speakers close to **ch** in **ch**urch	t^y	**chuť**	khoot^y
w	like **v** in **v**an; found only in foreign words	v	**víno**	veeno
ž	like **s** in plea**s**ure	zh	**žena**	**zhe**na

b, **d**, **f**, **g**, **k**, **m**, **n**, **p**, **t**, **v**, **z** are pronounced as in English

N.B.

1) **ě** makes the preceding consonant soft. A similar effect is produced by pronouncing **y** as in **y**et.

2) Voiced consonants (**b**, **d**, **d'**, **h**, **z**, **zh**, **v**) become voiceless (**p**, **t**, **t'**, **kh**, **s**, **sh**, **f** respectively) at the end of a word and before a voiceless consonant.
   Voiceless consonants within a word become voiced if followed by a voiced consonant (this involves particularly voiceless **k** becoming voiced **g**).

Vowels

Vowels in Czech can be either short (**a**, **e**, **i**, **o**, **u**, **y**) or long (**á**, **é**, **í**, **ó**, **ú**, **ů**, **ý**).

a	between the **a** in c**a**t and the **u** in c**u**t	a	**tam**	tam
á	like **a** in f**a**ther	ah	**máma**	**mah**ma
e	like **e** in m**e**t; this is always pronounced, even at the end of a word	e	**den**	den
é	similar to the **e** in b**e**d but longer	eh	**mléko**	**mleh**ko
i	like **i** in b**i**t	i	**pivo**	**pi**vo
í	like **ee** in s**ee**	ee	**bílý**	**bee**lee
o	like **o** in h**o**t	o	**slovo**	**slo**vo
ó	like **o** in sh**o**rt; found only in foreign words	o	**gól**	gol
u	like **oo** in b**oo**k	oo	**ruka**	**roo**ka
ú	like **oo** in m**oo**n	oo	**úkol**	**oo**kol
ů	like **ú** above	oo	**vůz**	vooz
y	like **i** above	i	**byt**	bit
ý	like **ee** in s**ee**	ee	**bílý**	**bee**lee

The letters **l** and **r** also operate as semi-vowels when they occur between two consonants or at the end of a word, following a consonant.

l	like **le** in cab**le**	^{u}l	**mohl**	**moh**^{u}l
r	like **ir** in b**ir**d	^{u}r	**krk**	k^{u}rk

Diphthongs

au	like **ow** in c**ow**	aoo	**auto**	**aoo**to
ou	like **ow** in m**ow**, or the exclamation **oh**	oh	**mouka**	**moh**ka

Estonian

Basic expressions *Pôhiväljendid*

Yes/No.	**Jaa (Jah)/Ei.**	yaa (yah)/ei
Please.	**Palun.**	**pa**lun
Thank you.	**Tänan.**	**tæ**nan
I beg your pardon?	**Kuidas, palun.**	**kui**das **pa**lun

Introductions *Tutvumine*

Good morning.	**Tere hommikust.**	**te**re **hom**mikust
Good afternoon.	**Tere päevast.**	**te**re **pæe**vast
Good night.	**Head ööd.**	head øød
Hello/Hi.	**Tere.**	**te**re
Good-bye.	**Head aega.**	head **ae**ga
My name is ...	**Minu nimi on …**	**mi**nu **ni**mi on
What's your name?	**Kuidas on teie nimi?**	**kui**das on **teie ni**mi
How are you?	**Kuidas läheb?**	**kui**das **læ**heb
Fine thanks.	**Tänan hästi.**	**tæ**nan **hæs**ti.
And you?	**Aga teil?**	**a**ga teil
Where do you come from?	**Kust te pärit olete?**	kust te **pæ**rit **o**lete
I'm from ...	**Ma olen pärit ...**	ma **o**len **pæ**rit
Australia	**Austraaliast**	aus**traaa**liast
Britain	**Suurbritanniast**	**suuur**bri**tannn**iast
Canada	**Kanadast**	**ka**nadast
USA	**USA-st**	uu ess**aaast**
I'm with my ...	**Ma olen koos oma ...**	ma **o**len kooos **o**ma
wife/husband	**abikaasaga**	**a**bikaasaga
family	**perekonnaga**	**pe**rekonnaga
children	**lastega**	**las**tega
boyfriend/girlfriend	**sôbraga**	s^{e}**bra**ga
I'm on my own.	**Ma olen üksinda.**	ma **o**len **ewk**sinda
I'm on holiday (vacation)/business.	**Ma olen puhkusel/ komandeeringus.**	ma **o**len **purh**kusel/ koman**dee**ringus

GUIDE TO PRONUNCIATION/EMERGENCIES, see page 79

Questions *Küsimused*

Where is/are ...?	**Kus on ...?**	kus on
When?/How?	**Millal?/Kuidas?**	**mil**lal/**kui**das
What?/Why?	**Mis?/Miks?**	mis/miks
Who?/Which?	**Kes?/Missugune?**	kes/**miss**sugune
Where can I get/find ...?	**Kust ma võiksin leida ...?**	kust ma **v^{e}ik**sin **lei**da
How far?	**Kui kaugel?**	kui **kau**gel
How long?	**Kui kaua?**	kui **kau**a
How much?	**Kui palju?**	kui **pal**yu
May I?	**Kas ma tohin?**	kas ma **to**hin
Can I have ...?	**Kas ma võin ...?**	kas ma v^{e}in
Can you help me?	**Kas te saate mind aidata?**	kas te **saa**te mind **ai**data
What does this mean?	**Mis see tähendab?**	mis seee **tæ**hendab
I understand.	**Ma saan aru.**	ma saaan **a**ru
I don't understand.	**Ma ei saa aru.**	ma ei saaa **a**ru
Can you translate this for me?	**Kas te oskate seda mulle tõlkida?**	kas te **os**kate **se**da **mull**le **t^{e}l**kida
Do you speak English?	**Kas te räägite inglise keelt?**	kas te **rææ**gite **ing**lise keeelt
I don't speak Estonian.	**Ma ei oska eesti keelt.**	ma ei **os**ka **ees**ti keeelt

A few useful words *Kasulikke sõnu*

beautiful/ugly	**ilus/kole**	**i**lus/**ko**le
better/worse	**parem/halvem**	**pa**rem/**hal**vem
big/small	**suur/väike**	suuur/**væi**ke
cheap/expensive	**odav/kallis**	**o**dav/**kal**lis
early/late	**vara/hilja**	**va**ra/**hil**ya
good/bad	**hea/halb**	hea/halb
hot/cold	**kuum/külm**	kuuum/kewlm
near/far	**lähedal/kaugel**	**læ**hedal/**kau**gel
next/last	**järgmine/viimane**	**yærg**mine/**vii**mane
old/new	**vana/uus**	**va**na/uuus
right/wrong	**õige/vale**	^{e}ige/**va**le
vacant/occupied	**vaba/kinni**	**va**ba/**kinn**ni

Hotel accommodation *Hotellis*

I've a reservation.	**Mul on tuba broneeritud.**	mul on **tu**ba bro**neer**itud
Here's the confirmation.	**Siin on kinnitus broneerimise kohta.**	siiin on **kin**nitus bro**neer**imise **kokh**ta
Do you have any vacancies?	**Kas teil on vabu kohti?**	kas teil on vabu **kokh**ti
I'd like a ... room.	**Ma sooviksin ... tuba**	ma **soo**viksin … **tu**ba
single/double	**ühelist/kahelist**	**ew**helist/**ka**helist
with twin beds	**kahe voodiga**	**ka**he **vooo**diga
with a double bed	**kaheinimese voodiga**	**ka**he**i**nimese **vooo**diga
with a bath	**vanniga**	**van**niga
with a shower	**duššiga**	**dush**shiga
We'll be staying ...	**Me peatume …**	me **pea**tume
overnight only	**vaid ühe öö**	vaid **ew**he øø
a few days	**mõned päevad**	**m^{e}**ned **pæe**vad
a week (at least)	**(vähemalt) nädala**	(**væ**hemalt) **næ**dala
Is there a campsite near here?	**Kas siin lähedal on kämping?**	kas siiin **læ**hedal on **kæm**ping

Decision *Otsustamine*

May I see the room?	**Kas ma saaksin tuba näha?**	kas ma **saaak**sin **tu**ba **næ**ha
That's fine. I'll take it.	**See sobib. Ma võtan selle.**	seee **so**bib. ma **v^{e}**tan **sel**le
No. I don't like it.	**Ei. See ei meeldi mulle.**	ei. seee ei **meeel**di **mull**le
It's too ...	**See on liiga ...**	seee on **liii**ga
dark/small	**pime/väike**	**pi**me/**væ**ike
noisy	**lärmakas**	**lær**makas
Do you have anything ...?	**Kas teil on midagi ...?**	kas teil on **mi**dagi
better/bigger	**paremat/suuremat**	**pa**remat **suu**remat
cheaper/quieter	**odavamat/vaiksemat**	odavamat **vaik**semat
May I please have my bill?	**Ma paluksin arvet?**	ma **pa**luksin **ar**vet
It's been a very enjoyable stay.	**Väga meeldiv oli teie juures viibida.**	**væ**ga **meeel**div **o**li teie **yuu**res **viii**bida

Eating out *Restoranis*

I'd like to reserve a table for 4.	**Ma sooviksin reserveerida laua neljale.**	ma **soo**viksin reser**vee**rida **laua nel**yale
We'll come at 8.	**Me tuleme kell kaheksa.**	me **tu**leme kelll **ka**heksa
I'd like breakfast/ lunch/dinner.	**Ma sooviksin hommikusööki/ lôunat/ôhtusööki.**	ma **soo**viksin **hom**mikusøøøki/ **l^{e}**unat/**^{e}kh**tusøøøki
What do you recommend?	**Mida te soovitate?**	**mi**da te **soo**vitate
Do you have vegetarian dishes?	**Kas teil on taimetoite?**	kas teil on **tai**me**toi**te

Breakfast *Hommikusööki*

I'd like an/some ...	**Ma sooviksin ...**	ma **soo**viksin
bread	**leiba**	**lei**ba
cheese	**juustu**	**yuuus**tu
egg	**muna**	**mu**na
ham	**sinki**	**sin**ki
jam	**keedist**	**kee**dist
rolls	**saiakesi**	**sai**akesi

Starters *Eelroad*

heeringas	**hee**ringas	herring
juustu-munasalat küüslauguga	**yuuus**tu**mu**na**sa**lat **kēw̄**slauguga	cheese and egg salad with garlic
kanalihasalat	**ka**nalihas**a**lat	chicken salad
kartulisalat	**kar**tuli**sa**lat	potato salad
krevetisalat	kre**ve**ti**sa**lat	prawn cocktail
rosolje	ro**sol**ye	salad of beet, potatoes, eggs and pickles
segasalat	**se**ga**sa**lat	mixed salad
soojad vôileivad	**sooo**yad **v^{e}**ileivad	hot sandwiches

NUMBERS, see page 78

baked	**küpsetatud**	**kewp**setatud
boilled	**keedetud**	**kee**detud
fried/grilled	**praetud/grillitud**	**prae**tud/**gril**litud
stewed	**hautatud**	**hau**tatud
underdone (rare)	**kergelt läbiküpsetatud**	**ker**gelt **læ**bi**küp**setatud
medium	**keskmiselt läbiküpsetatud**	**kesk**miselt **læ**bi**küp**setatud
well-done	**hästi läbiküpsetatud**	**hæs**ti **læ**bi**küp**setatud

Meat *Liha*

I'd like some ...	**Ma sooviksin ...**	ma **soo**viksin
beef/lamb	**loomaliha/lambaliha**	**loo**maliha/**lam**bali**ha**
pork/veal	**sealiha/vasikaliha**	**sea**liha/**va**sika**li**ha
biifsteek	**biii**fsteek	beefsteak
grillkana	**grilllka**na	grilled chicken
lambakarbonaad	**lam**baka**r**bonaaad	mutton-chop
loomalihafilee	**loo**malihafi**leee**	beef fillet
praetud vorst hapukapsaga	**prae**tud vorst **ha**pu**kap**saga	fried sausage with sauerkraut
sealiha karbonaad	**sea**liha **kar**bonaaad	pork chop
seapraad	**seapraaad**	roast pork
vasikaliha kotlet	**va**sika**li**ha **kot**let	veal cutlet

Fish & seafood *Kala- ja meretoidud*

eel	**angerjas**	**an**geryas
perch	**ahven**	**ah**ven
pike	**haug**	haug
keedetud kala	**kee**detud **ka**la	boiled fish
praetud kala	**prae**tud **ka**la	fried fish
praetud karpkala	**prae**tud **karp**kala	fried carp
praetud lest	**prae**tud lest	fried plaice

Vegetables *Juurvili*

beans	**oad**	oad
cabbage	**kapsas**	**kap**sas

gherkin	**väike marineeritud kurk**	**væi**ke mari**neer**itud kurk
leek	**lauk**	lauk
mushroom	**seen**	seeen
onion	**sibul**	**si**bul
peas	**herned**	**her**ned
potatoes	**kartulid**	**kar**tulid
tomato	**tomat**	**to**mat
omlett juurviljaga	om**lett yuuurvil**yaga	vegetable omelet
hautatud aedvili	**hau**tatud **aed**vili	stewed vegetables
aedviljasupp	**aed**vilya**suppp**	vegetable soup
värskekapsasupp	**vær**skekapsa**suppp**	fresh cabbage soup

Fruit & dessert *Puuvili ja magustoidud*

apple	**õun**	^{e}un
banana	**banaan**	ba**naaan**
lemon	**sidrun**	**sid**run
orange	**apelsin**	**a**pelsin
plum	**ploom**	plooom
strawberries	**maasikad**	**maa**sikad
jäätis	**yæææ**tis	ice-cream
kohupiimakook	kohupiima**koook**	cheesecake
puuviljakook	**puuu**vilya**koook**	fruit cake
rummikook	**rum**mi**koook**	rumcake
tarretis vahukoorega	**tar**retis **va**hu**koo**rega	jelly with whipped cream
tort	tort	gateau

Drinks *Joogid*

beer	**õlu**	^{e}lu
(hot) chocolate	**(kuum) kakao**	kuuum ka**kao**
coffee	**kohv**	kokhv
black/with milk	**must/piimaga**	must/**pii**maga
fruit juice	**puuviljamahl**	**puuu**vilya**maxl**
mineral water	**mineraalvesi**	mine**raaalve**si
tea	**tee**	teee
vodka	**viin**	viiin
red/white wine	**punane/valge vein**	**pu**nane/**val**ge vein

Complaints and paying *Pretensioonid*

This is too salty/sweet.	**See on liiga soolane/magus.**	seee on **liii**ga **soo**lane/**ma**gus
That's not what I ordered.	**Ma ei tellinud seda.**	ma ei **tell**linud **se**da
I'd like to pay.	**Ma sooviksin maksta.**	ma **soo**vikin **maks**ta
I think you made a mistake in the bill.	**Ma arvan, et arves on viga.**	ma **ar**van et **ar**ves on **vi**ga
Can I pay with this credit card?	**Kas ma saan maksta selle krediitkaardiga?**	kas ma saaan **maks**ta **sel**le kre**diiitkaar**diga
Is service included?	**Kas teenindus on sisse arvestatud?**	kas **tee**nindus on **sis**sse **ar**vestatud
We enjoyed it, thank you.	**Meile meeldis siin, suur tänu.**	**mei**le **meeel**dis siiin suuur **tæ**nu

Travelling around *Reisimine*

Plane *Lennuk*

Is there a flight to Kuressaare?	**Kas lennukiga saab minna Kuressaarde?**	kas **len**nukiga saaab **minn**na **ku**res**saaar**de
What time do I check in?	**Mis kell tuleb end lennukile registreerida?**	mis kelll **tu**leb end **len**nukile regis**treee**rida
I'd like to ... my reservation on flight no. ...	**Ma sooviksin ... oma broneeringut lennule number ...**	ma **soo**viksin ... **o**ma bro**nee**ringut **len**nule **num**ber
cancel	**tühistada**	**tü**histada
change	**muuta**	**muuu**ta
confirm	**kinnitada**	**kin**nitada

Train *Rong*

I want a ticket to Tartu.	**Ma sooviksin ühte piletit Tartusse.**	ma **soo**viksin **ükh**te **pi**letit **tar**tusse
single (one-way)	**üheotsa piletit**	ewheo**ts**a **pi**letit
return (roundtrip)	**edasi-tagasi piletit**	edasi**ta**gasi **pi**letit
first/second class	**esimese/teise klassi piletit**	esimese/**tei**se **klas**si **pi**letit

TELLING THE TIME, see page 77

How long does the journey (trip) take?	**Kui kaua sôit kestab?**	kui **kau**a s^{e}it **kes**tab
When is the … train to Tapa?	**Millal läheb … rong Tapale?**	**mil**lal **læ**heb … rong **ta**pale
first/next	**esimene/järgmine**	esimene/**yærg**mine
last	**viimane**	**vii**mane
Is this the right train to Riga?	**Kas see rong läheb Riiga?**	kas seee rong **læ**heb **riii**ga

Bus—Tam (streetcar) *Buss —Tramm*

What bus do I take to the centre?	**Missugune buss sôidab kesklinna?**	**miss**sugune busss s^{e}**i**dab **kesklinn**na
How much is the fare?	**Kui palju maksab pilet?**	kui **pal**yu **mak**sab **pi**let
Will you tell me when to get off?	**Palun öelge kus ma pean väljuma?**	**pa**lun **øel**ge kus ma pean **væl**yuma

Taxi *Takso*

How much is it to ...?	**Kui palju maksab sôit ...?**	kui **pal**yu **mak**sab s^{e}it
Take me to this address.	**Viige mind sel aadressil.**	**vii**ge mind sel **aad**ressil
Please stop here.	**Palun peatuge siin.**	**pa**lun **pea**tuge siiin

Car hire *Auto üürimine*

I'd like to hire (rent) a car.	**Ma sooviksin üürida autot.**	ma **soo**viksin **ew**da **au**tot
I'd like it for a day/week.	**Ma sooviksin seda üheks päevaks/ nädalaks.**	ma **soo**viksin **se**da **ew**heks **pæ**evaks/ **næ**dalaks
Where's the nearest filling station?	**Kus on lähim bensiinijaam?**	kus on **læ**him ben**sii**ni**yaaam**
Full tank, please.	**Täispaak, palun.**	**tæis**paaak **pa**lun
Give me … litres of petrol (gasoline).	**Andke mulle ... liitrit bensiini.**	**and**ke **mull**le ... **liii**trit ben**siii**ni
Where can I park?	**Kus ma vôin parkida?**	kus ma v^{e}in **par**kida
How do I get to …?	**Kuidas ma saan ...?**	**kui**das ma saaan
I've had a breakdown at ...	**Mul läks auto katki ...**	mul læks **au**to **kat**ki

NUMBERS, see page 78

Can you send a mechanic?	**Kas te saate saata mehaaniku?**	kas te **saa**te **saaa**ta me**khaa**niku
Can you mend this puncture (fix this flat)?	**Kas te saate selle kummi ära parandada?**	kas te **saa**te **sel**le **kum**mi æra **pa**randada

☞ You're on the wrong road. — **Te olete valel tänaval.**
Go straight ahead. — **Minge otse edasi.**
It's down there on the left/right — **See on siit edasi vasakul/paremal**
opposite/behind ... — **vastas/taga ...**
next to/after ... — **kôrval/pärast ...**
north/south/east/west — **pôhjas/lôunas/idas/läänes**

Sightseeing *Vaatamisväärsused*

Where's the tourist office?	**Kus asub turismibüroo?**	kus **a**sub **tu**rismibew**roo**
What are the main points of interest?	**Mis on peamised vaatamisväärsused?**	mis on **pea**mised **vaaa**tamis**væææ r**sused
Is there an English speaking guide?	**Kas teil on inglise keelt kônelev giid?**	kas teil on **ing**lise keeelt **k**[e]nelev giiid
Where is/are the ...?	**Kus on ...?**	kus on
beach	**rand**	rand
botanical gardens	**botaanikaaed**	bo**taa**nika**aed**
castle	**kindlus**	**kind**lus
cathedral	**katedraal**	kate**draaal**
city centre	**linnakeskus**	**lin**na**kes**kus
exhibition	**näitus**	**næi**tus
harbour	**sadam**	**sa**dam
market	**turg**	turg
museum	**muuseum**	**muuu**seum
shops	**poed**	poed
zoo	**loomaaed**	**loo**ma**aed**
When does it open/close?	**Mis kell see avatakse/suletakse?**	mis kelll seee **a**vatakse/**su**letakse
How much is the entrance fee?	**Kui palju on sissepääs?**	kui **pal**yu on **sisssepæææs**

TELLING THE TIME, see page 77

Entertainment *Meelelahutus*

What's playing at the ... Theatre?	**Mida mängitakse ... teatris?**	**mi**da **mæn**gitakse … **teat**ris
How much are the seats?	**Kui palju maksab pilet?**	kui **pal**yu **mak**sab **pi**let
Would you like to go out with me tonight?	**Kas te sooviksite täna koos minuga õhtut veeta?**	kas te **soo**viksite **tæ**na kooos **mi**nuga ^{e}**kh**tut **veee**ta
Is there a discotheque in town?	**Kas linnas on disko?**	kas **lin**nas on **dis**ko
Would you like to dance?	**Kas te soovite tantsida?**	kas te **soo**vite **tant**sida
Thank you. It's been a wonderful evening.	**Tänan. Oli suurepärane õhtu.**	**tæ**nan **o**li **suu**repærane ^{e}**kh**tu

Shops, stores and services *Poed, kauplused ja teenused*

Where's the nearest ...?	**Kus on lähim ...?**	kus on **læ**him
bakery	**leivapood**	**lei**va**poood**
bookshop	**raamatukauplus**	**raa**matu**kaup**lus
butcher's	**lihakauplus**	**li**ha**kaup**lus
chemist's	**apteek**	**ap**teeek
dentist	**hambaarst**	**hambaarst**
department store	**kaubamaja**	**kau**ba**ma**ya
grocery	**toidupood**	**toi**du**poood**
hairdresser	**juuksur**	**yuuuk**sur
liquor store	**alkoholikauplus**	**al**koholi**kaup**lus
newsagent	**ajaleheäri**	**a**yalehe**æ**ri
post office	**postkontor**	**postkon**tor
souvenir shop	**suveniiripood**	suve**niiripoood**
supermarket	**suur toidukauplus (supermarket)**	suuur **toi**du**kaup**lus (**su**permarket)

General expressions *Üldväljendid*

Where's the main shopping area?	**Kus on peamine ostukeskus?**	kus on **pea**mine **os**tu**kes**kus
Do you have any ...?	**Kas teil on ...?**	kas teil on
Can you show me this/that?	**Palun näidake mulle seda?**	**pa**lun **næi**dake **mull**le **se**da

NUMBERS, see page 78/DATE,see page 77

Do you have anything ...?	**Kas teil on midagi ...?**	kas teil on **mi**dagi
cheaper/better	**odavamat/paremat**	**o**davamat/**pa**remat
larger/smaller	**suuremat/väiksemat**	**suu**remat/**væik**semat
Can I try it on?	**Kas ma vôin seda selga proovida?**	kas ma v[e]in **se**da **sel**ga **proo**vida
How much is this?	**Kui palju see maksab?**	kui **pal**yu seee **mak**sab
Please write it down.	**Palun kirjutage see üles.**	**pa**lun **kir**yutage seee **ew**les
No, I don't like it.	**Ei, mulle see ei meeldi.**	ei **mull**le seee ei **meeel**di
I'll take it.	**Ma vôtan selle.**	ma **v[e]**tan **sel**le
Do you accept credit cards?	**Kas ma saan maksta krediitkaardiga?**	kas ma saaan **maks**ta kre**diiitkaar**diga

black	**must**	must	orange	**oranž**	o**ranzh**
blue	**sinine**	**si**nine	red	**punane**	**pu**nane
brown	**pruun**	pruuun	yellow	**kollane**	**kol**lane
green	**roheline**	**ro**heline	white	**valge**	**val**ge

I want to buy ...	**Ma soovin osta ...**	ma **soo**vin **os**ta
aspirin	**aspiriini**	aspi**riii**ni
batteries	**patareisid**	**pa**tareisid
film	**filmi**	**fil**mi
newspaper	**ajalehte**	**a**ya**lekh**te
English/American	**inglise/ameerika**	**ing**lise/a**mee**rika
shampoo	**šampooni**	sham**pooo**ni
sun-tan cream	**päevituskreemi**	**pæe**vitus**kreee**mi
soap	**seep**	**seee**p
toothpaste	**hambapastat**	**ham**ba**pas**tat
a half-kilo of apples	**pool kilo ôunu**	poool **ki**lo **[e]u**nu
a litre of milk	**ühe liitri piima**	**ew**he **liii**tri **piii**ma
I'd like ... film for this camera.	**Ma sooviksin ... filmi selle fotoaparaadi jaoks.**	ma **soo**viksin … **fil**mi **sel**le **fo**to**a**paraadi yaoks
black and white/colour	**must-valget/värvi**	must **val**get/**vær**vi
I'd like a hair-cut.	**Ma sooviksin lasta juukseid lôigata.**	ma **soo**viksin **las**ta **yuuuk**seid **l[e]**igata

Souvenirs *Suveniirid*

laudlina	**laudl**ina	tablecloth
linikute komplekt	**li**nikute kom**plekt**	set of cloth napkins
merevaigust kee	**me**re**vai**gust keee	amber necklace
postkaardid	**postkaar**did	postcards
rahvariietes poiss	**rakh**var**ii**etes poisss	male doll in folk costume
rahvariietes tüdruk	**rakh**var**ii**etes **tewd**ruk	female doll in folk costume
rätik	**ræ**tik	scarf
savinôud	**sa**vin^{e}ud	pottery

At the bank *Pangas*

Where's the nearest bank/currency exchange office?	**Kus on lähim pank/ valuutavahetus?**	kus on **læ**him pank/ va**luu**ta**va**hetus
I want to change some dollars/pounds into kroons.	**Ma soovin vahetada dollareid/naelu kroonideks.**	ma **soo**vin **va**hetada **dol**lareid/**nae**lu **kroo**nideks
What's the exchange rate?	**Mis on vahetuskurss?**	mis on **va**hetus**kursss**

At the post office *Postkontoris*

I want to send this by ...	**Ma soovin selle saata ...**	ma **soo**vin **sel**le **saaa**ta
airmail	**lennupostiga**	**len**nu**pos**tiga
express	**kiirpostiga**	**kiiirpos**tiga
registered mail	**tähitud kirjana**	**tæ**hitud **kir**yana
I want ...2-kroon stamps.	**Ma soovin ... kahekroonilisi marke.**	ma **soo**vin ... **ka**he**kroo**nilisi **mar**ke
What's the postage for a letter to the United States?	**Kui palju maksab mark kirjale USA-sse?**	kui **pal**yu **mak**sab mark **kir**yale uu ess **aaa**sse
Is there any mail for me? My name is ...	**Kas mulle on posti? Mu nimi on ...?**	kas **mull**le on **pos**ti. mu **ni**mi on
Can I send a telegram/fax.	**Ma soovin saata telegrammi/faxi.**	ma **soo**vin **saaa**ta **te**legrammmi/**fak**si

NUMBERS, see page 78

Telephoning *Helistamine*

Where's the nearest public phone?	**Kus on lähim avalik telefon?**	kus on **læ**him **a**valik **te**lefon
May I use your phone?	**Kas ma tohin kasutada teie telefoni?**	kas ma **to**hin **ka**sutada **teie** **te**lefoni
Hello. This is ... speaking.	**Hallo. Siin räägib.**	**hal**lo. siiin **ræ**ægib
I want to speak to ...	**Ma soovin rääkida ...**	ma **soo**vin **ræææ**kida
When will he/she be back?	**Millal ta tagasi tuleb?**	**mil**lal ta **ta**gasi **tu**leb
Will you tell him/her that I called?	**Palun öelge talle, et ma helistasin?**	**pa**lun **øel**ge **tall**le et ma **he**listasin

Time and date *Kellaaeg ja kuupäev*

It's ...	**Kell on ...**	kelll on
five past one	**viis minutit üks läbi**	viiis **mi**nutit ewks **læ**bi
quarter past three	**veerand neli**	**vee**rand **ne**li
twenty past five	**kakskümmend minutit viis läbi**	**kaks**kewmmend **mi**nutit viiis **læ**bi
half-past seven	**pool kaheksa**	poool **ka**heksa
twenty-five to nine	**kahekümne viie minuti pärast üheksa**	**kahekewm**ne **viie** **mi**nuti **pæ**rast **ø**heksa
ten to ten	**kümne minuti pärast kümme**	**kewm**ne **mi**nuti **pæ**rast **kewm**me
noon	**kaksteist päeval/**	**kaks**teist **pæe**val
midnight	**kaksteist öösel**	**kaks**teist **øøø**sel
in the morning	**hommikul**	**hom**mikul
during the day	**päeval**	**pæe**val
in the evening	**õhtul**	^{e}**kh**tul
at night	**öösel**	**øøø**sel
yesterday	**eile**	**ei**le
today/tomorrow	**täna/homme**	**tæ**na/**homm**me
spring/summer	**kevad/suvi**	**ke**vad/**su**vi
autumn/winter	**sügis/talv**	**sew**gis/talv

Sunday	**pühapäev**	**pew**hapæev
Monday	**esmaspäev**	**es**maspæev
Tuesday	**teisipäev**	**tei**sipæev
Wednesday	**kolmapäev**	**kol**mapæev
Thursday	**neljapäev**	**nel**yapæev
Friday	**reede**	**reee**de
Saturday	**laupäev**	**lau**pæev
January	**jaanuar**	**yaaa**nuar
February	**veebruar**	**veee**bruar
March	**märts**	mærts
April	**aprill**	ap**rilll**
May	**mai**	mai
June	**juuni**	**yuu**ni
July	**juuli**	**yuu**li
August	**august**	**au**gust
September	**september**	sep**tem**ber
October	**oktoober**	ok**tooo**ber
November	**november**	no**vem**ber
December	**dètsember**	det**sem**ber

Numbers *Arvud*

0	**null**	nul'l'l'	11	**üksteist**	**ewks**teist
1	**üks**	ewks	12	**kaksteist**	**kaks**teist
2	**kaks**	kaks	13	**kolmteist**	**kolm**teist
3	**kolm**	kolm	14	**neliteist**	**ne**liteist
4	**neli**	**ne**li	15	**viisteist**	**viiis**teist
5	**viis**	viiis	16	**kuusteist**	**kuuus**teist
6	**kuus**	kuuus	17	**seitseteist**	**seit**seteist
7	**seitse**	**seit**se	18	**kaheksateist**	**ka**heksateist
8	**kaheksa**	**ka**heksa	19	**üheksateist**	**ew**heksateist
9	**üheksa**	ewheksa	20	**kakskümmend**	**kaks**kewmmend
10	**kümme**	**küm**me	21	**kakskümmend üks**	**kaks**kewmmend ewks

30	**kolmkümmend**	**kolm**kewmmend
40	**nelikümmend**	**ne**likewmmend
50	**viiskümmend**	**viiis**kewmmend
60	**kuuskümmend**	**kuuus**kewmmend
70	**seitsekümmend**	**seit**sekewmmend
80	**kaheksakümmend**	**ka**heksakewmmend
90	**üheksakümmend**	**ew**heksakewmmend

100/1,000	**sada/tuhat**	sada/**tu**hat
first/second	**esimene/teine**	esimene/**tei**ne
once/twice	**ükskord/kaks korda**	**ewks**kord/**kaks kor**da
three time	**kolm korda**	**kolm kor**da
a half/one third	**pool/veerand**	poool/**vee**rand

Emergency *Hädaolukord*

Call the police	**Kutsuge politsei**	**kut**suge polit**sei**
Get a doctor	**Kutsuge arst**	**kut**suge arst
HELP	**Appi**	**appp**i
I'm ill	**Ma olen haige**	ma **o**len **hai**ge
I'm lost	**Ma olen ära eksinud**	ma **o**len **æ**ra **ek**sinud
Leave me alone	**Jätke mind rahule**	**yæt**ke mind **ra**hule
STOP THIEF	**Peatage varas**	**pea**tage **va**ras
My ... has been stolen.	**Minu ... on ära varastatud.**	**mi**nu ... on **æ**ra **va**rastatud
I've lost my ...	**Ma olen oma ... ära kaotanud.**	ma **o**len **o**ma ... **æ**ra **kao**tanud
handbag/wallet	**käekoti/rahakoti**	**kæe**koti/**ra**hakoti
Where can I find a doctor who speaks English?	**Kust ma võiksin leida arsti, kes räägib inglise keelt?**	kust ma **v^{e}ik**sin **lei**da **ars**ti kes **ræ**ægib **ing**lise keeelt

Guide to Estonian pronunciation

Notes

1) Estonian sounds can be short, long and overlong. Short, long and overlong sounds are indicated respectively by single, double and triple phonetic symbols. Overlong **ü** is indicated by $\overline{\textbf{ew}}$

2) Some Estonian consonants (**t**, **d**, **n**, **l**, **s**) are palatalized in certain words. Palatalization means that a consonant sound is modified by adding a short y-type sound to it. Palatalization is not indicated in Estonian spelling but is marked in this book by an apostrophe after the palatalized sound.

3) There are many diphthongs in Estonian (**ai**, **ei**, **oi**, **ui**, **õi**, **äi**, **öi**, **üi**, **ae**, **oe**, **õe**, **äe**, **öe**, **ao**, **eo**, etc.). The first vowel of the diphthong is always pronounced short.

TELEPHONING, see page 77

4) Certain letters (**c**, **f**, **q**, **š**, **w**, **y**, **ž**) appear only in loan words or proper names.

5) The main stress appears on the first syllable. In addition, words of three or more syllables have one or more secondary stresses, normally on the third or fifth syllable.

Consonants

Letter	Approximate pronunciation	Symbol	Example	
c	like **ts** in ca**ts**	ts	**Celsius**	**tsel**sius
g	like **g** in **g**as	g	**mage**	**ma**ge
h	1) like **h** in hind	h	**hobune**	**ho**bune
	2) like **ch** in Scottish lo**ch**	kh	**laht**	lakht
j	like **y** in **y**et	y	**jalg**	yalg
q	like **k** in kit	k	**Malmqvist**	**malm**kvist
r	rolled, like a Scottish r	r	**raha**	**ra**ha
s	like **s** in **s**it	s	**saun**	saun
š	like **sh** in **sh**out	sh	**šampoon**	sham**pooon**
w	like **v** in **v**ine	v	**Wiklar**	**vik**lar
x	like **x** in e**x**tra	ks	**Max**	maks
z	1) like **z** in **z**oology	z	**zen**	zenn
	2) like **ts** in ca**ts**	ts	**Zürich**	**tsü**rix
ž	like **s** in plea**s**ure	zh	**garaaž**	ga**raaazh**

b, **d**, **f**, **k**, **l**, **m**, **n**, **p**, **s**, **t**, **v**, **x** and **y** are pronounced as in English

Vowels

a	like **a** in p**a**lm	a	**abi**	abi
e	like **e** in b**e**t	e	**edu**	edu
i	like **ee** in s**ee**	i	**ise**	ise
o	like **a** in b**a**ll	o	**odav**	odav
u	like **oo** in l**oo**t	u	**uni**	uni
ô	no English equivalent; try to say **e** in g**e**t, as your tongue, slightly rounded, is retracted	^{e}	**örn**	^{e}rn
ä	like **a** in s**a**t	æ	**ära**	æra
ö	like **u** in f**u**r	ø	**öö**	øø
ü	like French **u** in **u**ne; round your lips and try to say **ea** as in m**ea**n	ew	**üks**	ewks

Hungarian

Basic expressions *Alapvető kifejezések*

Yes/No.	**Igen/Nem.**	**ee**gæn/næm
Please.	**Kérem.**	**kay**ræm
Thank you.	**Köszönöm.**	**kur**surnurm
I beg your pardon?	**Tessék?**	**tæsh**shayk

Introductions Bevezetés

Good morning.	**Jó reggelt!**	y$\overline{\text{aw}}$ **ræ**ggælt
Good afternoon.	**Jó napot!**	y$\overline{\text{aw}}$ **no**ppawt
Good night.	**Jó éjszakát!**	y$\overline{\text{aw}}$ **ay**^{y}sokkaat
Good-bye.	**Viszontlátásra!**	**vee**sawntlaataashro
My name is …	**… vagyok.**	**vo**d^{y}awk
Pleased to meet you.	**Örülök, hogy megismerhetem.**	**ur**rewlurk hawd^{y} **mæ**geeshmærhætæm
What's your name?	**Hogy hívják?**	hawd^{y} **h$\overline{\text{ee}}$**vzaak
How are you?	**Hogy van?**	hawd^{y} von
Fine thanks.	**Köszönöm jól.**	**kur**surnurm y$\overline{\text{aw}}$l.
And you?	**És ön?**	aysh urn
Where do you come from?	**Honnan jött?**	**hawn**-non jurt
I'm from …	**…-ból/ből jöttem.**	…-b$\overline{\text{aw}}$l/b$\overline{\text{ur}}$l **yur**tæm
Australia	**Ausztrália**	**o-oo**straaleeo
Britain	**Nagy-Britannia**	**nod**^{y}-breetonneeo
Canada	**Kanada**	**ko**nnoddo
USA	**Egyesült Államok**	**æ**d^{y}æshewlt **aa**llomawk
I'm with my …	**… vagyok.**	… **vo**d^{y}awk
wife	**A feleségemmel**	o **fæ**læshaygæm-mæl
husband	**A férjemmel**	o **fayr**^{y}æm-mæl
family	**A családommal**	o **cho**llaadawm-mol
boyfriend	**A barátommal**	o **bo**rraatawm-mol
girlfriend	**A barátnőmmel**	o **bo**rraatn$\overline{\text{ur}}$m-mæl
I'm on my own.	**Egyedül vagyok.**	æd^{y}ædewl vod^{y}awk

GUIDE TO PRONUNCIATION, see page 95/EMERGENCIES, see page 94

I'm on holiday (vacation)/ on business.	**Szabadságon/ Üzleti úton vagyok.**	**so**bbodshaagawn/ **ew**zlætee o͞otawn **vod**^{y}awk

Questions *Kérdések*

When?/How?	**Mikor?/Hogy?**	**mee**kawr/hawd^{y}
What?/Why?	**Mi?/Miért?**	mee/meeayrt
Who?/Which?	**Ki?/Melyik?**	kee/**mæ**^{y}eek
Where are/is …?	**Hol van …?**	hawl von
Where can I get/ find …?	**Hol találok/ kaphatok …?**	hawl **to**llaalawk/ **ko**phottawk
How far?	**Milyen messze?**	**mee**^{y}æn **mæs**-sæ
How long?	**Mennyi ideig?**	**mæn**^{y}ee **ee**dæeeg
How much?	**Mennyi?**	**mæn**^{y}ee
Can you help me?	**Segítene?**	**shæ**ghe͞etænæ
I understand.	**Értem.**	**ayr**tæm
I don't understand.	**Nem értem.**	næm **ayr**tæm
Can you translate this for me?	**Lefordítaná ezt nekem?**	**læf**awrde͞etonnaa æst **næ**kæm
May I?	**Kaphatok?**	**ko**phottok
Can I have …?	**Kaphatok …?**	**ko**phottok
Do you speak English?	**Beszél angolul?**	**bæ**sayl **on**gawlool
I don't speak (much) Hungarian.	**Nem tudok (jól) magyarul.**	næm **too**dawk (ya͞wl) **mod**^{y}orrool

A few useful words *Néhány hasznos szó*

better/worse	**jobb/rosszabb**	yawb/**raws**-sob
big/small	**nagy/kicsi**	nod^{y}/**kee**chee
cheap/expensive	**olcsó/drága**	**awl**cha͞w/**draa**go
early/late	**korán/későn**	**kaw**raan/**kay**shu͞rn
good/bad	**jó/rossz**	ya͞w/rawss
hot/cold	**meleg/hideg**	**mæ**læg/**hee**dæg
near/far	**közel/távol**	**kur**zæl/**taa**vawl
right/wrong	**helyes/helytelen**	**hæ**^{y}æsh/**hæ**^{y}tælæn
vacant/occupied	**szabad/foglalt**	**so**bbod/**fawg**lolt

Hotel–Accommodation *Szálloda*

I've a reservation.	**Előre foglaltam szobát.**	æl**u̅r̅**ræ **faw**gloltom **saw**baat
Do you have any vacancies?	**Van szabad szobájuk?**	von **so**bbod **saw**baazook
I'd like a … room.	**Szeretnék egy … szobát.**	særætnayk æd^{y} … **saw**baat
single	**egyágyas**	æd^{y}aad^{y}osh
double	**kétágyas**	**kay**taad^{y}osh
with twin beds	**ikerággyal**	**ee**kæraad^{y}-d^{y}ol
with a double bed	**franciaággyal**	**fron**tseeo-aad^{y}-d^{y}ol
with a bath	**fürdőszobás**	**fewr**du̅r̅sawbaash
with a shower	**zuhanyzós**	**zoo**hon^{y}awya̅w̅sh
We'll be staying …	**… maradunk.**	**mo**rroddoonk
overnight only	**Csak egy éjszakára**	chok æd^{y} **ay**^{y}ssokkaaro
a few days	**Néhány napig**	**nay**haan^{y} **no**ppeeg
a week	**Egy hétig**	æd^{y} **hay**teeg
Is there a campsite near here?	**Van a közelben kemping?**	von o **kur**yælbæn **kæm**peeng

Decision *Döntés*

May I see the room?	**Láthatnám a szobát?**	**laa**thotnaam o **saw**baat
That's fine. I'll take it.	**Ez jó lesz. Kiveszem.**	æy ya̅w̅ læs. **kee**væsæm
No. I don't like it.	**Nem. Ez nem tetszik.**	næm. æy næm **tæ**tseek
It's too …	**Túl …**	to̅o̅l
dark/small	**sötét/kicsi**	**shur**tayt/**kee**chee
noisy	**zajos**	**zo**yawsh
Do you have anything …?	**Volna valami …?**	**vaw**lno **vo**llommee
better/bigger	**jobb/nagyobb**	yawb/**no**d^{y}awb
cheaper	**olcsóbb**	**awl**cha̅w̅b
quieter	**csendesebb**	**chæn**dæshæb
May I please have my bill?	**Kérem a számlámat.**	**kay**ræm o **saam**laamot
It's been a very enjoyable stay.	**Nagyon jól éreztük magunkat.**	**no**d^{y}awn ya̅w̅l ayræztewk **mo**ggoonkot

Eating out *Étzezés*

I'd like to reserve a table for 4.	**Négy fő részére szeretnék asztalt foglalni.**	nayd^{y} f$\overline{ur}$ **ray**sayræ særætnayk **os**tolt **faw**glolnee
We'll come at 8.	**Nyolc órakor jövünk.**	n^{y}awlts **$\overline{aw}$**rokkawr **yur**vewnk
I'd like breakfast/ lunch/dinner.	**Reggelizni/ ebédelni/ vacsorázni szeretnék.**	**ræg**-gæleeynee/ æbaydælnee/ **vo**chawraaznee særætnayk
What do you recommend?	**Mit ajánlana?**	meet **o**yaanlonno
Do you have vegetarian dishes?	**Van vegetariánus ételük?**	von **væ**ghætaareeaanoosh **ay**tælewk

Breakfast *Reggeli*

I'd like (an/some) …	**Kérnék …**	**kayr**nayk
bread/butter	**kenyeret/vajat**	**kæn**^{y}æræt/**vo**yot
cheese	**sajtot**	**shoy**tawt
egg	**tojást**	**taw**yaasht
ham	**sonkát**	**shawn**kaat
jam	**lekvárt**	**læk**vaart
rolls	**zsemlét**	**zhæm**layt

Starters *Előételek*

alföldi saláta	**ol**furldee **shol**laato	sausage salad
levest	**læ**væsht	soup
libamáj rizottó	**lee**bommaay **ree**zawtt$\overline{aw}$	goose-liver risotto
rántott sajt	**raan**tawt shoyt	fried cheese

Meat Hús

I'd like some …	**… kérek.**	**kay**ræk
beef	**Marhahúst**	**mor**hoh$\overline{oo}$sht
chicken/duck	**Csirke/Kacsa**	**chær**kæ/**ko**cho
lamb	**Bárányhúst**	**baa**raan^{y}h$\overline{oo}$sht
pork	**Sertéshúst**	**shær**taysh-sh$\overline{oo}$sht

NUMBERS, see page 94

bécsi szelet	**bay**chee **sælæt**	breaded veal escalope
borjúpörkölt	**baw**ryoopurrkurlt	veal stew
cigányrostélyos	**tsee**gaanyrawshtayyawsh	steak in a brown sauce
erdélyi tokány	**ær**dayyee **taw**kaany	braised beef strips
gulyás	**goo**yaash	rich beef stew
rablóhús nyárson	**rob**lawhoosh **ny aar**shawn	roasted meat on a skewer

baked/boiled	**sült/főtt**	shewlt/furt
fried/grilled	**sült/roston sült**	shewlt/**rawsh**tawn shewlt
stewed	**főtt**	furt
underdone (rare)	**félig átsütve**	**fay**leeg **aat**shewtvæ
medium	**közepesen kisütve**	**kur**zæpæshæn **kee**shewtvæ
well-done	**jól megsütve**	yawl **mæg**shewtvæ

Fish *Halételek*

pike	**csuka/fogas**	**choo**ko/**faw**gosh
sterlet	**kecsege**	**kæ**chægæ
trout	**pisztráng**	**pee**straang
csuka tejfölben sütve	**choo**ko **tæy**furlbæn **shewtt**væ	pike fried and served with sour cream
halfatányéros	**hol**fottaanyayrawsh	fish with tartar sauce
Rác ponty	raats pawnty	carp with potatoes and sour cream dressing

Vegetables *Zöldségek*

beans	**bab**	bob
cabbage	**káposzta**	**kaa**pawsto
mushroom	**gomba**	**gawm**bo
onion	**hagyma**	**hody**mo
peas	**zöldborsó**	**zurld**bawrshaw
potatoes	**burgonya**	**boor**gawnyo
tomato	**paradicsom**	**po**rroddeechawm
galuska	**go**llooshko	dumplings
gombapaprikás	**gawm**bo **po**preekaash	mushrooms in paprika sauce
kaszinó tojás	**ko**sseenaw **tawy**aash	egg mayonnaise
tejfeles bableves	**tæy**fælæsh **bob**lævæsh	bean soup

Fruit–dessert *Gyümölcsök–édességek*

apple	**alma**	**ol**mo
banana	**banán**	**bon**naan
lemon	**citrom**	**tsee**trawm
orange	**narancs**	**no**rronch
plum	**szilva**	**seel**vo
strawberries	**eper**	**æ**pær
dobostorta	**daw**bawshtawrto	chocolate cream cake
fagylalt	**fod^{y}**lolt	ice-cream
Gundel palacsinta	**goon**dæl **po**llocheento	flambéd pancake
kapros túrós rétes	**ko**prawsh **too**rawsh **ray**tæsh	curd strudel with dill
torta	**tawr**to	gateau

Drinks *Italok*

beer	**sör**	shurr
(hot) chocolate	**kakaó**	**ko**kkoaw
coffee	**kávé**	**kaa**vay
black/with milk	**fekete/tejjel**	**fæ**kætæ/**tæ^{y}**-yæl
fruit juice	**gyümölcslé**	**d^{y}ew**murlchlay
mineral water	**ásványvíz**	**aash**vaan^{y}veeyz
tea	**tea**	tæo
wine	**bor**	bawr
red/white	**vörös/fehér**	**vu**rrush/**fæ**hayr

Complaints and paying *Panaszok és fizetés*

This is too …	**Túl …**	tool
bitter/sweet	**keserű/édes**	**kæ**shærew/**ay**dæsh
That's not what I ordered.	**Nem ezt rendeltem.**	næm æst **ræn**dæltæm
I'd like to pay.	**Fizetni szeretnék.**	**fee**yætnee **sæ**rætnayk
I think you made a mistake in the bill.	**Azt hiszem, hibás a számla.**	ost **hee**sæm **hee**baash o **saam**lo
Is service included?	**A kiszolgálás benne van?**	o **kee**sawlgaalaash **bæn**næ von
We enjoyed it, thank you.	**Nagyon ízlett, köszönjük.**	**nod^{y}**awn **ee**ylæt **kur**surn^{y}ewk

NUMBERS, see page 94

Travelling around *Utazás*

Plane *Repülőgép*

Is there a flight to Pécs?	**Van repülőjárat Pécsre?**	von ræpewlu̅r̅yaarot **petch**ræ
What time do I check in?	**Mikor kell bejelentkezni?**	**mee**kawr kæl **bæ**^{y}ælæntkæynæm
I'd like to ... my reservation.	**Szeretném ... a jegyfoglalásomat.**	særætnaym ... o **yæd**^{y}fawglollaashawmot
cancel	**töröltetni**	**tur**rurltætnee
change	**megváltoztatni**	**mæg**vaaltawstotnee
confirm	**megerősíteni**	**mæg**æru̅r̅shē̄ē̄tænee

Train *Vonat*

I want a ticket to Szeged.	**Szegedre kérek egy jegyet.**	sægædræ **kay**ræk æd^{y} **yæd**^{y}æt
single (one-way)	**csak oda**	chok **aw**do
return (roundtrip)	**oda-vissza**	**aw**do-**vees**-so
first class	**első osztályra**	**æl**shu̅r̅ **aws**taayro
second class	**másodosztályra**	**maa**shaw**aws**taayro
How long does the journey (trip) take?	**Mennyi ideig tart az út?**	**mæn**^{y}ee **ee**dæeeg tort oz o̅o̅t
When is the ... train to Siófok?	**Mikor indul ... vonat Siófokra?**	**mee**kawr **een**dool ... **vaw**not **shee**a̅w̅fawkro
first	**az első**	oz **æl**shu̅r̅
next	**a következő**	o **kur**vætkæzu̅r̅
last	**az utolsó**	oz **oo**tawlsha̅w̅
Is this the right train to Eger?	**Ez a vonat megy Egerbe?**	æz o **vaw**not mæd^{y} **æ**gærbæ

Bus—Tram (streetcar) *Autóbusz—Villamos*

What bus do I take to the centre/downtown?	**Melyik busz megy a városközpontba?**	**mæ**^{y}eek boos mæd^{y} o **vaa**rawshkurspawntbo
How much is the fare to ...?	**Mennyibe kerül a jegy ...?**	**mæn**^{y}eebæ **kæ**rewl o yæd^{y}
Will you tell me when to get off?	**Szólna mikor kell leszállnom?**	**sa̅w̅l**no **mee**kawr kæl **læ**saalnawm

TELLING THE TIME, see page 93/NUMBERS, see page 94

Taxi *Taxi*

How much is it to …?	**Mennyibe kerül …?**	**mæn^{y}**eebæ **kærew**
Take me to this address.	**Kérem, vigyen el erre a címre.**	**kay**ræm **veed^{y}**æn æl **ær**-ræ o **tseem**ræ
Please stop here.	**Kérem, itt álljon meg.**	**kay**ræm eet **aal**yawn mæg

Car hire *Autóbérlés*

I'd like to hire (rent) a car.	**Szeretnék bérelni egy autót.**	**sæ**rætnayk **bay**rælnee æd^{y} **o-oo**taw
I'd like it for a day/week.	**Egy napra/Egy hétre szeretném.**	æd^{y} **no**pro/æd^{y} **hay**træ **sæ**rætnaym
Where's the nearest filling station?	**Hol a legközeleb bi benzinkút?**	hawl o **læg**kurzælæb-bee **bæn**zeenkoot
Full tank, please.	**Tele kérem.**	**tæ**læ **kay**ræm
Give me … litres of petrol (gasoline).	**… liter benzint kérek.**	**lee**tær **bæn**zeent **kay**ræk
How do I get to …?	**Hogy jutok el … -ba/-be?**	hawd^{y} **yoo**tawk æl … -bo/-bæ
I've had a breakdown at …	**… nál/-nél elromlott a kocsim.**	… -naal/-nayl **æl**rawmlawt o **kaw**chem
Can you send a mechanic?	**Tudna küldeni egy szerelőt?**	**tood**no **kewll**dænee æd^{y} **sæ**rælur
Can you mend this puncture (fix this flat)?	**Meg tudná javítani ezt a defektes gumit?**	mæg **tood**naa **yo**vveetonnee est o **dæ**fæktæsh **goo**meet

☞ You're on the wrong road.	**Rossz irányban halad.** ☜
Go straight ahead.	**Egyenesen tovább.**
It's down there on the …	**Arra lefelé van …**
left/right	**balra/jobbra**
opposite/behind …	**… szemben/mögött**
next to/after …	**… mellett/után**
north/south/east/west	**észak/dél/kelet/nyugat**

NUMBERS, see page 94

Sightseeing *Városnézés*

Where's the tourist office?	**Hol van az utazási iroda?**	hawl von oz **oo**tozaashee **ee**rawdo
Is there an English-speaking guide?	**Van angolul beszélő idegenvezető?**	von **on**gawlool **bæ**saylur **ee**dægænvæzætur
Where is/are the …?	**Hol van/vannak …?**	hawl von/**von**-nok
beach	**a strand**	o shtrond
castle	**a vár**	o vaar
church	**a templom**	o **tæm**plawm
city centre/downtown	**a városközpont**	o **vaa**rawshkurzpawnt
harbour	**a kikötő**	o **kee**kurtur
market	**a piac**	o peeots
museum	**a múzeum**	o **moo**zæoom
shops	**az üzletek**	oz **ewz**lætæk
zoo	**az állatkert**	oz **aa**lotkært
When does it open/close?	**Mikor nyit/zár?**	**mee**kawr n^{y}eet/zaar
How much is the entrance fee?	**Mennyi a belépő?**	**mæn**^{y}ee o **bæ**laypur

Entertainment *Szórakozás*

What's playing at the … Theatre?	**Mi megy a … Színházban?**	mee mæd^{y} o … **see**haazbon
How much are the seats?	**Mennyibe kerül egy jegy?**	**mæn**^{y}eebæ **kæ**rewl æd^{y} yæd^{y}
I want to reserve 2 tickets for the show on Friday evening.	**Két jegyet szeretnék a péntek esti előadásra.**	kayt **yæd**^{y}æt **sæ**rætnayk o **payn**tæk **æsh**tee **æl**urddaashro
Would you like to go out with me tonight?	**Eljönne velem ma este valahová?**	**æl**yurn-næ **væ**læm mo **æsh**tæ **vol**lohawvo
Is there a discotheque in town?	**Van diszkó a városban?**	von **dees**kaw **vaa**rawshbon
Would you like to dance?	**Van kedve táncolni?**	von **kæd**væ **taan**tsawlnee
Thank you. It's been a wonderful evening.	**Köszönöm, csodálatos este volt.**	**kur**surnum **chaw**daalotawsh **æsh**tæ vawlt

DAYS OF THE WEEK, see page 93

Shops, stores and services *Üzletek–szolgáltatások*

Where's the nearest …?	**Hol a legközelebbi …?**	hawl o **læg**kurzælæb-bee
bakery	**pékség**	**payk**shayg
bookshop/store	**könyvesbolt**	**kurn^y**væshbawlt
butcher's	**hentes**	**hæn**tæsh
chemist's/drugstore	**gyógyszertár**	**d^{y}aw**d^{y}særtaar
dentist	**fogorvos**	**faw**gawrvawsh
grocery	**élelmiszerbolt**	**ay**lælmeesærbawlt
hairdresser	**fodrászat**	**faw**draasot
newsagent	**újságos**	**$\overline{oo}$y**shaagawsh
post office	**posta**	**pawsh**to
souvenir shop	**souvenir bolt**	**soo**væneer bawlt
supermarket	**ABC-áruház**	**aa**baytsay-**aa**roohaaz
toilets	**W.C.**	**vay**tsay

General expressions *Általános kifejezések*

Where's the main shopping area?	**Hol a vásárló negyed?**	hawl o **vaa**shaarl$\overline{aw}$ **næ**d^{y}æd
Do you have any …?	**Van …?**	von
Do you have anything …?	**Van valami …?**	von **vo**lomee
cheaper/better	**olcsóbb/jobb**	**awl**ch$\overline{aw}$b/y$\overline{aw}$b
larger/smaller	**nagyobb/kisebb**	**no**d^{y}awb/**kee**shæb
Can I try it on?	**Felpbóbálhatom?**	**fæl**pr$\overline{aw}$baalhottawm
How long will it take?	**Mennyi ideig tart?**	**mæ**n^{y}ee **ee**dæeeg tort
How much is this?	**Mennyibe kerül?**	**mæ**n^{y}eebæ **kæ**rewl
Please write it down.	**Kérem, írja le.**	**kay**ræm **eer**yo læ
No, I don't like it.	**Nem, nem tetszik.**	næm næm **tæ**tseek
I'll take it.	**Megveszem.**	**mæg**væsæm
Do you accept credit cards?	**Hitelkártyát elfogadnak?**	**hee**tælkaart^{y}aat **æl**fawgodnok
Can you order it for me?	**Meg tudná rendelni?**	mæg **tood**naa **ræn**dælnee

NUMBERS, see page 94

black	**fekete**	fækætæ	white	**fehér**	fæhayr
blue	**kék**	kayk	yellow	**sárga**	**shaar**go
brown	**barna**	borno	dark…	**sötét…**	**shur**taet
green	**zöld**	zurld	light…	**világos…**	**we**laagawsh
red	**piros**	**pee**rawsh			

I want to buy …	**… szeretnék venni.**	særætnayk **væn**-nee
aspirin	**Aszpirint**	**os**peereent
batteries	**Elemet**	ælæmæt
bottle opener	**Sörnyitót**	**shurrn**ʸeetaw
newspaper	**Újságot**	**oo**yshaag
English/American	**angol/amerikai**	**on**gawl/omæreekoee
shampoo	**Sampont**	**shom**pawnt
sun-tan cream	**Napozókrémet**	**no**ppawzawkraymæt
soap	**Szappant**	**so**ppont
toothpaste	**Fogkrémet**	**fawg**kraymæt
a half-kilo of apples	**Egy fél kiló almát**	ædʸ fayl **keelawol**maat
a litre of milk	**Egy liter tejet**	ædʸ **lee**tær **tæ**yæt
I'd like … film for this camera.	**Ehhez a fényképezőgéphez kérek … filmet.**	**æh**-hæz o **fa**nyʸkaypæyugayphæz **kay**ræk … **feel**mæt
black and white	**fekete-fehér**	**fæ**kætæ-fæhayr
colour	**színes**	**see**næsh
I'd like a hair-cut.	**Hajvágást kérek.**	**hoy**vaagaasht kayræk

Souvenirs *Souvenir*

barackpálinka	**bor**rotskpaaleenko	apricot brandy
herendi porcelán	**hæ**rændee **paw**rtsælaan	Herend china
hímzett asztelterítő	**heem**zæt **os**toltæreetur	embroidered tablecloth
hímzett blúz	**heem**zæt blooz	embroidered blouse
tokaji bor	**taw**koyee bawr	Tokay wine

At the bank *A bankban*

Where's the nearest currency exchange office/bank?	**Hol a legközelebbi valutabeváltó hely/bank?**	hawl o **læg**kurzælæb-bee **vo**llootobbævaaltaw hæʸ/bonk

HUNGARIAN

Magyar

I want to change some dollars/pounds into forint.	**Dollárt/Fontot szeretnék beváltani forintra.**	**dawl**-laart/**fawn**tawt særætnayk **bæ**vaaltonnee **faw**reentro
What's the exchange rate?	**Mi az átváltási árfolyam?**	mee oz **aat**vaaltaashee **aar**faw^{y}om

At the post office *A postán*

I want to send this by …	**Szeretném ezt … feladni.**	særætnaym æst … **fæ**odnee
airmail	**légipostán**	**lay**gheepawshtaan
express	**expressz**	**æks**præss
I want …-forint stamps.	**Egy … forintos bélyeget kérek.**	æd^{y} … **faw**reentawsh **bay**^{y}ægæt **kay**ræk
What's the postage for a postcard to America?	**Hány forintos bélyeg kell egy képeslapra az Amerikába?**	haan^{y} **faw**reentawsh **bay**^{y}æg kæl æd^{y} **kay**pæshlopro oz **o**mæreekaabo
Is there any mail for me? My name is …	**Van a számomra posta? … vagyok.**	von o **saa**mawmro **pawsh**to. … **vod**^{y}awk

Telephoning *Telefonálás*

Where's the nearest public phone?	**Hol van a legközelebbi telefonfülke?**	hawl von o **læg**kurzælæb-bee **tæ**læfawnfewlkæ
May I use your phone?	**Használhatom a telefonját?**	**hos**naalhottawm o **tæ**læfawnyaat
Hello. This is … speaking.	**Halló, itt … beszél.**	**hol-**lāweet … **bæ**sayl
I want to speak to …	**…-val/-vel szeretnék beszélni.**	…-vol/-væl **sær**ætnayk **bæ**saylnee
When will he/she be back?	**Mikor jön vissza?**	**mee**kawr yurn **vees**-so
Will you tell him/her that I called?	**Kérem, mondja meg neki, hogy kerestem.**	**kay**ræm **mawn**dyo mæg **næ**kee hawd^{y} **kæ**ræshtæm

NUMBERS, see page 94

Time and date *Idő és dátum*

It's …	**… van.**	… von
five past one	**egy óra öt perc**	ædʸ aw urt pærts
quarter past three	**negyed négy**	**næ**dʸæd naydʸ
twenty past five	**öt óra húsz perc**	urt aw hoos
half-past seven	**fél nyolc**	fayl nʸawlts
twenty-five to nine	**öt perccel múlt fél kilenc**	urt **pært**sæl moolt fayl **kee**lænts
ten to ten	**tíz perc múlva tíz**	tee pærts **moo**lvo tee
twelve o'clock noon/midnight	**tizenkét óra dél/éjfél**	**tee**zænkay aw del/**ey**fel
in the morning	**reggel**	**ræg**gæl
during the day	**napközben**	**nop**kurzbæn
in the evening/at night	**este/éjszaka**	**æsh**tæ/**ay**sokko
yesterday/today	**tegnap/ma**	**tæg**nop/mo
tomorrow	**holnap**	**hawl**nop
spring/summer	**tavasz/nyár**	**tov**vos/nʸaar
autumn/winter	**ősz/tél**	us/tayl

Sunday	**vasárnap**	**vosh**aarnop
Monday	**hétfő**	**hayt**fur
Tuesday	**kedd**	kæd
Wednesday	**szerda**	**sær**do
Thursday	**csütörtök**	**tshew**turrturk
Friday	**péntek**	**payn**tæk
Saturday	**szombat**	**sawm**bot
January	**január**	**yon**nooaar
February	**február**	**fæ**brooaar
March	**március**	**maar**tseeoosh
April	**április**	**aa**preeleesh
May	**május**	**maa**yoosh
June	**június**	**yoo**neeoosh
July	**július**	**yoo**leeoosh
August	**augusztus**	**o-oo**goostoosh
September	**szeptember**	**sæp**tæmbær
October	**október**	**awk**tawbær
November	**november**	**naw**væmbær
December	**december**	**dæ**tsæmbær

Numbers *Számok*

0	**nulla**	**nool**lo	11	**tizenegy**	**tee**zænæd^{y}
1	**egy**	æd^{y}	12	**tizenkettő**	**tee**zænkætt$\overline{\text{ur}}$
2	**kettő**	**kæt**t$\overline{\text{ur}}$	13	**tizenhárom**	**tee**zænhaarawm
3	**három**	**haa**rawm	14	**tizennégy**	**tee**zænnayd^{y}
4	**négy**	nayd^{y}	15	**tizenöt**	**tee**zænurt
5	**öt**	urt	16	**tizenhat**	**tee**zænhot
6	**hat**	hot	17	**tizenhét**	**tee**zænhayt
7	**hét**	hayt	18	**tizennyolc**	**tee**zænn^{y}awlts
8	**nyolc**	n^{y}awlts	19	**tizenkilenc**	**tee**zænkeelænts
9	**kilenc**	**kee**lænts	20	**húsz**	h$\overline{\text{oo}}$s
10	**tíz**	te$\overline{\text{e}}$	21	**huszonegy**	**hoo**sawnæd^{y}

30	**harminc**	**hor**meents
40	**negyven**	**næ**d^{y}væn
50	**ötven**	**urt**væn
60	**hatvan**	**hot**von
70	**hetven**	**hæt**væn
80	**nyolcvan**	**n^{y}awlts**von
90	**kilencven**	**kee**læntsvæn
100/1,000	**száz/ezer**	saaz/**æ**zær
first/second	**első/második**	**æl**sh$\overline{\text{ur}}$/**maa**shawdeek
once/twice	**egyszer/kétszer**	**æd^{y}**sær/**kayt**sær
a half	**egy fél**	æd^{y} fayl

Emergency *Szükséghelyzetek*

Call the police	**Hívja a rendőrséget**	**h$\overline{\text{ee}}$**yo o **ræn**d$\overline{\text{ur}}$sshaygæt
Get a doctor	**Hívjon orvost**	**h$\overline{\text{ee}}$**yawwn **awr**vawsht
Go away	**Távozzék**	**taa**vawzzayk
HELP	**SEGÍTSÉG**	**shæ**gh$\overline{\text{ee}}$shayg
I'm ill	**Beteg vagyok**	**bæ**tæg **vo**d^{y}awk
I'm lost	**Eltévedtem**	**æl**tayvædtæm
STOP THIEF	**FOGJÁK MEG, TOLVAY**	**faw**gyaak **mæg** **tawl**voy
My … has been stolen.	**Ellopták …**	**æl**lawptaak
I've lost my …	**Elvesztettem …**	**æl**væstættæm
handbag	**a kézitáskámat**	o **kay**zeetaashkaamot

TELEPHONING, see page 92

passport	**az útlevelemet**	oz **o͞ot**lævælæmæt
luggage	**a csomagomat**	o **chaw**moggawmot
wallet	**a pénztárcámat**	o **paynz**taartsaamot
Where can I find a doctor who speaks English?	**Hol találok angolul beszélő orvost?**	hawl **to**llaalawk **on**gawlool **bæ**saylu͞r **awr**vawsht

Guide to Hungarian pronunciation *Kiejtés*

Consonants

Letter	Approximate pronunciation	Symbol	Example	
c	like **ts** in ne**ts**	ts	**arc**	orts
cs	like **ch** in **ch**ap	ch	**kocsi**	**kaw**chee
g	always as in **g**o, never as in **g**in	g/gh	**gáz** **régi**	gaaz **ray**ghee
gy	like **di** in me**di**um, said fairly quickly	d^{y}	**ágy**	aad^{y}
j	like **y** in **y**es	y/^{y}	**jég**	yayg
ly	like **y** in **y**es	y/^{y}	**Károly**	**kaa**raw^{y}
ny	quite like **ni** in o**ni**on	n^{y}	**hány**	haan^{y}
r	pronounced with the tip of the tongue, like Scottish **r**	r	**ír**	e͞er
s	like **sh** in **sh**oot	sh	**saláta**	**sho**llaato
sz	like **s** in **s**o	s/ss	**szó, ész**	sa͞w ayss
ty	like **t y** in a fast pronunciation of pu**t y**our	t^{y}	**atya**	**o**t^{y}o
zs	like **s** in plea**s**ure	zh	**zsír**	zhe͞er

b, d, f, h, k, l, m, n, p, v, x, z as in English

Vowels

a	quite like **o** in n**o**t (British pronunciation)	o	**hat**	hot
á	like the explanation "**ah**!"	aa	**rág**	raag
e	quite like **e** in y**e**s, but with the mouth a little more open, i.e. a sound between **e** in yes and **a** in hat	æ	**te**	tæ

é	like **ay** in s**ay**, but a pure vowel, not a diphthong	ay	**mér**	mayr
i	like **ee** in f**ee**t (short)	ee	**hideg**	**hee**dæg
í	like **ee** in s**ee** (long)	e͞e	**míg**	me͞eg
o	quite like **aw** in s**aw** (British pronunciation) but shorter	aw	**bot**	bawt
ó	like **aw** in s**aw**, but with the tongue higher in the mouth	a͞w	**fotó**	**faw**ta͞w
ö	like **ur** in f**ur**, but without any **r**-sound and with rounded lips	ur	**örök**	**ur**rurk
ő	like **ur** in f**ur,** but without any **r**-sound, and with the lips tightly rounded	u͞r	**lő**	lu͞r
u	as in the British pronunciation of p**u**ll	oo	kulcs	koolch
ú	like **oo** in f**oo**d	o͞o	**kút**	ko͞ot
ü	as in French **u**ne; round your lips and try to say **ee**	ew	**körül**	**kurr**ewl
ű	the same sound as **ü**, but long and with the lips more tightly rounded	e͞w	**fűt**	fe͞wt

Note:

1) There are no silent letters in Hungarian, so all letters must be pronounced. This means that double consonants are pronounced long, though a double consonant appearing at the end of a word is pronounced short.
   Vowels standing next to each other are pronounced separately and do not combine to form diphthongs. The only exception is **j,** which sometimes combines with the preceding vowel and is then pronounced like a fleeting **y**, as in bo**y**.
2) When two or more consonants stand next to each other, the last one can influence the pronunciation of the others. If it is "voiceless" (**c, f, k, p, s, sz, t, ty**), it will make a preceding "voiced" consonant (**dz, v, g, b, zs, z, d, gy**) into a "voiceless" one, and vice versa.
3) In Hungarian, stress falls in the first syllable of each word.

Latvian

Basic expressions *Pamatizteicieni*

Yes/No.	**Jā/Nē.**	jah/neh
Please.	**Lūdzu.**	**looh**dzoo
Thank you.	**Paldies.**	**pal**deeass
I beg your pardon?	**Atvainojiet?**	**at**vainwa-yeeat

Introductions *Iepazīšanās*

Good morning.	**Labrīt.**	**lab**reet
Good afternoon.	**Labdien.**	**lab**deean
Good night.	**Ar labu nakti.**	ar **la**boo **na**kti
Good-bye.	**Uz redzēšanos.**	ooz **re**dzehshanwas
My name is ….	**Mani sauc ...**	**ma**ni sowts
What's your name?	**Kā jūs sauc?**	kah yoohss sowts
How are you?	**Kā jums klājas?**	kah yoomss **klah**yass
Fine thanks.	**Paldies, labi.**	**pal**deeass **la**bi
And you?	**Un jums?**	oon yoomss
Where do you come from?	**No kurienes jūs esat?**	nwa **koo**reeanes yoohss a'sat
I'm from …	**Es esmu no...**	ess **a'**smoo nwa
Australia	**Austrālijas**	**ow**strahliyas
Britain	**Lielbritānijas**	**leeal**britahniyas
Canada	**Kanādas**	**ka**nahdas
USA	**Amerikas Savienotām Valstīm**	amehrikas **sa**veea-nwatahm **val**steem
I'm with my …	**Es esmu kopā ar ...**	ess **a'**smoo **kwa**pah ar **sa**voo
wife/husband	**sievu/vīru**	**seea**voo/**vee**roo
family	**ģimeni**	**dyi**meni
boyfriend	**draugu**	**drow**goo
girlfriend	**draudzeni**	**drow**dzeni
I'm on my own.	**Es esmu viens pats (viena pati).**	ess **a'**smoo **veea**nss patss (**veea**na **pa**ti)
I'm on holiday (vacation)/ on business.	**Es esmu atvaļinājumā/ komandējumā.**	ess **a'**smoo **at**valyi-nahyoomah/ **ko**mandehyoomah

GUIDE TO PRONUNCIATION, see page 111/EMERGENCIES, see page 110

Questions *Jautājumi*

When?/How?	**Kad?/Cik?**	kad/tsik
What?/Why?	**Kas?/Kādēļ?**	kas/**kah**dehl'
Who?/Which?	**Kas?/Kurš?**	kas/koorsh
Where is/are …?	**Kur ir?**	koor ir
Where can I get/find …?	**Kur es varu dabūt/atrast ...?**	koor ess **va**roo **da**booht/**at**rast
How far?	**Cik tālu?**	tsik **tah**loo
How long?	**Cik ilgi?**	tsik **il**gi
How much?	**Cik daudz?**	tsik dowdz
May I?	**Vai es drīkstu?**	vai ess **dreek**stoo
Can I have …?	**Vai es varu ...?**	vai ess **va**roo
Can you help me?	**Vai jūs varat man palīdzēt?**	vai yoohss **va**rat man **pa**leedzeht
I understand.	**Es saprotu.**	ess **sa**prwatoo
I don't understand.	**Es nesaprotu.**	ess **ne**saprwatoo
Can you translate this for me?	**Vai jūs varat man šo pārtulkot?**	vai yoohss **va**rat man shwa **pahr**toolkwat
Do you speak English?	**Vai jūs runājat angliski?**	vai yoohss **roo**nahyat **an**gliski
I don't speak Latvian.	**Es nerunāju latviski.**	ess **ne**roonayoo **lat**viski

A few useful words *Daži noderīgi vārdiņi*

beautiful/ugly	**skaists/neglīts**	skaists/negleets
better/worse	**labāks/sliktāks**	**la**bahks/**slik**tahks
big/small	**liels/mazs**	leealss/mas
cheap /expensive	**lēts/dārgs**	le'tss/dahrgss
early/late	**agrs/vēls**	agrss/ve'lss
good/bad	**labs/slikts**	labss/sliktss
hot/cold	**karsts/auksts**	karstss/owkstss
near/far	**tuvs/tāls**	toovss/tahlss
old/young	**vecs/jauns**	va'tss/yownss
right/wrong	**pareizs/nepareizs**	**pa**reyss/**ne**pareyss
vacant/occupied	**brīvs/aizņemts**	breevss/**aiz**nya'mts

Hotel—Accommodation *Viesnīca—Apmešanās*

I've a reservation.	**Es esmu rezervējis (-jusi).**	ess **a**'smoo **re**zervehyis (-yoosi)
We've reserved two rooms.	**Mēs esam rezervējuši (-šas) divas istabas.**	mehss **a**'sam **re**zervehyooshi (-shas) **di**vass **is**tabas
Do you have any vacancies?	**Vai jums ir brīvas istabas?**	vai yoomss ir **bree**vass **is**tabas
I'd like a … room.	**Es vēlos ... istabu.**	ess **ve**'lwass ... **is**taboo
single	**vienai personai**	**veea**nai **pa**'rswanai
double	**divām personām**	**di**vahm **pa**'rswanahm
with twin beds	**ar divām gultām**	ar **di**vahm **gool**tahm
with a double bed	**ar dubultgultu**	ar **doo**booltgooltoo
with a bath	**ar vannas istabu**	ar **va**nnass **is**taboo
with a shower	**ar dušu**	ar **doo**shoo
We'll be staying …	**Mēs paliksim ...**	mehss **pa**liksim
overnight only	**tikai vienu nakti**	**ti**kai **veea**noo **nak**ti
a few days	**dažas dienas**	**da**zhass **dee**nass
a week (at least)	**nedēļu (vismaz)**	**ne**dehlyoo (**vis**maz)

Decision *Lēmumi*

May I see the room?	**Vai es varu redzēt istabu?**	vai ess **va**roo **re**dzeht **is**taboo
That's fine.	**Man patīk.**	man **pa**teek.
I'll take it.	**Es to ņemšu.**	ess twa **nyem**shoo
No. I don't like it.	**Nē, man tā nepatīk.**	neh man tah **ne**pateek
It's too …	**Tā ir par ...**	tah ir par
dark/small	**tumšu/mazu**	**toom**shoo/**ma**zoo
noisy	**trokšņainu**	**trwak**shnyainoo
Do you have anything …?	**Vai jums ir kāda ...?**	vai yoomss ir **kah**da
better/bigger	**labāka/lielāka**	**la**bahka/**leea**lahka
cheaper/quieter	**lētāka/klusāka**	**le**'tahka/**kloo**sahka
May I please have my bill?	**Lūdzu rēķinu.**	**looh**dzoo **reh**tyinoo
It's been a very enjoyable stay.	**Paldies, bija ļoti patīkami.**	**pal**deeass **bi**ya **lywa**ti **pa**teekami

Eating out *Restorāni un kafejnīcas*

I'd like to reserve a table for 4.	**Es vēlos rezervēt galdu četrām personām.**	ess **ve**'lwass **re**zerveht **gal**doo **chet**rahm **pa**'rswanahm
We'll come at 8.	**Mēs būsim astoņos.**	mehss **boo**sim **a**stwanywas
I'd like breakfast/ lunch/dinner.	**Es vēlos brokastis/pusdienas/ vakariņas.**	ess **ve**'lwass **brwa**-kastis/**poo**zdeeanas **va**karinyas
What do you recommend?	**Ko jūs ieteicat?**	kwa yoohss **eea**teytsat?
Do you have vegetarian dishes?	**Vai jums ir veģetārie ēdieni?**	vai yoomss ir **ve**dyetahreea **eh**deeani

Breakfast *Brokastis*

I'd like …	**Es vēlos ...**	ess **ve**'lwass...
bread/butter	**maizi/sviestu**	**mai**zi/**svee**astoo
cheese	**sieru**	**seea**roo
egg/ham	**olu/šķiņķi**	**wa**loo/**shtyin**'tyi
jam	**ievārījumu**	**eea**vahreeyoomoo
rolls	**maizīti**	**mai**zeeti

Starters *Priekšēdieni*

marinētas sēnes	**ma**rina'tas **seh**ness	pickled mushrooms
nēģi	**neh**dyi	lamprey
šprotes	**shprwa**tess	smoked sprats
žāvēts lasis	**zhah**ve'ts **la**siss	smoked salmon
žāvēts zutis	**zhah**ve'ts **zoo**tiss	smoked eel

baked	**krāsnī cepts**	**krahs**nee tsa'pts
boilled/fried	**vārīts/cepts**	**vah**reets/tsa'pts
grilled	**grillēts**	**gril**le'tss
roast	**krāsnī cepts**	**krahs**nee tsa'pts
stewed	**sautēts**	**sau**ta'tss
underdone (rare)	**pajēls**	**pa**-ye'lss
medium	**vidējs**	**vi**dehyss
well-done	**labi izcepts**	**la**bi **iz**tsa'pts

NUMBERS, see page 109

Meat *Gaļa*

I'd like some …	**Es vēlos ...**	ess **ve**'lwass
beef	**vēršgaļu**	**vehr**shgalyoo
chicken/duck	**vistu/pīli**	**vis**too/**pee**li
lamb	**jērgaļu**	**ye'r**galyoo
pork	**cūkgaļu**	**tsoohk**galyoo
veal	**teļgaļu**	**tel'**galyoo
karbonāde	**kar**bonahde	pork chop
kotletes	**kot**letess	meat balls
mežcūkas cepetis	**mezh**tsoohkas **tse**petis	wild boar steak
sautēta vista	**sow**te'ta **vis**ta	braised chicken
sīpolu sitenis	**see**pwaloo **si**tenis	steak (beef) with onions
teļgaļas cepetis	**tel'**galyas **tse**petis	roast veal

Fish and seafood *Zivis un zivju ēdieni*

cepts lasis	tsa'ptss **la**siss	fried/grilled salmon
cepta forele	**tsa'**pta **fo**rele	fried/grilled trout
cepta bute	**tsa'**pta **boo**te	fried plaice
sālīta siļķe	**sah**leeta **sil'**tye	salt herring
cepta karpa	**tsa'**pta **kar**pa	fried carp
zivju kotletes	**ziv**yoo **kot**letes	fish cakes
līdaka želējā	**leeh**daka **zhe**lehyah	pike in jelly

Vegetables *Dārzeņi/saknes*

beans	**pupiņas**	**poo**pinyass
cabbage	**kāposti**	**kah**pwasti
carrots	**burkāni**	**boor**kahni
mushroom	**sēnes**	**seh**ness
onion	**sīpoli**	**see**pwali
peas	**zirņi**	**zir**nyi
potatoes	**kartupeļi**	**kar**toopelyi
tomato	**tomāti**	**to**mahti
burkānu pankūkas	**boor**kahnoo **pan**kookass	carrot pancakes
omlete ar sēnēm	**om**lete ar **seh**nehm	mushroom omelet
omlete ar sieru	**om**lete ar **see**aroo	cheese omelet
sautētas saknes ar mērci	**sow**te'tas **sak**ness ar **mehr**tsi	stewed vegetables with cream sauce

Fruit & dessert *Augļi & saldēdieni*

apple/banana	**āboli/banāni**	**ah**bwali/**ba**nahni
plum/lemon	**plūmes/citroni**	**plooh**mess/**tsit**rwani
orange/strawberries	**apelsīni/zemenes**	**a**pelseeni/**ze**menes
ābolkūka	**ah**bwalkoohka	apple-tart
buberts	**boo**bertss	egg mousse with fruit sauce
maizes zupa	**mai**zess **zoo**pa	rye bread soup with fruit and spices
saldējums	**sal**dehyooms	ice-cream
torte	**tor**te	gateau

Drinks *Dzērieni*

beer	**alus**	**a**looss
(hot) chocolate	**(karsts) kakao**	(karsts) ka**ka**o
coffee	**kafija**	**ka**fiya
black	**melna**	**ma'**lna
with milk	**ar pienu**	ar **pee**anoo
fruit juice	**augļu sula**	**ow**glyoo **soo**la
mineral water	**minerālūdens**	**mi**nerahloodens
tea	**tēja**	**teh**ya
wine	**vīns**	veenss
red/white	**sarkanvīns/ baltvīns**	**sar**kanveens/ **balt**veenss
vodka	**degvīns**	**da'g**veenss

Complaints and paying *Sūdzības un maksājumi*

This is too salty/sweet.	**Tas (tā) ir par sālītu/saldu.**	tass (tah) ir par **sah**leetoo/**sal**doo
That's not what I ordered.	**Es to nepasūtināju.**	ess twa **ne**pasoohtinahyoo
I'd like to pay.	**Lūdzu rēķinu.**	**looh**dzoo **reh**tyinoo
I think you made a mistake in the bill.	**Man liekas, ka rēķinā ir kļūda.**	man **leea**kass ka **reh**tyinah ir **klyoo**da
Can I pay with this credit card?	**Vai varu maksāt ar šo kredītkarti?**	vai **va**roo **mak**saht ar shwa **kre**deetkarti
We enjoyed it, thank you.	**Paldies, viss bija ļoti garšīgs.**	**pal**deeass viss **bi**ya lyoti **gar**sheegss

NUMBERS, see page 109

Travelling around *Ceļojumi*

Plane *Lidmašīna*

Is there a flight to Vilnius?	**Vai ir lidojums uz Viļņu?**	vai ir **lid**wayooms ooz **vil**'nyoo
What time do I check in?	**Cikos man ir jāreģistrējas?**	**tsi**kwas man ir **yah**redyistrehyas
I'd like to … my reservation on flight no. …	**Es vēlos ... savu biļeti uz lidojumu ...**	ess **ve**'lwass … **sa**voo **bi**lyeti ooz **li**dwayumoo
cancel	**atteikt**	**at**teykt
change	**mainīt**	**mai**neet
confirm	**apstiprināt**	**ap**stiprinaht

Train *Vilciens*

I want a ticket to Tallin.	**Es vēlos biļeti uz Tallinu.**	ess **ve**'lwass **bi**lyeti ooz **tal**linoo
single (one-way)	**vienā virzienā**	**vee**anah **vir**zeeanah
return (roundtrip)	**turp un atpakaļ**	toorp oon **at**pakal'
first/second class	**pirmā/otra klasē**	**pir**mah/**wa**trah **kla**sseh
How long does the journey (trip) take?	**Cik ilgi ir jābrauc?**	tsik **il**gi ir **jah**browts
When is the … train to Ventspils?	**Kad atiet ... vilciens uz Ventspili?**	kad **a**teeat ... **vil**tseeanss ooz **ve**'**n**tspili
first	**pirmais**	**pir**mais
next	**nākošais**	**nah**kwashais
last	**pēdējais**	**peh**dehyais
Is this the right train to Cēsis?	**Vai šis ir pareizais vilciens uz Cēsīm?**	vai shiss ir **pa**reizaiss **vil**tseeanss uz **tse**'seem

Bus—Tram (streetcar) *Autobuss - Tramvajs*

What bus do I take to the centre/downtown?	**Ar kādu autobusu man jābrauc uz centru?**	ar **kah**doo **ow**toboosoo man **yah**browts ooz **tsen**troo
How much is the fare to …?	**Cik maksā biļete līdz ...?**	tsik **mak**sah **bi**lyete leedz
Will you tell me when to get off?	**Lūdzu pasakiet, kad jāizkāpj.**	**looh**dzoo pasakeeat kad **yahis**kahpy

TELLING THE TIME, see page 109

Taxi *Taksometrs*

How much is it to …?	**Cik maksā līdz ...?**	tsik **mak**sah leedz
Take me to this address.	**Lūdzu brauciet uz šo adresi.**	**looh**dzoo **brow**tseeat ooz shwa **a**dresi
Please stop here.	**Lūdzu apstājieties šeit.**	**looh**dzoo **ap**stahyeeateeas sheyt

Car hire (rental) *Automašīnas īre*

I'd like to hire (rent) a car.	**Es vēlos īrēt automašīnu.**	ess **ve**'lwass **ee**reht **ow**tomasheenoo
For a day/week.	**Uz dienu/ nedēļu.**	ooz **dee**anoo/ **ne**dehlyoo
Where's the nearest filling station?	**Kur ir tuvākā degvielu uzpildes stacija?**	koor ir **too**vahkah **da**'gveealoo **oo**spildes **sta**tsiya
Full tank, please.	**Pilnu tanku, lūdzu.**	**pil**noo **tan**koo, **looh**dzoo
Give me … litres of petrol (gasoline).	**Dodiet man ... litrus degvielas.**	**dwa**deeat man ... **li**trooss **deg**weealas
How do I get to …?	**Kā es varu nokļūt uz ...?**	kah ess **va**roo **no**klyooht ooz
I've had a breakdown at …	**Man salūzusi mašīna ...**	man **sa**loohzoosi **ma**sheena
Can you send a mechanic?	**Vai jūs varat atsūtīt mehāniķi.**	vai yoohss **va**rat **at**sooteet **me**-hahnityi
Can you mend this puncture (fix this flat)?	**Vai jūs varat salāpīt riepu.**	vai yoohss **va**rat **sa**lahpeet **reea**poo

☞ You're on the wrong road.	**Jūs esat uz nepareizā ceļa.** ☜
Go straight ahead.	**Brauciet taisni uz priekšu.**
It's down there on the	**Tas ir tur ...**
left/right	**pa kreisi/pa labi**
opposite/behind …	**pretī/aiz**
next to/after …	**blakus/pēc**
north/south/ east/west	**uz ziemeļiem/uz dienvidiem/ uz austrumiem/uz rietumiem**

NUMBERS, see page 109

Sightseeing *Ekskursijas*

Where's the tourist office?	**Kur atrodas tūrisma birojs?**	koor **at**rwadas **too**risma **bi**royss
Is there an English-speaking guide?	**Vai ir pieejams angliski runājošs gīds?**	vai ir **peea**-eyams **an**gliski **roo**nahywash geedss
Where is/are the …?	**Kur ir ...?**	koor ir
beach	**pludmale**	**plooh**dmale
botanical gardens	**botāniskais dārzs**	**bo**tahniskais dahrss
castle	**pils**	pilss
cathedral	**katedrāle**	**ka**tedrahle
city centre/downtown	**pilsētas centrs**	**pilsa**'tas tsentrss
harbour	**osta**	**wa**sta
market	**tirgus**	**tir**gooss
museum	**muzejs**	**moo**zeysss
shops	**veikali**	**vey**kali
zoo	**zooloģiskais dārzs**	**zo**-olodyiskais dahrss
When does it open?	**No cikiem tas ir vaļā?**	nwa **tsi**keeam tass ir **va**lyah
When does it close?	**Cikos to slēdz?**	**tsi**kwass twa sla'dz
How much is the entrance fee?	**Cik maksā ieeja?**	tsik **mak**sah **eea**-eya

Entertainment *Izklaidēšanās*

What's playing at the … Theatre?	**Kāda izrāde ir ... teātrī?**	**kah**da **iz**rahde ir ... **tey**ahtree
How much are the seats?	**Cik maksā biļetes?**	tsik **mak**sah **bi**lyetes
Would you like to go out with me tonight?	**Vai jūs vēlētos ar mani kopā šovakar kautkur iziet?**	vai yoohss **ve**'le'twas ar **ma**ni **kwa**pah **sho**vakar **kowt**koor izeeat
Is there a discoteque in town?	**Vai pilsētā ir diskotēka?**	vai **pil**sa'tah ir **dis**kotehka
Would you like to dance?	**Vai jūs vēlaties dejot?**	vai yoohss **ve**'lateeas **de**-ywat
Thank you. It's been a wonderful evening.	**Paldies. Bija ļoti patīkams vakars.**	**pal**deeass. **bi**ya **lywa**ti **pa**teekams **va**karss

TELLING THE TIME, see page 109

Shops, stores and services *Veikali un pakalpojumi*

Where's the …?	**Kur ir …?**	koor ir
baker's	**maizes veikals**	**mai**zess **vey**kalss
bookshop/store	**grāmatveikals**	**grah**matveykals
butcher's	**gaļas veikals**	**gal**yass **vey**kalss
chemist's	**aptieka**	**apt**eeaka
dentist	**zobārsts**	**zwa**bahrsts
department store	**universālveikals**	**oo**niversahlveykals
grocery	**pārtikas veikals**	**pahr**tikas **vey**kalss
hairdresser	**frizieris**	**fri**zeearis
liquor store	**dzērienu veikals**	**dzeh**reeanoo **vey**kalss
newsagent	**avīžu kiosks**	**a**veezhoo **ki**osks
post office	**pasts**	pastss
souvenir shop	**suvenīru veikals**	**soo**veneeroo **vey**kalss
supermarket	**pārtikas lielveikals**	**pahr**tikass **leeal**veiykalss
toilets	**tualetes**	**too**aletes

General expressions *Vispārēji izteicieni*

Where's the main shopping area?	**Kur ir galvenais iepirkšanās centrs?**	koor ir **gal**va'nais **ee**apirkshanahs tsentrs
Do you have …?	**Vai jums ir...?**	vai yoomss ir
Can you show me this/that?	**Lūdzu parādiet man šo/to.**	**looh**dzoo **pa**rahdeeat man shwa/twa
Do you have anything …?	**Vai jums ir kas ...?**	vai yoomss ir kass
cheaper/better	**lētāks/labāks**	**le**'tahks/**la**bahks
larger/smaller	**lielāks/mazāks**	**leea**lahks/**ma**zahks
Can I try it on?	**Vai es varu uzmēģināt?**	vai ess **va**roo **ooz**mehdyinaht
How much is this?	**Cik tas maksā?**	tsik tass **mak**sah
Please write it down.	**Lūdzu uzrakstiet.**	**looh**dzoo **ooz**raksteeat
No, I don't like it.	**Nē, man tas nepatīk.**	neh man tass **ne**pateek
I'll take it.	**Es to ņemšu.**	ess twa **nyem**shoo
Do you accept credit cards?	**Vai varu maksāt ar kredītkarti?**	vai **va**roo **mak**saht ar **kre**deetkarti

TELLING THE TIME, see page 109

black	**melns**	ma'lnss	brown	**brūns**	broonss
orange	**oranžs**	oranzhss	yellow	**dzeltens**	**dza'**lta'nss
blue	**zils**	zilss	green	**zaļš**	zal'sh
red	**sarkans**	**sar**kanss	white	**balts**	baltss

I want to buy …	**Es vēlos pirkt ...**	ess **ve'**lwass pirkt
aspirin	**aspirīnu**	**as**pireenoo
batteries	**baterijas**	**ba**teriyas
film	**filmu**	**fil**moo
newspaper	**avīzi**	**a**veezi
English	**angļu**	**an**glyoo
American	**amerikāņu**	**a**merikahnyoo
postcard	**pastkarti**	**past**karti
shampoo	**šampūnu**	**sham**poohnoo
sun-tan cream	**sauļošanās krēmu**	**sow**lyoshanahs **kreh**moo
soap	**ziepes**	**zeea**pess
toothpaste	**zobu krēmu**	**zwa**boo **kreh**moo
a half-kilo of apples	**puskilogramu ābolu**	**poos**kilogramoo **ah**bwaloo
a litre of milk	**litru piena**	**li**troo **peea**na
I'd like … film for this camera.	**Es vēlos ... filmu šim fotoaparātam.**	ess **ve'**lwass ... **fil**moo shim **fo**toaparahtam
black and white	**melnbaltu**	**ma'ln**baltoo
colour	**krāsu**	**krah**soo
I'd like a hair-cut.	**Es vēlos apgriest matus.**	ess **ve'**lwass **ab**greeast **ma**tooss

Souvenirs *Suvenīri*

adījumi	**a**deeyoomi	knitwear
audumi	**ow**doomi	textiles and embroidery
dzintars	**dzin**tarss	amber jewellery
keramika	**ke**ramika	ceramics and pottery
kokgriezumi	**kwak**greeazoomi	wood carvings
tautiskas lelles	**tow**tiskas **lel**less	dolls in national costume

At the bank *Bankā*

Where's the nearest bank/ currency exchange office?	**Kur ir tuvākā banka/naudas apmaiņas birojs?**	koor ir **too**vahkah **ban**ka/**now**dass **ap**mainyass **bir**ways
I want to change some dollars/ pounds into lats.	**Es vēlos apmainīt dažus dolārus/ mārciņas latos.**	ess **ve**'lwass **ap**maineet **da**zhooss **do**lahrooss/ **mahr**tsinyas **lat**wass
What's the exchange rate?	**Kāds ir maiņas kurss?**	kahdss ir **mai**nyass koorss

At the post office *Pastā*

I want to send this by …	**Es vēlos nosūtīt šo pa ...**	ess **ve**'lwass **nwa**soohteet shwa pa
airmail	**gaisa pastu**	pa **gai**sa **pas**too
express	**ar ekspresi**	ar **eks**presi
I want …-latu/ santīmu stamps.	**Es vēlos ... latu/ santīmu pastmarkas.**	ess **ve**'lwass ... **la**too/ **san**teemoo **past**markas
What's the postage for a letter to England?	**Cik maksā vēstule uz Angliyu?**	kwa **mak**sah **ve**'stoole ooz **an**gleeyoo
Is there any mail for me?	**Vai man ir pienācis kāds pasta sūtījums?**	vai man ir **pee**anahtsis kahdss **pas**ta **soo**teeyooms

Telephoning *Telefona sarunas*

Where's the nearest public phone?	**Kur ir tuvākais telefona automāts?**	koor ir **too**vahkais **te**lefona **ow**tomahts
May I use your phone?	**Vai es drīkstu lietot jūsu telefonu?**	vai ess **dreek**stoo **leea**twat **yooh**soo **te**lefonoo
Hello. This is … speaking.	**Hallo. Te runā ...**	**hal**lo. te **roo**nah
I want to speak to …	**Es vēlos runāt ar ...**	ess **ve**'lwass **roo**naht ar
When will he/she be back?	**Kad viņš/ viņa atgriezīsies?**	kad vin'sh/**vi**nya **ad**greeazeeseeas
Will you tell him/her that I called?	**Lūdzu pasakiet viņam/viņai, ka es zvanīju.**	**looh**dzoo **pa**sakeeat **vi**nyam/**vi**nyai ka ess **zva**neeyoo

NUMBERS, see page 109

Time and date *Laiks un datums*

It's ...	**Tagad ir...**	**ta**gad ir
five past one	**piecas minūtes pāri vieniem**	**pea**tsass **mi**nootes **pah**ri **veea**neeam
quarter past three	**ceturksnis pāri trijiem**	**tsa**'toorksnis **pah**ri **tri-**yeeam
twenty past five	**divdesmit minūtes pāri pieciem**	**div**desmit **mi**nootes **pah**ri **peea**tseeam
half-past seven	**pusastoņi**	**poos**sastwanyi
twenty-five to nine	**divdesmit piecas minūtes pirms deviņiem**	**diw**desmit **peea**tsas **mi**nootes pirmss **de**vinyeeam
ten to ten	**desmit pirms desmitiem**	**des**mit pirmss **des**miteeam
noon/midnight	**divpadsmit dienā/pusnakts**	**div**patsmit **dee**anah/**poos**snakts
in the morning	**no rīta**	nwa **ree**ta
during the day	**pa dienu**	pa **dee**anoo
in the evening	**vakarā**	**va**karah
at night	**naktī**	**nak**tee
yesterday/today	**vakar/šodien**	**va**kar/**shwa**deean
tomorrow	**rīt**	reet
spring/summer	**pavasaris/vasara**	**pa**vasaris/**va**sara
autumn/winter	**rudens/ziema**	**roo**denss/**zeea**ma

Numbers *Skaitļi*

0	**nulle**	**nool**le	11	**vienpadsmit**	**veean**patsmit
1	**viens**	veeanss	12	**divpadsmit**	**div**patsmit
2	**divi**	**di**vi	13	**trīspadsmit**	**trees**patsmit
3	**trīs**	treess	14	**četrpadsmit**	**chetr**patsmit
4	**četri**	**chet**ri	15	**piecpadsmit**	**peeats**patsmit
5	**pieci**	**peea**tsi	16	**sešpadsmit**	**sesh**patsmit
6	**seši**	**se**shi	17	**septiņpadsmit**	**sep**tin'patsmit
7	**septiņi**	**sep**tinyi	18	**astoņpadsmit**	**as**twan'patsmit
8	**astoņi**	**as**twanyi	19	**deviņpadsmit**	**de**vin'patsmit
9	**deviņi**	**de**vinyi	20	**divdesmit**	**div**desmit
10	**desmit**	**des**mit	21	**divdesmit viens**	**div**desmit veeanss

30	**trīsdesmit**	**treez**desmit
40	**četrdesmit**	**chetr**desmit
50	**piecdesmit**	**peeats**desmit
60	**sešdesmit**	**sesh**desmit
70	**septiņdesmit**	**sep**tin'desmit
80	**astoņdesmit**	**as**twan'desmit
90	**deviņdesmit**	**de**vin'desmit
100/1,000	**simts/tūkstots**	simts/**toohk**stwats
first/second	**pirmais/otrais**	**pir**maiss/**wat**raiss
once/twice	**vienreiz/divreiz**	**veean**reyz/**di**vreyz
a half/a quarter	**puse/ceturtdaļa**	**poo**sse/**tsa**'toordalya

Sunday	**svētdiena**	**sveh**deeana
Monday	**pirmdiena**	**pirm**deeana
Tuesday	**otrdiena**	**watr**deeana
Wednesday	**trešdiena**	**trezh**deeana
Thursday	**ceturtdiena**	**tsa'**toordeeana
Friday	**piektdiena**	**peeag**deeana
Saturday	**sestdiena**	**sez**deeana
January	**janvāris**	**yan**vahris
February	**februāris**	**feb**roahris
March	**marts**	martss
April	**aprīlis**	**a**preeliss
May	**maijs**	maiyss
June	**jūnijs**	**yooh**niyss
July	**jūlijs**	**yooh**liyss
August	**augusts**	**ow**goostss
September	**septembris**	**sep**tembris
October	**oktobris**	**ok**tobris
November	**novembris**	**no**vembris
December	**decembris**	**det**sembris

Emergency *Steidzīgi nepieciešama palīdzība*

Call the police	**Izsauciet policiju.**	**i**ssowtseeat **po**litseeyoo
Get a doctor	**Izsauciet ārstu.**	**i**ssowtseeat **ahr**sstoo
Go away	**Ejiet projām.**	**e-**yeeat **prwa-**yahm
HELP	**PALĪGĀ!**	**pa**leegah

TELEPHONING, see page 108

I'm ill	**Es esmu slims (slima)**	ess **a**'smoo slimss (**sli**ma)
I'm lost	**Es nezinu kur atrodos.**	ess **ne**zinoo koor **at**rwadwas
STOP THIEF	**ĶERIET ZAGLI**	**tye**reeat **zag**li
My … have been stolen.	**Mans ... ir nozagts**	manss ... ir **nwa**zakts
I've lost my …	**Es esmu pazaudējis (-jusi) savu ...**	ess **a**'smoo **pa**zowdehyis (-yoosi) **sa**voo
handbag	**rokas somu**	**rwa**kass **swa**moo
passport/luggage	**pasi/bagāžu**	**pa**ssi/**ba**gahzhoo
wallet	**naudas maku**	**now**dass **ma**koo
Where can I find a doctor who speaks English?	**Kur es varu atrast ārstu, kas runā angliski?**	koor ess **va**roo **at**rast **ahr**stoo kass **roo**nah **an**gliski

Guide to Latvian pronunciation

Notes

1) Latvian makes a clear difference between long (**ā**, **ē**, **ī**, **ū**) and short (**a**, **e**, **i**, **u**) vowels.
2) Stress is Latvian always falls on the first syllable of a word.
3) The soft consonants (**ğ**, **ķ**, **ļ**, **ņ**) are palatalized before vowels by pressing the top of the tongue hard against the palate.

Consonants

Letter	Approximate pronunciation	Symbol	Example	
c	like **ts** in ca**ts**	ts	**cik**	tsik
č	like **ch** in **ch**urch	ch	**četri**	**che**tri
dz	like **ds** in la**ds**	dz	**daudz**	dowdz
dž	like **j** in **j**oy	dzh	**džins**	dzhinss
ğ	like **d** in **d**uty	dy	**ğimene**	**dyi**mene
h	like **h** in **h**ymn	h	**mehāniķis**	**me**-hahnityis
j	like **y** in **y**ell	y	**jūnijs**	**yooh**niyss
ķ	like **t** in **t**une	ty	**rēķins**	**reh**tyinss

ļ	softened like **li** in million; at the end of word or between consonants the **y** sound is not heard	ly l’	**gaļa** **kādēļ**	**gal**ya **kah**dehl’
ņ	softened **n** as in English **n**ew; at the end of words or between consonants the **y** sound is not heard	ny n’	**ņemt** **šķiņķi**	nyemt **shkyin**’kyi
r	rolled like a Scottish **r**	r	**roka**	**rwa**ka
s	like **s** in sit	s ss	**sieva** **slims**	**seea**va slimss
š	like **sh** in **sh**e	sh	**šodien**	**shwa**deean
ž	like **s** in plea**s**ure	zh	**daži**	**da**zhi

b, **d**, **f**, **g**, **k**, **l**, **m**, **n**, **p**, **t**, **v**, **z** are pronounced as in English

Vowels

a	like **u** in s**u**n	a	**balts**	balts
ā	like **a** in c**a**r	ah	**ābols**	**ahb**walss
e	1) short, like **e** in g**e**t	e	**zemenes**	**ze**menes
	2) longer, like **a** as in h**a**t	a’	**vecs**	va’tss
ē	1) short, like **ai** in **ai**r	eh	**ēdiens**	**eh**deenanss
	2) longer, like **a** in b**a**d	e’	**vēlos**	**ve**’lwass
i	like **i** in l**i**p	i	**ilgi**	**il**gi
ī	like **ee** in k**ee**n	ee	**vīrs**	veerss
o	1) as in the diphthong **u+o**, like **wa** in **wa**llet	wa	**ola**	**wa**la
	2) in words of foreign origin, like **o** in c**o**rn	o	**opera**	**o**pera
u	like **u** in p**u**t	oo	**kur**	koor
ū	like **oo** in s**oo**n	ooh	**lūdzu**	**looh**dzoo

Diphthongs

ai	like **i** in f**i**ne	ai	**maize**	**mai**ze
au	like **ow** in c**ow**	ow	**sauc**	sowts
ei	like **ey** in pr**ey**	ey	**sveiki**	**svey**ki
ie	like a combination of **ee+a**, like **ea** in d**ea**r	eea	**paldies**	**pal**deeass

Lithuanian

Basic expressions *Pagrindiniai pasakimai*

Yes/No.	**Taip/Ne.**	taip/ne
Please.	**Prašau.**	pra**sha^{oo}**
Thank you.	**Ačiū.**	**aa**ch^{y}ioo
I beg your pardon.	**Atsiprašau.**	ahts^{y}iprah**sha^{oo}**

Introductions *Supažindinimai*

Good morning.	**Labas rytas.**	**laa**bahs **ree**tahs
Good afternoon.	**Laba diena.**	lah**bah** die**nah**
Good night.	**Labąnakt.**	lah**baa**nahkt
Good-bye.	**Viso gero.**	**v^{y}**iso **g^{y}**ero
My name is …	**Mano vardas yra …**	**mah**no **vahr**dahs ee**rah**
What's your name?	**Koks Jūsų vardas?**	koks **yoo**soo **vahr**dahs
How are you?	**Kaip gyvenate?**	kaip gee**v^{y}**anahte
Fine, thanks.	**Ačiū, gerai.**	**aa**ch^{y}ioo g^{y}**erai**
And you?	**O Jūs kaip?**	o yoos kaip
Where do you come from?	**Iš kur Jūs?**	ish kur yoos
I'm from …	**Aš iš …**	ahsh ish
Australia	**Australijos**	a^{oo}**straa**l^{y}iyos
Britain	**Britanijos**	br^{y}**itaa**n^{y}iyos
Canada	**Kanados**	kah**naa**dos
USA	**JAV**	yaav
I'm with my …	**Aš su …**	ahsh su
wife/husband	**žmona/vyru**	zhmoh**nah**/**vee**ru
family	**šeima**	sh^{y}ei**mah**
children	**vaikais**	vai**kais**
parents	**tėvais**	teh**vais**
boyfriend/girlfriend	**draugu/drauge**	dra^{oo}**gu**/dra^{oo}**g^{y}e**
I'm on my own.	**Aš vienas (viena).**	ahsh **vie**nas (**vie**nah)
I'm on holiday (vacation)/on business.	**Aš atostogauju/ komandiruotėje.**	ahsh ahtosto**ga^{oo}**yu/ komahndi**ruo**tehyeh

GUIDE TO PRONUNCIATION/EMERGENCIES, see page 127

Questions *Klausimai*

When?/How?	**Kada?/Kaip?**	kah**dah**/kaip
What?/Why?	**Kas?/Kodėl?**	kahs/kod**ehl**
Who?/Which?	**Kas?/Kuris?**	kahs/kur^{y}**is**
Where is/are …?	**Kur yra …?**	kur ee**rah**
Where can I get/ find …?	**Kur aš galėčiau nusipirkti/rasti …?**	kur ahsh gah**l^{y}eh**chia^{oo} nus^{y}i**p^{y}irk**ti/**rah**sti
How far?	**Ar toli?**	ahr **toh**l^{y}i
How long?	**Ar ilgai?**	ahr il**gai**
How much?	**Kiek?**	k^{y}iek
May I …?	**Ar galėčiau …?**	ahr gah**l^{y}eh**chia^{oo}
Can I have …?	**Ar galėčiau …?**	ahr gah**l^{y}eh**chia^{oo}
Can you help me?	**Ar negalėtumėte man padėti?**	ahr negah**l^{y}eh**tum^{y}ete mahn pah**deh**ti
What does this mean?	**Ką tai reiškia?**	kaa tai **reish**k^{y}a
I understand.	**Suprantu.**	su**prahn**tu
I don't understand.	**Nesuprantu.**	nesu**prahn**tu
Can you translate this for me?	**Ar negalėtumėte man tai išversti?**	ahr negah**l^{y}eh**tum^{y}ete mahn tai ish**ver**sti
Do you speak English?	**Ar Jūs kalbate angliškai?**	ahr yoos **kahl**bahte **ahng**l^{y}ishkai
I don't speak Lithuanian.	**Gerai negaliu kalbėti lietuviškai.**	g^{y}**erai** negah**l^{y}iu** kal**beht**^{y}i l^{y}ie**tu**v^{y}ishkai

A few useful words *Keli naudingi žodžiai*

better/worse	**geresnis/blogesnis**	g^{y}**ereh**snis/blo**g^{y}eh**snis
big/small	**didelis/mažas**	**di**delis/**maa**zhahs
cheap/expensive	**pigus/brangus**	p^{y}**igus**/brahng**gus**
early/late	**ankstyvas/vėlus**	ahngk**stee**vahs/v^{y}eh**lus**
good/bad	**geras/blogas**	**g^{y}a**rahs/**bloh**gahs
hot/cold	**karštas/šaltas**	**kahr**shtahs/**shahl**tahs
near/far	**artimas/tolimas**	**ahr**timahs/**toh**limahs
next/last	**kitas/paskutinis**	**k^{y}i**tahs/pahsku**ti**nis
right/ wrong	**teisingas/ neteisingas**	tei**sing**gahs/ netei**sing**gahs
vacant/occupied	**laisvas/užimtas**	**lai**svahs/uzh^{y}**im**tahs

Hotel–Accommodation *Apsistojimas viešbutyje*

I've a reservation.	**Aš esu užsakęs užsakiusi.**	ahsh **e**su ushsahkas ush**saak**^{y}oosi
Do you have any vacancies?	**Ar turite laisvų kambarių?**	ahr **tur**^{y}ite lais**voo** kahmbah**r^{y}oo**
I'd like a … room.	**Aš norėčiau kambario …**	ahsh no**r^{y}eh**chia^{oo} **kahm**bahrio
single	**vienviečio**	v^{y}ien**v^{y}ie**ch^{y}o
double	**dviviečio**	dv^{y}i**v^{y}ie**ch^{y}o
with twin beds	**su dviem viengulėm lovom**	su dviem vien**gul**^{y}ehm **loh**vom
with a double bed	**su dvigule lova**	dv^{y}igu**l^{y}a loh**vah
with a bath/shower	**su vonia/dušu**	su vohn**^{y}ah/**dus**hu**
We'll be staying …	**Mes apsistosime …**	m^{y}as ahps^{y}**istohs**^{y}imeh
overnight only	**tik vienai nakčiai**	tik **vie**nai **naak**ch^{y}ei
a few days	**keliom dienom**	**k^{y}e**l^{y}ohm **die**nohm
a week	**savaitei**	sah**vai**tei

Decision *Sprendimai*

May I see the room?	**Ar galiu pamatyti kambarį?**	ahr gah**l^{y}iu** pahmah**tee**ti **kahm**bahree
That's fine. I'll take it.	**Puiku. Aš apsistosiu jame.**	pui**ku**. ahsh ahps^{y}**istohs**^{y}u yah**m^{y}e**
No. I don't like it.	**Ne. Man jis nepatinka.**	ne. mahn yis nepah**ting**kah
It's too …	**Jis per …**	yis p^{y}er
dark/small	**tamsus/mažas**	tahm**sus/maa**zhahs
noisy	**triukšmingas**	tr^{y}uk**shming**gahs
Do you have anything …?	**Ar Jūs turite ką nors …?**	ahr yoos **tur**^{y}ite kaa nors
better/bigger	**geresnio/didesnio**	g^{y}a**r^{y}as**nyo/di**das**nyo
cheaper/	**pigesnio**	p^{y}i**g^{y}as**nyo
quieter	**ramesnio**	rah**m^{y}as**nyo
May I please have my bill?	**Prašau sąskaitos.**	**prasha^{oo} saa**skaitos
It's been a very enjoyable stay.	**Man buvo labai malonu čia apsistoti.**	mahn buv**o** lah**bai** mahlo**nu** ch^{y}eh aps^{y}**istoh**ti

NUMBERS, see page 126

Eating out *Valgymas ne namie*

I'd like to reserve a table for 4.	**Aš norėčiau stalo keturiems.**	ahsh nor^{y}**eh**chia^{oo} **staa**lo k^{y}etu**riems**
We'll come at 8.	**Mes ateisime aštuntą.**	m^{y}as ah**teis**^{y}imeh ash**tun**taa
What do you recommend?	**Ką Jūs pasiūlitumėte?**	kaa yoos pah**sioo**litum^{y}ete
Do you have vegetarian dishes?	**Ar Jūs turite vegetariškų valgių?**	ahr yoos **tur**^{y}ite veg^{y}e**tah**rishkoo vahl**g^{y}oo**

Breakfast *Pusryčiai*

I'd like some…	**Aš norėčiau…**	ahsh nor^{y}**eh**chia^{oo}
bread/butter	**duonos/sviesto**	**duo**nohs/**svie**stoh
cheese	**sūrio**	**soor**^{y}oh
egg	**kiaušinio**	**k^{y}a^{oo}**shin^{y}oh
ham	**kumpio**	**kump**^{y}oh
jam	**uogienės**	wuo**gie**nehs
rolls	**bandėlių**	bahn**dehl**^{y}oo

Starters *Užkandžiai*

ikrai	ikrai	caviar
kumpis	**kump**^{y}is	ham
marinuoti grybai	mahr^{y}i**nuo**ti **gree**bai	pickled mushrooms
mišrainė	mish**rain**^{y}eh	salad
rūkyta dešra	**rook^{y}ee**tah d^{y}esh**rah**	smoked sausage
silkė	**silk**^{y}eh	herring

baked	**keptas krosnyje**	**kep**tahs **kros**neeyeh
boiled	**virtas**	**vir**tahs
fried	**keptas keptuvėje**	**kep**tahs keptuveh**yeh**
grilled	**keptas ant grotelių**	**kep**tahs ahnt gro**tal**^{y}oo
roast	**kepsnys**	**kep**snees
underdone (rare)	**ne visai iškeptas**	ne vi**sai** ish**kep**tahs
medium	**viduriniai iškeptas**	vidur^{y}i**n^{y}ei** ish**kep**tahs
well-done	**labai sukepintas**	lah**bai** su**k^{y}ah**pintahs

NUMBERS, see page 126

Meat *Mėsa*

I'd like some …	**Norėčiau …**	nor^{y}**eh**chia^{oo}
beef/lamb	**jautienos/avienos**	**ya^{oo}**tienos/ah**vie**nos
chicken	**vištienos**	v^{y}ish**tie**nos
duck	**antienos**	ahn**tie**nos
pork	**kaulienos**	k^{y}a^{oo}**l^{y}ie**nos
veal	**veršienos**	ver**shie**nos
balandeliai	bahlahn**deh**l^{y}ei	stuffed cabbage rolls
galkos	**gahl**kos	meat balls
karbonadas su kopūstais	kahrbo**nah**dahs su ko**poo**stais	pork chop with cabbage
pyragas	pee**rah**gahs	meat pie
troškinta mėsa	trosh**k^{y}in**tah **m^{y}e**sah	meat stew

Fish and seafood *Žūvis ir jūros maistas*

keptas karpis	**k^{y}ap**tahs **kahr**p^{y}is	fried carp
marinuotos žuvys su bulvėmis	mahr^{y}i**nuo**tos zhu**vees** su **bul**v^{y}ehmis	marinated fish with potatoes
silkių ir daržovių sriuba	**s^{y}il**k^{y}oo ir dahr**zho**v^{y}oo sriu**bah**	herring and vegetable soup
troškinta žuvis	trosh**k^{y}in**tah zhu**v^{y}ees**	fish stew
žuvų blyneliai	zhu**voo** blee**neh**l^{y}ei	fish pancakes
žuvų galkos	zhu**voo** **gahl**kos	fried fish dumplings

Vegetables *Daržovės*

beans	**pupos**	**pu**pos
cabbage	**kopūstas**	ko**poo**stahs
mushroom	**grybas**	**gree**bahs
onions	**svogūnai**	svo**goo**nai
peas	**žirniai**	**zhir**n^{y}ei
potatoes	**bulvės**	**bul**vehs
tomato	**pomidoras**	pomi**do**rahs
bulviniai blynai	bulv^{y}in^{y}ei **blee**nai	potato pancakes
kopustu sriuba	ko**pus**too sr^{y}u**bah**	cabbage soup
šaltibarščiai	shahlti**bahr**shch^{y}ei	cold beetroot soup
varškėčiai	vahrsh**k^{y}e**ch^{y}ei	curd cheese pancakes
varškės/grybų virtinukai	**vahr**shk^{y}ehs/**gree**boo virti**nu**kai	curd cheese/mushroom dumplings

Fruit & dessert *Vaisiai ir desertai*

apple	**obuolys**	ohbuo**lees**
banana	**bananas**	bah**nah**nahs
lemon	**citrina**	ts^{y}itree**nah**
orange	**apelsinas**	ahp^{y}el**see**nahs
plum	**slyva**	sl^{y}ee**vah**
strawberries	**žemuogės**	zh^{y}em**uo**g^{y}ehs
blyneliai	bli**nehl**^{y}ei	small pancakes
grietininiai ledai	gr^{y}ietinin^{y}ei **l**^{y}**a**dai	ice-cream
obuolinis pyragas	ohbuo**l**^{y}inis pee**rah**gahs	apple pie
tortas	**tor**tahs	gateau
uogų virtinukai	**wuo**goo virti**nu**kai	fruit dumplings

Drinks *Gėrimai*

beer	**alus**	ah**lus**
(hot) chocolate	**kakava**	kahkah**vah**
coffee	**kava**	kah**vah**
black/with milk	**juoda/su pienu**	**yuo**dah/su p^{y}ie**nu**
fruit juice	**vaisių sultys**	**vai**s^{y}oo **sul**t^{y}ees
mineral water	**mineralinis vanduo**	m^{y}ine**rah**l^{y}inis vahnd**uo**
tea	**arbata**	ahrbah**tah**
wine	**vynas**	**vee**nahs
red/white	**raudonas/baltas**	ra^{oo}**doh**nahs/**bahl**tahs
vodka	**degtinė**	deg**ti**ne

Complaints and paying *Nusiskundimai ir atsilyginimai*

This is too …	**Tai per …**	tai p^{y}er
bitter/sweet	**kartu/saldu**	kahr**tu**/sahl**du**
That's not what I ordered.	**Tai nėra pagal mano užsakymą.**	tai **neh**ra pahg**ahl** **mah**no ush**sah**keemaa
I'd like to pay.	**Aš norėčiau užmokėti.**	ahsh nor^{y}**eh**chia^{oo} ushmoh**k**^{y}**ehti**
I think you made a mistake in the bill.	**Aš manau, kad Jūs sąskaita yra neteisinga.**	ahsh mana^{oo} kahd yoos **saa**skaitah ee**rah** neteis^{y}**ing**ah
We enjoyed it, . thank you	**Ačiu, tai mums patiko.**	**aa**chiu, tai mums pah**ti**ko

NUMBERS, see page 126

Travelling around *Keliavimas*

Plane *Lėktuvas*

Is there a flight to Vilnius?	**Ar yra reisas į Vilnių?**	ahr ee**rah rei**sahs ee **v^{y}il**nyoo
What time do I check in?	**Kurią valandą man reikės registruotis?**	**ku**riaa **vaa**lahndaa mahn r^{y}ei**k^{y}as** reg^{y}**istruo**tis
I'd like to … my reservation.	**Aš norėčiau rezervuoti vietą reisui …**	ahsh no**reh**chia^{oo} rezer**vuo**ti **vie**taa **rei**sui
cancel	**anuliuoti**	ahnu**liuo**ti
change	**mainyti**	mai**nee**ti
confirm	**patvirtinti**	pah**tv^{y}ir**tinti

Train *Traukinys*

I want a ticket to Shiauliai.	**Aš norėčiau bilieto į Šiaulius.**	ahsh no**r^{y}eh**chia^{oo} **b^{y}**ilieto ee **shya^{oo}**l^{y}ius
single (one-way)	**į vieną galą**	ee **vie**naa **gah**laa
return (roundtrip)	**grįžtamasio bilieto**	**greezh**tahmahsio **b^{y}**ilieto
first/second class	**pirma/antra klasė**	**pir**mah/**aan**trah klahs^{y}eh
How long does the journey (trip) take?	**Ar ilga kelionė?**	ahr **il**gah k^{y}**elioh**neh
When is the … train to Kaunas?	**Kada išeina … traukinys į Kauną?**	kah**dah** ish**ei**nah … tra^{oo}k^{y}**inees** ee **ka^{oo}**naa
first/next	**pirmasis/sekantis**	p^{y}ir**mah**sis/**s^{y}a**kahntis
last	**paskutinis**	pahsku**tin^{y}**is

Bus—Tram (streetcar) *Autobusas–Troleibusas*

What bus do I take to the centre (downtown)?	**Kokiu autobusu važiuoti į miesto centrą?**	**koh**kiu a^{oo}to**bu**su vah**zhiuo**ti ee **mies**to **tsen**traa
How much is the fare to …?	**Kiek kainuoja bilietas …?**	kiek kai**nuo**ya **b^{y}i**lietahs
Will you tell me when to get off?	**Prašau man pasakyti kur išlipti.**	prash**a^{oo}** mahn pahsah**kee**ti kur ish**l^{y}ipti**

TELLING THE TIME, see page 125

Taxi *Taksi*

How much is it to …?	**Kiek kainuoja važiuoti į …?**	kiek kai**nuo**yah vah**zhiuo**ti ee
Take me to this address.	**Nuvežkite mane į šį adresą.**	nuv^{y}**ezh**k^{y}ite mah**ne** ee shee **aad**resaa
Please stop here.	**Prašau čia sustoti.**	prasha^{oo} ch^{y}eh su**stoh**ti

Car hire (rental) *Automobilių nuoma*

I'd like to hire (rent) a car.	**As norėčiau išnuomoti automobilį.**	ash nor^{y}**eh**chia^{oo} ish**nuo**mohti a^{oo}tomo**b^{y}**ilee
I'd like it for a day/week.	**Aš norėčiau jį išnuomoti per dieną/savaitę.**	ahsh nor^{y}**eh**chia^{oo} yee ish**nuo**mohti p^{y}er **die**naa/sah**vai**teh
Where's the nearest filling station?	**Kur yra artimiausia degalinė?**	kur ee**rah** ahrti**mia^{oo}**siah degahl^{y}**in**^{y}eh
Full tank, please.	**Prašau pilną benzino baką.**	prasha^{oo} **p^{y}il**naa b^{y}en**zee**no **baa**kaa
Give me … litres of petrol (gasoline).	**Prašau … benzino litrų.**	prasha^{oo} … b^{y}en**zee**no **l^{y}i**troo
How do I get to …?	**Kaip patekti į …?**	kaip pah**tek**ti ee …
I've had a breakdown at …	**Mano automobilis sugedo prie …**	**mah**no a^{oo}tomo**b^{y}i**lis sug^{y}**a**doh prie
Can you send a mechanic?	**Ar galite atsiųsti mechaniką?**	ahr **gah**l^{y}ite **ats^{y}oo**sti me**haa**n^{y}ikaa
Can you mend this puncture (fix this flat)?	**Ar galite pataisyti pradurtą skytę?**	ahr **gah**l^{y}ite pahtai**see**ti prah**dur**taa **skee**ta

☞ You're on the wrong road.	**Tas yra netikras kelias.** ☜
Go straight ahead.	**Važiuokite pirmyn.**
It's down there …	**Tai yra ten …**
on the left/right	**į kairę/į dešinę**
opposite/next to/after …	**priešais/šalia/paskui …**
north/south/east/west	**į šiaurę/į pietus/į rytus/į vakarus**

NUMBERS, see page 126

Sightseeing *Įžymybių apžiūrėjimas*

Where's the tourist office?	**Kur yra turistų biuras?**	kur ee**rah** tur[y]**is**too **biu**rahs
Is there an English-speaking guide?	**Ar yra gidas, kuris kalba angliškai?**	ahr eerah **gi**dahs **ku**ris **kahl**bah **ahng**l[y]ishkai
Where is/are the …?	**Kur yra …?**	kur ee**rah**
beach	**pliažas**	**pliah**zhahs
botanical gardens	**botanikos sodas**	bo**taa**n[y]ikos **soh**dahs
castle	**pilis**	p[y]il[y]**is**
cathedral	**katedra**	**kaa**tedrah
city centre (downtown)	**miesto centras**	**mie**sto **ts[y]an**trahs
exhibition	**paroda**	pahro**dah**
harbour	**uostas**	**uo**stahs
market	**turgus**	**tur**gus
museum	**muziejus**	mu**zie**yus
shops	**parduotuvės**	pahrduo**tu**v[y]ehs
zoo	**zoologijos sodas**	zo-o**loh**g[y]iyos **soh**dahs
When does it open/close?	**Kada atsidaro/užsidaro?**	kah**dah** ahtsi**dah**ro/ uzhsi**dah**ro
How much is the entrance fee?	**Kiek kainuoja mokestis už įėjimą?**	kiek kai**nuo**jah **moh**k[y]estis ush ee-eh**yi**maa

Entertainment *Linksminimas*

What's playing at the … Theatre?	**Kokia pjesė bus …teatre?**	ko**k[y]ah pye**seh bus … te-ah**tre**
How much are the seats?	**Kiek kainuoja vietos?**	kiek kai**nuo**yah **vie**tos
Would you like to go out with me tonight?	**Ar norėtumete su manimi šį vakarą pasivaikščioti?**	ahr no**r[y]eh**tumete su mahni**mi** shee **vah**kahraa pahsi**vaik**shchuoti
Is there a discotheque in town?	**Ar yra diskotėka mieste?**	ahr ee**rah** disko**teh**kah mies**te**
Would you like to dance?	**Ar norėtumete pašokti?**	ahr no**r[y]eh**tumete **pah**shohkti
Thank you. It's been a wonderful evening.	**Ačiū. Buvo puikus vakaras.**	**aa**chioo/**bu**vo pui**kus vah**kahrahs

TELLING THE TIME/DAYS OF THE WEEK, see page 125

Shops, stores and services *Parduotuvės ir aptarnavimas*

Where's the nearest …?	**Kur yra artimiausia …?**	kur ee**rah** ahrti**mia^{oo}**siah
baker's	**duonos parduotuvė**	**duo**nos pahrduo**tu**veh
bookshop/store	**knygynas**	kn^{y}ee**gee**nahs
chemist's/drugstore	**vaistinė**	**vai**stineh
dentist	**dantų gydytojas**	dahn**too gee**deetoyahs
department store	**universaline parduotuvė**	un^{y}iver**saal**^{y}ine pahrduo**tu**veh
grocery	**bakalejos krautuvė**	bahkah**l^{y}eh**yos **kra^{oo}**tuveh
hairdresser	**kirpejas**	k^{y}ir**peh**yahs
newsagent	**laikraščių pardavėjas**	**lai**krahshch^{y}oo pahrdah**veh**yahs
post office	**paštas**	**pah**shtahs
supermarket	**savitarnos parduotuvė**	sah**v^{y}i**tahrnos pahrduo**tu**veh

General expressions *Bendros frazes*

Where's the main shopping area?	**Kur yra pagrindinis parduotuvių centras?**	kur ee**rah** pahgr^{y}in**di**nis pahrduo**tu**v^{y}oo **ts^{y}an**trahs
Do you have any …?	**Ar turite …?**	ahr **tur**^{y}ite
Can you show me this/that?	**Ar galėtumete man parodyti …?**	ahr gah**l^{y}eh**tum^{y}ete mahn pah**roh**deeti
Do you have anything …?	**Ar turite ką nors …?**	ahr **tur**^{y}ite kaa nors
cheaper/better	**pigesnį/geresnį**	pig^{y}esnee/g^{y}**er**^{y}esnee
larger/smaller	**didesnį/mažesnį**	di**des**nee/mah**zhes**nee
Can I try it on?	**Ar galėčiau jį pasrimatuoti?**	ahr gah**l^{y}eh**chia^{oo} yee pahsrimah**tuo**ti
How much is this?	**Kiek tai kainuoja?**	kiek tai kai**nuo**ya
Please write it down.	**Prašau užrašyti.**	pra**sha^{oo}** uzhrah**shee**ti
No, I don't like it.	**Ne, tai man nepatinka.**	ne, tai mahn nepah**ting**kah
I'll take it.	**Aš perku.**	ash p^{y}er**ku**

NUMBERS, see page 126

Do you accept credit cards?	**Ar priimate kredito kortelės?**	ahr **pree**mahte kre**di**to kor**te**lehs

black	**juodas**	**juo**dahs	brown	**rudas**	**ru**dahs
orange	**oranžinis**	o**rahn**zhinis	white	**baltas**	**bahl**tahs
blue	**melynas**	**meh**leenahs	green	**žalias**	**zhaa**lias
red	**raudonas**	ra^{oo}**doh**nahs	yellow	**geltonas**	g^{y}el**toh**nahs

I want to buy …	**Aš norėčiau pirkti …**	ahsh no**reh**chia^{oo} **pirk**ti
aspirin	**aspiriną**	ahspi**ri**naa
batteries	**baterijas**	bah**te**riyahs
film	**fotofilmą**	fotofil**maa**
newspaper	**laikraštį**	**laik**rahshtee
American	**amerikietišką**	ahmer^{y}**ikie**tishkaa
English	**angliška**	**ahngl**^{y}ishkaa
shampoo	**šampuną**	shahm**poo**naa
sun-tan cream	**saulės įdegimo kremą**	**sa^{oo}**l^{y}ehs eede**g^{y}i**mo **kr^{y}**emaa
soap	**muilą**	**mui**laa
toothpaste	**dantų pastą**	dahn**too** pah**staa**
a half-kilo of apples	**pusę kilograma obuolių**	pus^{y}**a** kilo**graa**mah ohbuol^{y}**oo**
a litre of milk	**litrą pieno**	**l^{y}it**raa **pie**no
I'd like … film for this camera.	**Aš norėčiau … filmo šiam fotoaparatui.**	ahsh nor^{y}**eh**chia^{oo} … **fil**mo shyam fotoahpah**rah**tui
black and white	**nespalvoto**	nespahl**vo**to
colour	**spalvoto**	spahl**vo**to
I'd like a hair-cut.	**Aš norėčiau apkirpimo.**	ahsh nor^{y}**eh**chia^{oo} ahp**k^{y}ir**p^{y}imo

Souvenirs *Suvenyrai*

gintariniai karoliai	g^{y}intah**r^{y}in**^{y}ei kah**ro**l^{y}ei	amber necklace
medžio dirbiniai	**meh**dzhio dirbi**n^{y}ei**	wood carvings
šalikas	**shahl**^{y}ikahs	shawl
tautiška lėlė	**ta^{oo}**tishkah l^{y}eh**l^{y}eh**	national doll
vario sage	**vaa**r^{y}o sah**g^{y}eh**	copper brooch

At the bank *Banke*

Where's the nearest bank/currency exchange office?	**Kur yra artimiausias bankas/valiutos keitimo punktas?**	kur ee**rah** ahrtim**ia^{oo}**sias bahng**kahs**/vah**liu**tos kei**ti**mo **pung**tahs
I want to change some dollars/pounds into Lits.	**Aš norėčiau iškeisti dolerius/ svarus sterlingų į litus.**	ahsh nor^{y}**ah**chia^{oo} ish**k^{y}ei**sti **do**lerius/ svah**rus sterl**^{y}ingoo ee l^{y}**itus**
What's the exchange rate?	**Koks yra valiutos kursas?**	koks ee**rah** vah**liu**tos **kur**sahs

At the post office *Pašte*

I want to send this by …	**Aš norėčiau šį pasiusti …**	ahsh nor^{y}**eh**chia^{oo} shee pahs^{y}**oo**sti
airmail	**oro paštu**	**oh**ro pahsh**tu**
express	**skubu persiuntimu**	sku**bu p^{y}er**siuntimu
I want …	**Aš norėčiau …**	ahsh nor^{y}**eh**chia^{oo} …
10-lit stamps.	**dešimties litų pašto ženklų.**	dashimties **l^{y}i**too **pahsh**to zh^{y}eng**kloo**
What's the postage for a letter/postcard to the United States?	**Kiek kainuoja pašto ženklų laiškui/atvirukai į Ameriką?**	kiek kai**nuo**ya **pahsh**to **zh^{y}eng**kloo **laish**kui/ahtvi**ru**kai ee ah**meri**kaa
Is there any mail for me?	**Ar man yra atsiustas paštas?**	ahr mahn ee**rah** ahts^{y}**oo**stahs **pahsh**tahs

Telephoning *Telefonas*

Where's the nearest public phone?	**Kur yra artimiausias auto-matas telefonas?**	kur ee**rah** ahrti**mia^{oo}**s^{y}ahs a^{oo}to-**mah**tahs tele**foh**nahs
Hello. This is … speaking.	**Alio. Čia kalba …**	ah**l^{y}io.** ch^{y}eh **kahl**bah
I want to speak to …	**Aš norėčiau kalbėtis su …**	ahsh nor^{y}**eh**chia^{oo} kahl**beh**tis su
When will he/she be back?	**Kada jis/ji bus namie?**	kah**dah** yis/yi bus nah**mieh**
Will you tell him/her that I called?	**Prašau pasakyti jam/jai kad aš skambinau?**	prah**sha^{oo}** pahsah**keeti** yahm/yai kahd ahsh **skahm**b^{y}ina^{oo}

Time and date *Laikas ir data*

It's …	**Dabar …**	dah**baar**
five past one	**penkios minutės po pirmos**	**pang**kios m^{y}i**nu**tehs poh **p^{y}ir**mos
quarter past three	**penkiolika minučių po trijų**	peng**k^{y}o**likah m^{y}**inooch**^{y}oo poh **tri**yoo
twenty past five	**dvidešimt minučių po penkių**	**dv^{y}i**deshimt m^{y}**inooch**^{y}oo poh **pang**kioo
half-past seven	**pusė aštuonių**	**pu**seh ashtuo**n^{y}oo**
twenty-five to nine	**aštuonios trisdešimt penkios**	ash**tuo**n^{y}os **tris**deshimt **pang**kios
ten to ten	**be dešimt minučių desimt**	beh **dash**imt m^{y}**inooch**^{y}oo **dash**imt
noon	**vidurdienis**	v^{y}**idur**dienis
midnight	**vidurnaktis**	v^{y}**idur**nahktis

Sunday	**sekmadienis**	s^{y}ek**maa**dienis
Monday	**pirmadienis**	p^{y}ir**maa**dienis
Tuesday	**antradienis**	ahn**traa**dienis
Wednesday	**trečiadienis**	tre**chiah**dienis
Thursday	**ketvirtadienis**	k^{y}etv^{y}ir**taa**dienis
Friday	**penktadienis**	penk**taa**dienis
Saturday	**šeštadienis**	sh^{y}esh**taa**dienis
January	**sausio**	**sa^{oo}**s^{y}o
February	**vasario**	vah**sahr**^{y}o
March	**kovo**	**koh**voh
April	**balandžio**	bah**lahn**dzh^{y}o
May	**gegužės**	g^{y}egu**zh^{y}ehs**
June	**birželio**	b^{y}ir**zhal**^{y}o
July	**liepos**	**lie**pos
August	**rugpiučio**	rug**p^{y}iu**ch^{y}o
September	**rugsėjo**	rugs**^{y}eh**yo
October	**spalio**	**spah**lio
November	**lapkričio**	**laap**kr^{y}ich^{y}o
December	**gruodžio**	**gruo**dzh^{y}o

NUMBERS, see page 126

in the morning	**rytą**	**ree**taa
during the day	**po pietų**	poh pie**too**
in the evening	**vakare/vakarą**	vahkah**reh/vaa**kahraa
at night	**nakties**	nahk**ties**
yesterday/today	**vakar/šiandien**	**vaa**kahr/**sh^{y}en**dien
tomorrow	**rytoj**	ree**toy**
spring	**pavasaris**	pah**vaa**sahr^{y}is
summer	**vasara**	**vaa**sahrah
autumn/winter	**ruduo/žiema**	ru**duo**/zhie**mah**

Numbers *Skaičiai*

0	**nulis**	**nul**^{y}is	11	**vienuolika**	vie**nuo**l^{y}ikah
1	**vienas**	**vie**nahs	12	**dvylika**	**dvee**l^{y}ikah
2	**du/dvi**	du/dv^{y}i	13	**trylika**	**tree**l^{y}ikah
3	**trys**	treess	14	**keturiolika**	ketu**r^{y}o**l^{y}ikah
4	**keturi**	ketu**r^{y}i**	15	**penkiolika**	peng**k^{y}o**l^{y}ikah
5	**penki**	peng**k^{y}i**	16	**šešiolika**	sh^{y}e**sh^{y}o**l^{y}ikah
6	**šeši**	she**sh^{y}i**	17	**septyniolika**	septee**n^{y}o**l^{y}ikah
7	**septyni**	septee**n^{y}i**	18	**aštuoniolika**	ashtu**n^{y}o**l^{y}ikah
8	**aštuoni**	ashtuo**n^{y}i**	19	**devyniolika**	devee**n^{y}o**l^{y}ikah
9	**devyni**	devee**n^{y}i**	20	**dvidešimt**	**dv^{y}i**deshimt
10	**dešimt**	**dash**imt	21	**dvidešimt vienas**	**dv^{y}i**deshimt **vie**nahs

30	**trisdešimt**	**tr^{y}is**deshimt
40	**keturiasdešimt**	**ka**turiasdeshimt
50	**penkiasdešimt**	**peng**kiasdeshimt
60	**šešiasdešimt**	**sh^{y}a**shiasdeshimt
70	**septyniasdešimt**	sep**tee**niasdeshimt
80	**aštuoniasdešimt**	ash**tuo**niasdeshimt
90	**devyniasdešimt**	de**vee**niasdeshimt
100/1,000	**šimtas/tūkstantis**	**sh^{y}im**tahs/**took**stahntis

first	**pirmas**	**p^{y}ir**mahs
second	**antras**	**ahn**trahs
third	**trečias**	**tr^{y}a**chias
once/twice	**kartą/dukart**	**kahr**taa/**du**kahrt
a half/a quarter	**pusė/ketvirtis**	**pu**seh/k^{y}e**tv^{y}ir**tis

Emergency *Krastutinis atvėjis*

Call the police.	**Pakvieskite policiją.**	pah**kvie**sk^{y}ite pol^{y}**i**tsiyaa
Get a doctor.	**Pakvieskite gydytoją.**	pah**kvie**sk^{y}ite **gee**deetoyaa
Go away.	**Eikit šalin.**	**ei**kit **chah**lin
HELP!	**GELBĖKITE!**	**g^{y}el**behk^{y}ite
I'm ill.	**Aš nes veikuoju/sergu.**	ash nesvei**kuo**yu/**s^{y}er**gu
I'm lost.	**Aš esu paklydęs (paklydusi).**	ash **esu** pah**klee**das (pah**klee**dus^{y}i)
LOOK OUT!	**SAUGOKITĖS!**	**sa^{oo}**gok^{y}itehs
STOP THIEF!	**LAIKYKITE VAGĮ!**	lai**keek**^{y}ite **vaa**gee
My … has been stolen.	**Mano … yra pavogtas.**	**mah**no …ee**rah** **pah**vohgtahs
I've lost my …	**Pamėčiau … savo.**	pah**m^{y}eh**chia^{oo} … **sah**vo
handbag	**rankinę**	**rahng**k^{y}ina
passport/luggage	**pasą/bagažą**	**paa**saa/bah**gaa**zhaa
wallet	**piniginę**	p^{y}inig^{y}**i**na
Where can I find a doctor who speaks English?	**Kur galiu rasti gydytoją, kuris kalba angliškai?**	kur gah**liu** **rah**sti **gee**deetoyaa, ku**ris** **kahl**bah **ahng**lishkai

Guide to Lithuanian pronunciation

Notes

1) Lithuanian vowels are of two distinct kinds, either short and long.
2) The consonants often pronounced softer than in English. The more emphatic forms of palatalization sound similar to a short **y**-sound between the consonants and the vowel following it (in our transcription, shown ^{y}).

Consonants

Letter	Approximate pronunciation	Symbol	Example	
c	like **ts** in cats	ts	**colis**	**tsol**^{y}is
č	like **ch** in **church**	ch	**čia**	cheh
d	as in English **deed**, with the tip of the tongue against the back of the teeth	d	**kada**	**kah**dah

TELEPHONING, see page 124

g	like **g** in **go**	g	**draugas**	dra^{oo}**gahs**
h, ch	as English **h** but more emphatic	h	**humoras**	**hu**mor**ahs**
j	like **y** in **yes**	y	**jūsu**	**yoo**soo
r	rolled, like a Scottish **r**	r	**rytas**	**ree**tahs
š	like **sh** in **shut**	sh	**iš**	ish
ž	like s in pleasure	zh	**žmona**	zhmoh**nah**
dž	like **j** in English **jam**	dzh	**medžio**	**meh**dzhio

b, f, k, l m, n, p, s, t, v, z are pronounced as in English, with the exception that most have soft forms

Vowels

a	1) short, like **u** in **cut**	ah	**aš**	ahsh
	2) long when stressed, like **a** in barn	aa	**ačiu**	**aach**^{y}iu
ą	like long **a** above	aa	**ką**	kaa
e	1) short, like **e** in pet	e	**ne**	ne
	2) broad, like **a** in cat	ah	**senas**	**s**^{y}**a**nahs
ę	long, like **a** in man	a	**pusę**	pus^{y}**a**
ė	similar to English **are**	eh	**tėvais**	**teh**vais
i	short, like English pig	i	**kuris**	kur^{y}**is**
į	long, like **ee** in seen	ee	**šį**	shee
y	like long **i** above	ee	**rytas**	**ree**tahs
o	1) short, like **o** in English hot	o	**viso**	**v**^{y}iso
	2) long, like **o** in more	oh	**blogas**	**bloh**gahs
u	short, like **u** in put	u	**dušas**	dush**ahs**
ū	long, like **oo** in loot	oo	**jūs**	yoos
ų	like long **u** above	oo	**laisvų**	lais**voo**

Diphthongs

au	like **ow** in **cow**	a^{oo}	**prašau**	**pra**sha^{oo}
ai	like **i** in mine	ai	**maistas**	**mai**stahs
iai	**ai** in main	ei, ^{y}ei	**vaisiai**	**vais**^{y}ei
ei	like **ai** in main	ei	**šeima**	sh^{y}ei**mah**
uo	**oo** followed by a short **o** sound	uo	**obuolys**	ohbuo**lees**
ui	roughly like **ooey**	ui	**puiku**	**pui**ku
ie	roughly like **eea**	ie	**kiek**	k^{y}iek

Polish

Basic Expressions *Podstawe wyrazy*

Yes/No.	**Tak/Nie.**	tahk/n^{y}eh
Please.	**Proszę.**	**pro**sheh
Thank you.	**Dziękuję.**	dzhen^{y}**koo**yeh
I beg your pardon?	**Przepraszam.**	.psheh**prah**shahm

Introductions *Przedstawianie się*

Good morning.	**Dzień dobry.**	dzhehn^{y} **do**bri
Good afternoon.	**Dzień dobry.**	dzhehn^{y} **do**bri
Good night.	**Dobranoc.**	do**brah**nots
Goodbye.	**Do widzenia.**	do vee**dzhen**^{y}ah
My name is …	**Nazywam się …**	nah**zi**wahm s^{y}eh
What's your name?	**Jak się pan[i] nazywa?**	yahk s^{y}eh pahn [**pah**n^{y}ee] nah**zi**vah
How are you?	**Jak się pan[i] miewa?**	yahk s^{y}eh pahn [**pah**n^{y}ee] **myeh**vah
Very well, thanks. And you?	**Bardzo dobrze, dziękuję. A pan[i]?**	**bahr**dzo **do**bzheh, dzhen^{y}**koo**yeh. a pahn [**pah**n^{y}ee]
Where do you come from?	**Skąd pan[i] pochodzi?**	skont pahn [**pah**n^{y}ee] po**ho**dzhee
I'm from …	**Jestem z …**	**yeh**stehm s
Australia	**Australia**	ah**wstrah**lyah
Britain	**Wielka Brytania**	**vyeh**lkah bri**tah**n^{y}ah
Canada	**Kanada**	kah**nah**dah
United States	**Stany Zjednoczone**	**stah**ni syehdno**cho**neh
Are you on your own?	**Czy jest pan[i] sam[a]?**	chi yehst pahn [**pah**n^{y}ee] sahm [**sah**mah]
I'm with my …	**Jestem z …**	**yeh**stehm s
wife	**żoną**	**zho**nawng
husband	**mężem**	**meh**zhehm
family	**rodziną**	ro**dzhee**nawng
boyfriend	**dziewczyną**	dzheh**fchi**nawng
girlfriend	**chłopakiem**	hwo**pah**kyehm

GUIDE TO PRONUNCIATION, see page 143/EMERGENCIES, see page 143

Questions *Pytania*

When?/How?	**Kiedy?/Jak?**	**kyeh**di/yahk
What?/Why?	**Co?/Dlaczego?**	tso/dlah**cheh**go
Who?/Which?	**Kto?/Który?/Która?**	kto/**ktoo**ri/**ktoo**rah
Where is/are…?	**Gdzie jest/są…?**	gdzheh yehst/sawng
Where can I find/get …?	**Gdzie mogę znaleźć …?**	gdzheh **mo**geh **znah**les^{y}tsh
How far?	**Jak daleko?**	yakh da**leh**koh
How long?	**Jak długo?**	yakh **dhwoo**goh
How much?	**Ile?**	eeleh
Can/May …?	**Czy mogę …?**	chi **mo**geh
Can I have …?	**Czy mogę dostać …?**	chi **mo**geh **do**stahtsh
Can you help me?	**Czy może mi pan[i] pomóc?**	chi **mo**zheh mee pahn [**pah**n^{y}ee] po**vyeh**dzhehtsh
I understand.	**Rozumiem.**	ro**zoo**myehm
I don't understand.	**Nie rozumiem.**	n^{y}eh ro**zoo**myehm
Can you translate this for me?	**Proszę to przetłumaczyć.**	**pro**sheh to pshehtwoo**mah**chitsh
Do you speak English?	**Czy mówi pan[i] po angielsku?**	chi **moo**vee pahn [**pah**n^{y}ee] po ahn**gyeh**lskoo
I don't speak (much) Polish.	**Nie mówię (zbyt dobrze) po-polsku.**	n^{y}eh **moo**veh (zhbit po **dob**zheh) **pol**skoo

A few useful words *Kilka innych pożytecznych wyrazów*

better/worse	**lepsze/gorsze**	**leh**psheh/**gor**sheh
big/small	**duże/małe**	**doo**zheh/**mah**weh
cheap/expensive	**tanie/drogie**	**tah**n^{y}eh/**dro**gyeh
early/late	**wczesne/późne**	**fcheh**sneh/**pooz**^{y}neh
good/bad	**dobre/złe**	**do**breh/zweh
hot/cold	**ciepłe/zimne**	**tsheh**pweh/**zee**mneh
near/far	**bliskie/dalekie**	**blee**skyeh/dah**leh**kyeh
right/wrong	**dobre/złe**	**do**breh/zweh
vacant/occupied	**wolne/zajęte**	**vo**lneh/zah**yeh**teh

Hotel—Accomodation *Hotel*

I have a reservation.	**Mam rezerwację.**	mahm rehzeh**rvah**tsyeh
We've reserved two rooms.	**Zarezerwowaliśmy dwa pokoje.**	zahrehzehvo**vah**lees^{y}mi dvah po**ko**yeh
Do you have any vacancies?	**Czy są jakieś wolne pokoje?**	chi sawng **ya**kyehs^{y} **vo**lneh po**ko**yeh
I'd like a …	**Chciał(a)bym …**	**htshah**w(ah)bim
single room	**pokój jednoosbowy**	**po**kooy yehdnooso**bo**vi
double room	**pokój dwuosobowy**	**po**kooy dvoooso**bo**vi
with twin beds	**z dwoma łóżkami**	z **dvo**mah woozh**kah**mee
with a double bed	**z podwójnym łóżkiem**	spod**voo**ynim **woo**zhkyehm
with a bath	**z łazienką**	z wah**zyeh**nkawng
with a shower	**z prysznicem**	spri**shn^{y}ee**tsehm
We'll be staying …	**Zostaniemy …**	zostah**nyeh**mi
overnight	**przez jedną noc**	pshez **jehd**nawng nots
a few days	**kilka dni**	**kee**lkah dn^{y}ee
a week	**tydzień**	**ti**dzhehn^{y}

Decision *Decyzja*

May I see the room?	**Czy mogę zobaczyć pokój?**	chi **mo**geh zo**bah**chitsh **po**kooy
I'll take it.	**Wezmę go.**	**veh**zmeh go
I don't like it.	**Nie podoba mi się.**	n^{y}eh po**do**bah mee s^{y}eh
It's too …	**Jest zbyt …**	yehst sbit
dark/small	**ciemny/mały**	**tsheh**mni/**mah**wi
noisy	**hałaśliwy**	hahwah**s^{y}lee**vi
Do you have anything …?	**Czy ma pan[i] coś …?**	chi mah pahn [**pah**n^{y}ee] tsos^{y}
cheaper	**tańszego**	tahn^{y}**sheh**go
quieter	**spokojniejszego**	spokoyn^{y}eh**sheh**go
May I have my bill, please?	**Czy mogę prosić o rachunek?**	chi **mo**geh **pro**s^{y}eetsh o rah**hoo**nehk
It's been a very enjoyable stay.	**Bardzo miło spędziliśmy tutaj czas.**	**bahr**dzo **mee**wo spehn^{y}dzhee**lee**symi **too**tigh chahs

Eating out *Restauracja*

I'd like to reserve a table for 4.	**Chciał(a)bym zarezerwować stolik na cztery osoby.**	**htshah**w(ah)bim zahrehzehr**vo**vahtsh **sto**leek nah **chteh**ri os**o**bi
We'll come at 8.	**Przyjdziemy o ósmej.**	pshi**ydzheh**mi o **oo**smehy
I'd like …	**Poproszę…**	po**pro**sheh
What do you recommend?	**Co by nam pan [pani] polecił[a] ?**	co bi nahm pahn [**pahn**yee] po**leh**tsheew[ah]
Do you have any vegetarian dishes?	**Czy są dania wegetariańskie/ bezmięsne?**	chi sawng **dah**nyah vehgehtahryah**nysk**yeh/ behsm**yeh**sneh

Breakfast *Śniadanie*

I'll have some …	**Poproszę …**	po**pro**sheh
bread/cheese	**chleb/ser**	hlehb/sehr
eggs/ham	**jajka/szynka**	**yah**ykah/**shin**kah
jam	**dżem**	jehm
rolls	**bułki**	**boo**wkee

Starters *Przystawki*

befsztyk tatarski	**beh**fshtik tah**tah**rskee	steak tartar
jaja faszerowane pieczarkami	**yah**yah fahshehro**vah**neh pyehchahr**kah**mee	eggs stuffed with mushrooms
sandacz po polsku z jajkami	**sah**ndahch po **po**lskoo z yahy**kah**mee	Polish-style perch with eggs
śledź w oleju	sylehdzh w o**leh**yoo	herring in oil
węgorz wędzony	**veh**gozh veh**dzo**ni	smoked eel

Meat *Dania mięsne*

I'd like some …	**Poproszę …**	po**pro**sheh
beef	**wołowinę**	vowo**vee**neh
chicken/duck	**roorczę/raczrę**	**roor**cheh/**rah**chreh
lamb	**baraninę**	bahrah**nyee**neh
pork	**wieprzowinę**	vyehpsho**vee**neh
veal	**cielęcinę**	tshehleh**tshee**neh

NUMBERS, see page 142

baked	**zapiekane**	zahpyeh**kah**neh
boiled/fried	**gotowane/smażone**	goto**vah**neh/smah**zho**neh
grilled/stewed	**z rusztu/duszone**	**sroo**shtoo/doo**sho**neh
underdone (rare)	**mało wysmażone**	**mah**wo wismah**zho**neh
medium	**średnio wysmażone**	s[y]**reh**dn[y]o vismah**zho**neh
well-done	**mocno wysmażone**	**mo**tsno vismah**zho**neh

pieczony schab	pyeh**cho**ni shahb	roast loin of pork
sznycel cielęcy	**shni**tsehl tsheh**leh**tsi	breaded veal escalope
sztuka mięsa	**shtoo**kah **myeh**sah	boiled beef
zrazy	**srah**si	pound steak
zeberka	zheh**beh**rkah	ribs

Fish *Dania rybne*

cod/plaice/trout	dorsh/**flon**drah/pstrong	**dorsz/flądra/pstrąg**
ryba zapiekana z migdałami	**ri**bah zahpyeh**kah**nah z meegdah**wah**mee	baked fish with almonds
karp gotowany w jarzynach	kahrp goto**vah**ni v ja**zhi**nahh	steamed carp in vegetables
pstrągi panierowane	**pstron**gee pahn[y]ehro**vah**neh	trout in breadcrumbs

Vegetables and salads *Jarzyny i sałatki*

beans	**fasola**	fah**so**lah
cabbage	**kapusta**	kah**poo**stah
carrots	**marchew**	**mah**rhehf
mushrooms	**pieczarki**	pyeh**chah**rkee
onions	**cebula**	tseh**boo**lah
potatoes	**ziemniaki**	z[y]eh**mn[y]ah**kee
tomatoes	**pomidory**	pomee**do**ri
naleśniki ze serem	nahleh**s[y]n[y]ee**kee zeh **seh**rehm	white cheese pancakes
omlet z pieczarkami	**o**mleht spyehchahr**kah**mee	pancake with mushrooms
pierogi z grzybami	pyeh**ro**gee sgzhi**bah**mee	dumplings stuffed with mushrooms
pierogi z kapustą	pyeh**ro**gee skah**poo**stawng	dumplings stuffed with boiled cabbage

Fruit and dessert *Owoce i desery*

apple	**jabłko**	**yah**bwko
lemon	**cytryna**	tsi**tri**nah
orange	**pomarańcza**	pomah**rah**n^{y}chah
pear	**gruszka**	**groo**shkah
strawberries	**truskawki**	troo**skah**fkee
galaretka	gahlah**reh**tkah	jelly
krem waniliowy	krehm vahn^{y}ee**lyo**vi	vanilla cream
lody	**lo**di	ice-cream
pączek	**pon**chehk	doughnut
piernik	**pyeh**rn^{y}eek	honey cake

Drinks Napoje

beer	**piwo**	piwo
coffee	**kawa**	**kah**vah
black	**czarna**	chahrnah
with milk	**z mlekiem**	smlehkyehm
fruit juice	**sok owocowy**	sok ovo**co**vi
mineral water	**woda mineralna**	**vo**dah meeneh**rah**lnah
tea	**herbata**	heh**rbah**tah
wine	**wina**	**vee**nah
red/white	**czerwone/białe**	chehr**vo**neh/**byah**weh

Complaints—Bill (check) *Zazalenia—Rachunek*

This is too salty/ sweet.	**To jest zbyt słone/ słodkie.**	to yehst zbit **swo**neh/ **swo**tkyeh
That's not what I ordered.	**Tego nie zamawiałem (zamawiałam).**	**teh**go n^{y}eh zahmah**vyah**wehm (zahmah**vyah**wahm)
I'd like to pay.	**Chciał(a)bym zapłacić.**	**htshah**w(ah)bim zah**pwah**tsheetsh
I think there's a mistake in this bill.	**Wydaje mi się że w tym rachunku jest błąd.**	vi**dah**yeh mee s^{y}eh zheh v tim rah**hoo**nkoo yehst bwont
We enjoyed it, thank you.	**Dziękuję, smakowało nam.**	**dzheh**kooyeh smahko**vah**wo nahm

NUMBERS, see page 142

Travelling around *Podróże*

Plane *Samolot*

Is there a flight to Kraków?	**Czy są jakieś loty do Krakowa?**	chi sawng **yah**kyehs^{y} **lo**ti do krah**ko**vah
What time should I check in?	**O której godzinie mam się zgłosić do odprawy?**	o **ktoo**reh go**dzhee**n^{y}eh mahm s^{y}eh **sgwo**-s^{y}eetsh do o**tprah**vi
I'd like to … my reservation.	**Chciał(a)bym … moją rezerwację.**	**htshah**w(ah)bim **… mo**yawng rehsehr**vah**tsyeh
cancel	**odwołać**	od**vo**wahtsh
change	**zmienić**	**smyeh**n^{y}eetsh
confirm	**potwierdzić**	po**tfyeh**rdzheetsh

Train *Pociąg*

I'd like a ticket . to Toruń.	**Poproszę bilet do Torunia.**	po**pro**sheh **bee**leht to to**roo**n^{y}ah
single (one-way)	**w jedną stronę**	v **yeh**dnawng **stro**neh
return (roundtrip)	**tam i z powrotem**	tahm ee spov**ro**tehm
first class	**pierwszej klasy**	**pyhe**rfshehy **klah**si
second class	**drugiej klasy**	**droo**gyehy **klah**si
How long does the journey (trip) take?	**Jak długo trwa podróż?**	yahk **dwoo**go trfah **po**droozh
When is the … train to Poznań?	**Kiedy jest … pociąg do Poznania?**	**kyeh**di yehst … **po**tshawngg do po**snah**n^{y}ah
first/last	**pierwszy/ostatni**	**pyeh**rfshi/o**stah**tn^{y}ee
next	**następny**	nah**steh**pni
Is this the right train to Przemyśl?	**Czy to jest pociąg do Przemyśla?**	chi to yehst **po**tshawngg do psheh**mi**s^{y}lah

Bus—Tram (streetcar) *Autobus—Tramwaj*

Which tram goes to the town centre/ downtown?	**Którym tramwajem mogę dojechać do centrum?**	**ktoo**rim trahm**vah**yehm **mo**geh do**yeh**hahtsh do **tseh**ntroom
Will you tell me when to get off?	**Proszę mi powiedzieć kiedy wysiąść?**	**pro**sheh mee po**vyeh**dzhehtsh **kyeh**di **vi**s^{y}ons^{y}tsh

TELLING THE TIME, see page 141/NUMBERS, see page 142

Taxi *Taksówka*

What's the fare to …?	**Ile wynosi opłata do …?**	eeleh vi**nos**^{y}ee o**pwah**tah do
Take me to this address.	**Proszę mnie zawieźć na ten adres.**	**pro**sheh mnyeh **zah**vyehs^{y}tsh nah tehn **ah**drehs
Please stop here.	**Proszę się tu zatrzymać.**	**pro**sheh s^{y}eh too zat**zhi**mahtsh

Car hire (rental) *Wynajem samochodów*

I'd like to hire (rent) a car.	**Chciał(a)bym wynająć samochód.**	**htshah**w(ah)bim vi**nah**yontsh sah**mo**hoot
I'd like it for a day/a week.	**Chciał(a)bym/ go na jeden dzień/ tydzień.**	**htshah**w(ah)bim go nah **yeh**dehn dzhehn^{y}/ **ti**dzhehn^{y}
Where's the nearest filling station?	**Gdzie jest najbliższa stacja benzynowa?**	gdzheh yehst nahy**blee**zhshah **stah**tsyah behnzi**no**vah
Fill it up, please.	**Proszę do pełna.**	**pro**sheh do **peh**wnah
Give me … litres of petrol (gasoline).	**Poproszę … litrów benzyny.**	po**pro**sheh … **lee**troof beh**nzi**ni
How do I get to …?	**Jak mogę się dostać do …?**	yahk **mo**geh s^{y}eh **do**stahtsh do
I've had a breakdown at …	**Samochód mi się zepsuł w …**	sah**mo**hood mee s^{y}eh **zeh**psoow v
Can you send a mechanic?	**Czy może tu przyjechać mechanik?**	chi **mo**zheh too pshi**yeh**hahtsh meh**hah**n^{y}eek

☞ You're on the wrong road.	**Źle pan[i] jedzie.** ☜
Go straight ahead.	**Proszę jechać prosto.**
It's down there on the left/right.	**To jest tam dalej po lewej/prawej.**
opposite/behind …	**naprzeciw/za**
next to/after …	**obok/za**
north/south	**na północ/na południe**
east/west	**na wschód/na zachód**

Sightseeing *Zwiedzanie*

Where's the tourist office?	**Gdzie jest informacja turystyczna?**	gdzheh yehst eenfor**maht**syah toori**sti**chnah
Is there an English-speaking guide?	**Czy jest przewodnik mówiący po angielsku?**	chi yehst pshe**vo**dn^{y}eek moo**vyon**tsi po ah**ngyeh**lskoo
Where is/are the …?	**Gdzie jest/są …?**	gdzheh yehst/sawng
botanical gardens	**ogród botaniczny**	**o**grood botah**n^{y}ee**chni
castle	**zamek**	**zah**mehk
cathedral	**katedra**	kah**teh**drah
city centre	**centrum miasta**	**tseh**ntroom **myah**stah
exhibition	**wystawa**	vi**stah**vah
harbour	**port/przystań**	port/**pshi**stahn^{y}
market	**rynek**	**ri**nehk
museum	**muzeum**	moo**zeh**oom
park	**park**	pahrk
zoo	**zoo**	zoo
What are the opening hours?	**Jakie są godziny otwarcia?**	**yah**kyeh sawng go**dzhee**ni ot**fah**rtshah
How much is the entrance fee?	**Ile kosztuje wstęp?**	**ee**leh ko**shtoo**yeh fstehp

Entertainment *Odpoczynek*

What's playing at the theatre?	**Co dzisiaj grają w teatrze?**	tso **dzhee**s^{y}ah **grah**yawng f**tehah**tzheh
How much are the seats?	**Ile kosztują bilety?**	**ee**leh ko**shtoo**yawng bee**leh**ti
Would you like to go out with me tonight?	**Czy możemy się umówić na wieczór?**	chi **mo**zhemi s^{y}eh oo**moo**vetsh nah **vyeh**choor
Is there a discotheque in town?	**Czy jest tu gdzieś dyskoteka?**	chi yehst too gdzhehs^{y} disko**teh**kah
Shall we go to the cinema (movies)?	**Może poszlibyśmy do kina?**	**mo**zheh poshlee**bis^{y}**mi do **kee**nah
Thank you, it's been a wonderful evening.	**Dziękuję, to był cudowny wieczór.**	**dzheh**kooyeh to biw tsoo**do**vni **vyeh**choor

DAYS OF THE WEEK, see page 142

Shops, stores and services *Sklepy i zakłady usługowe*

Where's the nearest …?	**Gdzie jest najbliższy …?**	gdzheh yehst nahy**blee**zhshi
baker's	**piekarnia**	pye**kah**rn^{y}ah
bookshop	**księgarnia**	ks^{y}ehn**gah**rn^{y}ah
butcher's	**sklep mięsny**	sklehp **myehn**sni
chemist's	**apteka**	ah**pteh**kah
dentist	**gabinet dentystyczny**	gah**bee**neht dehntis**ti**chni
department store	**dom towarowy**	dom tovah**ro**vi
grocer's	**sklep spożywczy**	sklehp spo**zhi**vchi
newsagent's	**kiosk**	kyosk
post office	**poczta**	**po**chtah
souvenir shop	**sklep z pamiątkami**	sklehp spamyon**tkah**mee
supermarket	**sam spożywczy**	sahm spo**zhi**fchi
wine merchant	**sklep monopolowy**	sklehp monopo**lo**vi

General expressions *Zwroty ogólne*

Where's the main shopping area?	**Gdzie jest główne centrum handlowe?**	gdzheh yehst **gwoo**vneh **tseh**ntroom hahnd**lo**veh
Do you have any …?	**Czy są …?**	chi sawng
Don't you have anything …?	**Czy nie ma pan[i] czegoś …?**	chi n^{y}eh mah pahn [**pah**n^{y}ee] **cheh**gos^y
cheaper	**tańszego**	tah**n^{y}sheh**go
better	**lepszego**	leh**psheh**go
larger	**większego**	vyeh**ksheh**go
smaller	**mniejszego**	mn^{y}eh**sheh**go
Can I try it on?	**Czy mogę to przymierzyć?**	chi **mo**geh do pshi**myeh**zhitsh
How much is this?	**Ile to kosztuje?**	**ee**leh to ko**shtoo**yeh
Please write it down.	**Proszę to napisać.**	**pro**sheh to nah**pee**sahtsh
No, I don't like it.	**Nie, nie podoba mi się to.**	n^{y}eh n^{y}eh po**do**bah mee s^{y}eh to
I'll take it.	**Wezmę to.**	**veh**smeh to

NUMBERS, see page 142

Do you accept credit cards?	**Czy mogę zapłacić kartą kredytową?**	chi **mo**geh zah**pwah**tsheetsh **kah**rtawng krehdi**to**vanwg

black	**czarny**	**chah**rni	brown	**brązowy**	bron**zo**vi
blue	**niebieski**	n^{y}eh**byeh**skee	white	**biały**	**byah**wi
grey	**szary**	**sha**ri	green	**zielony**	z^{y}eh**lo**ni
red	**czerwony**	cheh**rvo**ni	yellow	**żółty**	**zhoo**wti

I want to buy …	**Chcę kupić …**	htseh **koo**peetsh
aspirin	**aspirynę**	ahspee**ri**neh
battery	**baterię**	bah**teh**ryeh
bottle opener	**otwieracz do butelek**	ot**fyeh**rahch do boo**teh**lehk
newspaper	**gazetę**	gah**zeh**teh
American/English	**amerykańską/ angielską**	ahmehri**kah**n^{y}skawng/ ah**ngyeh**lskawng
shampoo	**szampon**	**shah**mpon
soap	**mydło**	**mi**dwo
suntan cream	**krem do opalania**	krehm do opah**lah**n^{y}ah
toothpaste	**pasta do zębów**	**pah**stah do **zeh**boof
a kilo of apples	**kilo jabłek**	**kee**lo **yah**bwehk
a litre of milk	**litr mleka**	**lee**tr **mleh**kah
I'd like a … film for this camera.	**Proszę film do tego aparatu.**	**pro**sheh feelm do **teh**go ahpah**rah**too
black and white	**czarnobiały**	**chah**rno**byah**wi
colour	**kolorowy**	kolo**ro**vi

Souvenirs *Upominki*

bursztyn	**boo**rshtin	amber
ceramika	kerah**mee**kah	ceramics
koronki	ko**ron**ki	lace
laleczki z Cepelii	lah**leh**chkee stseh**peh**lyee	dolls in folk costume
lichtarze	leeh**tah**zheh	candlesticks
pościel wyszywana	pos^{y}ts^{y}el vishi**vah**nah	embroidered linen
srebro	**sreh**bro	silver goods

TELLING THE TIME, see page 141

At the bank *W banku*

Where's the bank/ currency exchange office?	**Gdzie jest najbliższy bank/ kantor wymiany walut?**	gdzheh yehst nahy**blee**zhshi bahnk/ **kah**ntor vi**myah**ni **vah**loot
I want to change some dollars/pounds.	**Chciał(a)bym wymienić trochę dolarów/funtów.**	**htshah**w(ah)bim vi**myeh**n^{y}eetsh **tro**heh do**lah**roof/**foon**toof
What's the exchange rate?	**Jaki jest kurs wymiany?**	**yah**kee yehst koors vi**myah**ni

At the post office *Na poczcie*

I'd like to send this (by) …	**Chciał(a)bym wysłać to …**	**htshah**w(ah)bim **vi**swahtsh to
airmail	**pocztą lotniczą**	**po**chtawng lot**n^{y}ee**chawng
express	**ekspresem**	eh**ksprehs**ehm
A …łotowy stamp, please.	**Proszę znaczek za … złote.**	**pro**sheh **znah**chehk zah … **zwo**teh
What's the postage for a postcard to Los Angeles?	**Ile kosztuje znaczek na kartkę do Los Angeles?**	**ee**leh kosh**too**yeh **znah**chehk na **kah**rtkeh do los ahn**jeh**lehs
Is there any mail for me?	**Czy są dla mnie jakieś listy.**	chi sawng dlah mnyeh **yah**kyehs^{y} **lee**sti.

Telephoning *Telefonowanie*

Where's the nearest telephone booth?	**Gdzie jest najbliższa budka telefoniczna?**	gdzheh yehst nahy**blee**zhshah **boo**dkah tehlehfo**nee**chnah
Hello. This is …	**Halo. Tu mówi …**	**hah**lo. too **moo**vee
I'd like to speak to …	**Czy mogę rozmawiać z …**	chi **mo**geh ros**mah**vyahtsh s
When will he/ she be back?	**Kiedy wróci?**	**kyeh**di **vroo**tshee

NUMBERS, see page 142

Time and date *Czas i daty*

It's …	**Jest …**	yehst
five past one	**pięć po pierwszej**	pyehntsh po **pyeh**rfshehy
a quarter past three	**kwadrans po trzeciej**	**kfah**drahns po **chsheh**tsheh
twenty past four	**dwadzieścia po czwartej**	dvadvah**dzheh**s^{y}tshah po **chvah**rtehy
half-past six	**wpół do siódmej**	fpoow do **s^{y}oo**dmehy
twenty-five to seven	**pięć po wpół do siódmej**	pyehntsh po fpoow do **s^{y}oo**dmehy
ten to ten	**za dziesięć dziesiąta**	zah **dzheh**s^{y}ehntsh **dzheh**s^{y}ontah
twelve o'clock	**dwunasta**	**dvoo**nastah
in the morning	**rano**	**rah**no
during the day	**w ciągu dnia**	**fthson**goo dn^{y}ah
at night	**w nocy**	**vno**tsi
yesterday	**wczoraj**	**fcho**rahy
today	**dzisiaj/dziś**	**dzhee**s^{y}ahy/dzhees^y
tomorrow	**jutro**	**yoo**tro
spring/summer	**wiosna/lato**	**vyo**snah/**lah**to
autumn/winter	**jesień/zima**	**yeh**s^{y}ehn^y/**z^{y}ee**mah

January	**styczeń**	**sti**chehn^y
February	**luty**	**loo**ti
March	**marzec**	**mah**shehts
April	**kwiećień**	**kfyeh**tshehn^y
May	**maj**	mahy
June	**czerwiec**	**cheh**rvyehts
July	**lipiec**	**lee**pyehts
August	**sierpień**	**s^{y}eh**rpyehn^y
September	**wrzesień**	**vsheh**s^{y}ehn^y
October	**październik**	pahz^y**dzheh**rn^{y}eek
November	**listopad**	lees**to**pahd
December	**grudzień**	**groo**dzhehn^y

Sunday	**niedziela**	n^{y}eh**dzheh**lah
Monday	**poniedziałek**	pon^{y}eh**dzhah**wehk
Tuesday	**wtorek**	**fto**rehk
Wednesday	**środa**	s^{y}**ro**dah
Thursday	**czwartek**	**chfah**rtehk
Friday	**piątek**	**pyon**tehk
Saturday	**sobota**	so**bo**tah

Numbers *Liczby*

0	**zero**	**zeh**ro	11	**jedenaście**	yehdeh**nah**s^{y}tsheh
1	**jeden**	**yeh**dehn	12	**dwanaście**	dvah**nah**s^{y}tsheh
2	**dwa**	dvah	13	**trzynaście**	chshi**nah**s^{y}tsheh
3	**trzy**	chshi	14	**czternaście**	chtehr**nah**s^{y}tsheh
4	**cztery**	**chteh**ri	15	**piętnaście**	pyeht**nah**s^{y}tsheh
5	**pięć**	pyehntsh	16	**szesnaście**	shehs**nah**s^{y}tsheh
6	**sześć**	shehs^{y}tsh	17	**siedemnaście**	s^{y}ehdehm**nah**s^{y}tsheh
7	**siedem**	**s^{y}eh**dehm	18	**osiemnaście**	os^{y}ehm**nah**s^{y}tsheh

8	**osiem**	**o**s^{y}ehm
9	**dziewięć**	**dzheh**vyehntsh
10	**dziesięć**	**dzheh**s^{y}ehntsh
19	**dziewiętnaście**	dzhehvyehnt**nah**s^{y}tsheh
20	**dwadzieścia**	dvah**dzheh**s^{y}tshah
21	**dwadzieścia jeden**	dvah**dzheh**s^{y}tshah **yeh**dehn
30	**trzydzieści**	chshi**dzheh**s^{y}tshee
40	**czterdzieści**	chtehr**dzheh**s^{y}tshee
50	**pięćdziesiąt**	pyehntsh**dzheh**s^{y}ont
60	**sześćdziesiąt**	shehs^{y}tsh**dzheh**s^{y}ont
70	**siedemdziesiąt**	s^{y}ehdehm**dzheh**s^{y}ont
80	**osiemdziesiąt**	os^{y}ehm**dzheh**s^{y}ont
90	**dziewięćdziesiąt**	dzhehvyehtsh**dzheh**s^{y}ont
100/1000	**sto/tysiąc**	sto/**ti**s^{y}onts

first/second	**pierwszy/drugi**	**pyeh**rvshi/**droo**gee
once/twice	**raz/dwa razy**	rahs/dvah **rah**zi
a half	**połowa/pół**	po**wo**vah/poow

Emergency *Nagły wypadek*

Call the police	**Proszę wezwać policję**	**pro**sheh **veh**svahtsh po**lee**tsyeh
HELP	**RATUNKU**	rah**too**nkoo
I'm ill	**Jestem chory**	**yeh**stehm **ho**ri
I'm lost	**Zgubiłem (Zgubiłam) się**	sgoo**bee**wehm (sgoo**bee**wahm) s^{y}eh
Leave me alone	**Proszę mnie zostawić w spokoju**	**pro**sheh mn^{y}eh zo**stah**veetsh fspo**ko**yoo
STOP THIEF	**ŁAPAĆ ZŁODZIEJA**	**wah**pahtsh zwo**dzheh**yah
My … has been stolen.	**Skradziono mi …**	skrah**dzho**no mee
I've lost my …	**Zgubiłem (Zgubiłam) …**	zgoo**bee**wehm (zgoo**bee**wahm)
handbag/wallet	**torebkę/portfel**	to**reh**bkeh/**por**tfehl
Where can I find a doctor who speaks English?	**Gdzie mogę znaleźć lekarza, który mówi po angielsku?**	gdzheh **mo**geh **znah**lehs^{y}tsh leh**kah**zhah, **ktoo**ri **moo**vi po ah**ngyeh**lskoo

Guide to Polish pronunciation

Consonants

Letter	Approximate Pronunciation	Symbol	Example	
b, f, k, l, m, p, z are pronounced as in English				
cz	as **ch** in **ch**urch	ch	**czy**	chi
dz	as **j** in **j**am	j	**dżem**	jehm
g	as in **g**irl	g	**guma**	**goo**mah
j	as the **j** in **y**et	y	**jak**	yahk
ł	as **w** in **w**in	w	**ładny**	**wah**dni
n, t, d	as in English but the tongue	n	**na**	nah
	is against the front teeth	t	**tak**	takh
	not the teeth ridge	d	**dom**	dom
s	as **s** in **s**it	s	**sam**	sahm
sz	as **sh** in **sh**ine	sh	**szal**	shahl

TELEPHONING, see page 140

w	as **v** in **v**an	v	**woda**	**vod**ah
ż or **rz**	as **s** in plea**s**ure	zh	**żelazo**	zheh**lah**zo
			rzeka	**zheh**kah

Sounds distinctly different

c	like the sequence **ts** in **tsets**e pronounced quickly	ts	**co**	tso
ć or **ci**	like the Polish **c** but much softer	tsh	**pić**	peetsh
		tsh	**ciało**	**tshah**wo
dz	like the sequence **ds** in be**ds** pronounced quickly	dz	**dzwonek**	**dzvo**nek
dź or **dzi**	like the Polish **dz** but much softer	dzh	**dział**	dzhahw
h or **ch**	similar to English **h** but with much more friction	h	**herbata**	hehr**bah**tah
			chudy	**hoodi**
ń or **ni**	like English **n** with considerable softening	n^y	**nie**	n^ye
r	like the Scottish **r**	r	**rak**	rahk
ś or **si**	like English **s** but much softer	s^y	**się**	s^yeh
			ktoś	$ktos^y$
ź or **zi**	like English **z** but much softer	z^y	**zielony**	z^yeh**loni**

Vowels

a	as **u** in c**u**lt	ah	**tak**	tahk
e	like **e** of t**e**n	eh	**lek**	lehk
i	as **i** in f**i**t	i	**ty**	ti
o	as **o** in c**o**t	o	**kot**	kot
u or **ó**	a sound between the **u** of p**u**t and **oo** of b**oo**ts	oo	**drut**	droot
ą	1) pronounced **on** before a consonant;	on	**prąd**	pront
	2) when it's the final letter, as in the French word fi**an**cé	awng	**są**	sawng
ę	1) pronounced **en** before a consonant	ehn	**pęd**	pehnt
	2) like **e** in b**e**d when it is the final letter	eh	**tę**	teh

Romanian

Basic expressions *Expresii curente*

Yes/No.	**Da/Nu.**	da/noo
Please.	**Vă rog.**	ver rog
Thank you.	**Mulţumesc.**	mooltsoo**mesc**
I beg your pardon?	**Poftim?**	pof**teem**

Introductions *Prezentări*

Good morning.	**Bună dimineaţa.**	**boo**ner deemee**na**tsa
Good afternoon.	**Bună ziua.**	**boo**ner **zee**wah
Good night.	**Noapte bună.**	**nwap**teh **boo**ner
Good-bye.	**La revedere.**	la reve**de**reh
My name is …	**Mă numesc …**	mer noo**mesc**
What's your name?	**Cum vă numiţi?**	coom ver noo**meets**^{y}
How are you?	**Ce mai faceţi?**	cheh migh **fa**chets^{y}
Fine thanks. And you?	**Mulţumesc bine, şi dumneavoastră?**	mooltsoo**mesc** **bee**neh shee doomna**vwas**trer
Where do you come from?	**De unde veniţi?**	deh **oon**deh ve**neets**^{y}
I'm from …	**Vin din …**	veen deen
Australia	**Australia**	a^{oo}**stra**lya
Britain	**Marea Britanie**	**ma**reh-a bree**ta**nyeh
Canada	**Canada**	ca**na**da
USA	**Statele Unite**	**sta**teleh oo**nee**teh
I'm with my …	**Sînt cu …**	sınt coo
wife	**soţia mea**	so**tsee**a meh-**a**
husband	**soţul meu**	**so**tsool me^{oo}
family	**familia mea**	fa**mee**lya meh-**a**
boyfriend	**prietenul meu**	pree-**e**tenool me^{oo}
girlfriend	**prietena mea**	pree-**e**tena meh
I'm on my own.	**Sînt singur.**	sınt **seen**goor
I'm here on holiday/vacation.	**Sînt aici în vacanţă.**	sınt a**eech**^{y} ın va**can**tser

GUIDE TO PRONUNCIATION/EMERGENCIES, see page 159/158

Questions *Întrebări*

When?/How?	**Cînd?/Cum?**	cind/coom
What?/Why?	**Ce?/De ce?**	cheh/de cheh
Who?/Which?	**Cine?/Care?**	**chee**neh/**ca**reh
Where is/are …?	**Unde este/sint …?**	**oon**deh **yest**eh/sint
Where can I get/find …?	**De unde pot lua …?**	deh **oon**deh pot lwa
Is it far?	**Este departe?**	**ye**steh de**par**teh
How long?	**Cît timp durează?**	cit teemp doo**ra**zer
How much?	**Cîţi?**	cits[y]
May I …?	**Imi permiteţi …?**	**imi** permi**te**tsi
Can I have …?	**Pot avea …?**	pot aveh-**a**
Can you help me?	**Puteţi să mă ajutaţi?**	poo**tets**[y] ser mer azhoo**tats**[y]
What does this mean?	**Ce înseamnă aceasta?**	cheh in**sam**ner a**chas**ta
I understand.	**Înţeleg.**	intse**leg**
I don't understand.	**Nu înţeleg.**	noo intse**leg**
Can you translate this for me?	**Puteţi să-mi traduceţi, vă rog, asta?**	poo**tets**[y] serm[y] tra**doo**chets[y] ver rog **a**sta
Do you speak English?	**Vorbiţi englezeşte?**	vor**beets**[y] engle**zesh**teh
I don't speak Romanian.	**Nu vorbesc româneşte.**	noo vor**besc** romi**nehsh**teh

A few useful words *Alte cuvinte utile*

better/worse	**mai bine/mai rău**	migh **bee**neh/migh roh
big/small	**mare/mic**	**ma**reh/meec
cheap/expensive	**ieftin/scump**	**yef**teen/scoomp
early/late	**devreme/tîrziu**	de**vre**meh/tir**zyoo**
good/bad	**bun/rău**	boon/roh
hot/cold	**cald/rece**	cald/**re**cheh
near/far	**aproape/departe**	a**prwa**peh/de**par**teh
right/wrong	**bine/rău**	**bee**neh/rohfree
vacant/occupied	**liber/ocupat**	**lee**ber/ocoo**pat**

Hotel—Accommodation *Hotel*

I've a reservation.	**Am o rezervare.**	am o rezer**va**reh
We've reserved two rooms/ an apartment.	**Am rezervat două camere/ un apartament.**	am rezer**va**toon do-wer **ca**mereh/ aparta**ment**
Do you have any vacancies?	**Aveţi camere libere?**	a**vets**^{y} **ca**mereh **lee**bereh
I'd like a … room	**Aş vreao cameră …**	ash vreh-**a** **ca**merer …
single	**cu un pat**	coo oon pat
double	**cu două paturi**	coo do-wer **pa**toor^{y}
with twin beds	**cu două paturi**	coo do-wer **pa**toor^{y}
with a double bed	**cu pat dublu**	coo pat **doo**bloo
with a bath/shower	**cu baie/cu duş**	coo **ba**yeh/coo doosh
We'll be staying …	**O să stăm …**	o ser sterm
overnight only	**numai o noapte**	**noo**migh o **nwap**teh
a few days	**cîteva zile**	**ci**teva **zee**leh
a week	**o săptămînă**	o serpter**mi**ner
Is there a campsite near here?	**Există un teren de camping?**	eg**zee**ster oon te**ren** deh **cam**peeng

Decision *Decizie*

May I see the room?	**Pot să văd camera, vă rog?**	pot ser verd **ca**mera ver rog
It's fine. I'll take it.	**E bine, o iau.**	yeh **bee**neh o ya^{oo}
No. I don't like it.	**Nu-mi place.**	noom^{y} **pla**cheh
It's too …	**Este prea …**	**yes**teh preh-**a**
dark/small	**intunecoasă/mică**	intoone**cwa**ser/**mee**cer
noisy	**zgomotoasă**	zgomo**twa**ser
Do you have anything …?	**Aveţi ceva …?**	a**vets**^{y} che**va**
better/bigger	**mai bun/mai mare**	migh boon/migh **ma**reh
cheaper/quieter	**yefteen/liniştit**	yefteen/leeneesh**teet**
May I please have my bill?	**Nota de plată, vă rog?**	**no**ta deh **pla**ter ver rog
It's been a very enjoyable stay.	**Am avut un sejur minunat.**	am a**voot** oon se**zhoor** meenoo**nat**

NUMBERS, see page 158/DAYS OF THE WEEK, see page 157

Eating out *Restaurant*

I'd like to reserve a table for 4.	**Doresc să rezerv o masă pentru patru persoane.**	do**resc** ser re**zerv** o **m**aser **pen**troo **pa**troo pers**wa**neh
We'll come at 8.	**O să venim la ora opt.**	o ser ve**neem** la ora opt
I'd like breakfast/ lunch/dinner.	**Aş vrea micul dejun/masa de prînz/cina.**	ash vreh-**a mee**cool de**zhoon/ma**sa deh prinz/**chee**na
What do you recommend?	**Ce ne recomandaţi?**	cheh neh recoman**dats**ʸ
Do you have vegetarian dishes?	**Aveţi mîncăruri pentru vegetarieni?**	a**vets**ʸ min**cer**roorʸ **pen**troo vejetar**yen**ʸ

Breakfast *Micul dejun*

I'd like …	**Aş dori …**	ash do**ree**
bread/butter	**pîine/unt**	**pi**yneh/oont
egg	**un ou**	oon oh
ham	**nişte şuncă**	**neesh**teh**shoon**cer
jam	**nişte gem**	**neesh**teh jem
rolls	**chifle**	**keef**leh

Starters *Antreuri*

borş	borsh	richly flavoured soup
chifteluţe	keefte**loo**tseh	fried meat balls
ciorbă	**chy**orber	soured soup
ghiveci	gee**vech**ʸ	vegetable stew
icre	**ee**creh	fish roe
mezeluri	meze**loor**ʸ	cold meats
mititei/mici	meetee**tay**/meechʸ	small, meat rissoles

baked/boiled	**copt/fiert**	copt/fyert
fried/grilled	**prăjit/la grătar**	prer**zheet**/la grer**tar**
roast	**prăjit la cuptor**	prer**zheet** la coop**tor**
stewed	**fiert inăbuşit**	fyert inerboo**sheet**
underdone (rare)	**cu puţin sînge**	coo poot**seen sin**jeh
medium	**potrivit**	potree**veet**
well-done	**bine prăjit**	**bee**neh prer**zheet**

NUMBERS, see page 158

Meat *Carne*

I'd like some …	**Aş vrea nişte …**	ash vreh-**a neesh**teh
beef/lamb	**carne de vacă/miel**	**car**neh deh **va**cer/myel
pork/veal	**carne de porc/viţel**	**car**neh deh porc/**veet**sel
rabbit/duck	**iepure/raţă**	**ye**pooreh/**rat**ser
biftec	beef**tec**	beef steak
cîrnaţi	cir**nats**^{y}	sausage
frigărui de porc	freeger**rooy** deh porc	grilled pork kebabs
friptură cu sos	freep**too**rer coo sos	roast meat with sauce
slănină	sler**nee**ner	bacon
stufat	stoo**fat**	beef in a rich marinade
şniţel	**shnee**tsel	breaded escalope
tocană de miel	to**ca**ner deh myel	lamb and vegetable stew

Fish and seafood *Peşte şi fructe de mare*

carp	**crap**	crahp
trout	**păstrăv**	**per**strerv
pike	**ştiucă**	**shtyoo**cer
ciorbă pescărească	**chy**orber pescer**reh**-ascer	fish soup with vegetables
ghiveci de peşte	gee**vech**^{y} deh **pesh**teh	typical fish stew
saramură de peşte	sara**moo**rer deh **pesh**teh	grilled fish seasoned with paprika

Vegetables and salads *Legume şi salate*

beans	fa**so**leh	**fasole**
cabbage	**var**zer	**varză**
lettuce	sa**la**ter **ver**deh	**salată verde**
mushroom	chyoo**perch**^{y}	**ciuperci**
onion	**cha**per	**ceapă**
potatoes	car**tof**^{y}	**cartofi**
rice	o**rez**	**orez**
tomatoes	**ro**shee	**roşii**
cartofi prăjiţi	car**tof**^{y} prer**zheets**^{y}	chips (fries)
mămăligă	mermer**lee**ger	cornmeal mush
salata orientală	sa**la**ta oryen**ta**ler	potato salad with fish
sarmale de post	sar**ma**leh deh post	rice in vine leaves
tocinei	tochee**nay**	grated potato rissoles

Fruit & dessert *Fructe şi nuci*

apple	**măr**	merr
banana	**banană**	ba**na**ner
lemon	**lămîie**	ler**mɨ**yeh
orange	**portocală**	porto**ca**ler
plum	**prune**	**proo**neh
strawberries	**căpşuni**	cerp**shoon**^{y}
baclava	bacla**va**	a flaky pastry pie
clătite	cler**tee**teh	pancake
cozonac	cozo**nac**	traditional sweet loaf
îngheţată	ɨnge**tsa**ter	icecream
prăjitură	prerzhee**too**rer	small sponge torte

Drinks *Băuturi*

beer	**bere**	**be**reh
coffee	**cafea**	cafeh-**a**
black/with milk	**neagra/cu lapte**	neh-**a**grer/coo **lap**teh
sugar	**zahăr**	**za**herr
fruit juice	**suc de fructe**	sooc deh **frooc**teh
hot chocolate	**lapte cald cu cacao**	**lap**teh cald coo ca**ca**o
mineral water	**apă minerală**	**a**per meene**ra**ler
tea	**ceai**	chay
red/white wine	**roşu/alb vin**	**ro**shoo/alb vin

Complaints—Bill (check) *Reclamaţii—Nota de plată*

This is too …	**Aceasta este prea …**	a**chas**ta **yes**teh preh-**a**
bitter/sweet	**amarășdulce**	a**ma**rer/**dool**cheh
That's not what I ordered.	**Aceasta nu este ce am comandat.**	a**chas**ta noo **yes**teh cheh am coman**dat**
I'd like to pay.	**Aş vrea să plătesc.**	ash vreh-**a** ser pler**tesc**
I think there's a mistake in the bill.	**Cred că este o greşeală în nota de plată.**	cred cer **yes**teh o gre**sha**ler ɨn deh **pla**ter
Is service included?	**Serviciul este inclus?**	ser**vee**chyool **yes**teh een**cloos**
We enjoyed it, thank you.	**Ne-a plăcut foarte mult, mulţumesc.**	na pler**coot** **fwar**teh moolt mooltsoo**mesc**

NUMBERS, see page 158

Travelling around *A călţori*

Plane *Avion*

Is there a flight to Constanţa?	**Există un zbor pentru Constanţa?**	eg**zees**ter oon zbor **pen**troo con**stan**tsa
What time do I check in?	**La ce ora trebuie să înregistrez bagajele?**	la cheh **o**rer **tre**booyeh ser ɨnrejees**trez** ba**ga**zheleh
I'd like to … my reservation.	**Aş vrea să … rezervarea.**	ash vreh-**a** ser … rezer**va**reh-a
cancel	**anulez**	anoo**lez**
change	**schimb**	skeemb
confirm	**confirm**	con**feerm**

Train *Tren*

I want a ticket to Bucharest.	**Vreau un bilet pentru Bucureşti.**	vra^{oo} oon bee**let** **pen**troo boocoo**resht**^{y}
single (one-way)	**dus**	doos
return (roundtrip)	**dus-întors**	doos-ɨn**tors**
first class	**clasa întîi**	**cla**sa ɨnt**iy**
second class	**clasa a doua**	**cla**sa a **do**wa
How long does the journey (trip) take?	**Cît durează călătoria?**	cɨt doo**ra**zer cerlerto**reea**
When is the … train to Suceava?	**La ce ora pleacă … tren spre Suceava?**	la cheh **o**rer pleh-**a**cer … tren spreh soo**cha**va
first/last	**primul/ultimul**	**pree**mool/**ool**teemool
next	**urmatorul**	oormer**to**rool
Is this the right train to Predeal?	**Trenul acesta merge la Predeal?**	**tre**nool a**ches**ta **mer**jeh la pre**deh-al**

Bus—Tam (streetcar) *Autobuz—Tramvai*

What tram do I take to the centre?	**Ce tramvai merge în centru?**	cheh tram**vigh mer**jeh ɨn **chen**troo
How much is the fare to …?	**Cît costă pîna la …?**	cɨt **co**ster **pi**ner la…
Will you tell me when to get off?	**Puteţi să-mi spuneţi cînd să cobor?**	poo**tets**^{y} serm^{y} **spoo**nets^{y} cɨnd ser co**bor**

TELLING THE TIME, see page 156

Taxi *Taxi*

How much is it to …?	**Cît costă pînă la …?**	cit **cos**ter **pî**ner la
Take me to this adress.	**Vreau să merg la adresa aceasta.**	vrau ser merg la a**dre**sa a**cha**sta
Please stop here.	**Vă rog, opriţi aici.**	ver rog o**preets**ʸ **aeech**ʸ

Car hire *Inchirieri auto*

I'd like to hire (rent) a car.	**Aş vrea să închiriez o masinăž.**	ash vreh-**a** ser înkeeree-**ez** o ma**shee**ner
I'd like it for a day/ week.	**Pentru o zi/ o săptămînă.**	**pen**troo o zee/ o serpter**mî**ner
Where's the nearest filling station?	**Unde este cea mai apropiată staţie Peco?**	**oon**deh **yes**teh cha migh pro**pya**ter **sta**tsyeh Peco
Full tank, please.	**Faceţi plinul, vă rog.**	**fa**chetsʸ **plee**nool ver rog
Give me … litres of petrol (gasoline).	**Puneţi … litri de benzină.**	**poo**netsʸ … **lee**trʸ deh ben**zee**ner
Where can I park?	**Unde se poate parca?**	**oon**deh seh **pwa**teh par**ca**
How do I get to …?	**Cum ajung la …?**	coom a**zhoong** la
I've had a breakdown at …	**Sînt în pană la …**	sînt în **pa**ner la …
Can you send a mechanic?	**Puteţi să trimiteţi un mecanic?**	poo**tets**ʸ ser tree**mee**tetsʸ oon me**ca**neec
Can you mend this puncture (fix this flat)?	**Puteţi vulcaniza roata aceasta?**	poo**tets**ʸ voolcanee**za** **rwa**ta a**cha**sta

☞ You're on the wrong road.	**Sînteţi pe un drum greşit.** ☜
Go straight ahead.	**Mergeţi drept înainte.**
It's down there on the …	**E mai jos pe …**
left/right	**stînga/dreapta**
opposite/behind …	**vis-a-vis/în spate**
next to/after …	**lîngă/după**
north/south/east/west	**nord/sud/est/vest**

NUMBERS, see page 158

Sightseeing *Excursii turistice*

Where's the tourist office?	**Unde se află oficiul de turism?**	**oon**deh seh **a**fler **ofee**chyool deh too**reesm**
Is there an English-speaking guide?	**Aveţi un ghid care vorbeşte englezeşte?**	avets^y oon geed **ca**reh vor**besh**teh engle**zesh**teh
Where is/are the …?	**Unde este/sînt …?**	**oon**deh **yes**teh/sɨnt
beach	**plajă**	**pla**zher
botanical gardens	**grădina botanică**	grer**dee**na bo**ta**neecer
castle	**castelul**	cas**te**lool
cathedral	**catedrala**	cate**dra**la
city centre	**centrul oraşului**	**chen**trool o**ra**shoolooy
harbour	**portul**	**por**tool
market	**piaţa**	**pya**tsa
museum	**muzeul**	moo**ze**ool
shops	**centrul comercial**	**chen**trool comer**chyal**
zoo	**grădina zoologică**	grer**dee**na zoo**lo**jeecer
When does it open/close?	**La ce oră deschideţi/închideţi?**	la cheh **o**rer des**kee**dets^y/ɨn**kee**dets^y
How much is the entrance fee?	**Cît costă intrarea?**	cɨt **cos**ter een**tra**reh-a

Entertainment *Destindere*

What's playing at the … Theatre?	**Ce piesă se joacă la Teatrul …?**	cheh **pye**ser seh **zhwa**cer la teh-**a**trool
How much is a ticket?	**Cît costă un bilet?**	cɨt **cos**ter oon bee**let**
Would you like to go out with me tonight?	**Putem ieşi împreună deseară?**	poo**tem** ye**shee** ɨmpre**oo**ner de**sa**rer
Is there a discotheque in town?	**Exista o discotecă în oraş?**	eg**zees**ter o deesco**te**cer ɨn o**rash**
Would you like to dance?	**Vreţi să dansăm?**	vrets^y ser dan**serm**
Thank you. It's been a wonderful evening.	**Mulţumesc, a fost o seară minunată.**	mooltsoo**mesc** a fost o seh-**a**rer meenoo**na**ter

TELLING THE TIME, see page 156/DATE, see page 157

Shops, stores and services *Magazine şi servicii*

Where's the nearest ...?	**Unde este prin apropiere ...?**	**oon**deh **yes**teh preen apro**pye**reh
bakery	**o brutărie**	o brooter-**ree**-eh
bookshop/store	**o librărie**	o leebrer-**ree**-eh
butcher's	**o măcelărie**	o mercheler-**ree**-eh
chemist's/drugstore	**o farmacie**	o farma**chee**-eh
dentist	**un cabinet dentar**	oon cabee**net** den**tar**
department store	**un magazin universal**	oon maga**zeen** ooneever**sal**
grocery	**o băcănie**	o bercer**nee**-eh
newsagent	**un chioşc de ziare**	oon kyoshc deh **zya**reh
post office	**o poşta**	o **posh**ta
souvenir shop	**un magazin de suveniruri**	oon maga**zeen** deh soove**neer**oor^{y}
supermarket	**un magazin alimentar**	oon maga**zeen** aleemen**tar**
toilets	**toaleta**	to-**aleta**

General expressions *Expresii de uz general*

Where's the main shopping area?	**Unde este centrul comercial principal?**	**oon**deh **yes**teh **chen**trool comer**chyal** preenchee**pal**
Do you have ...?	**Aveţi ...?**	**avets^{y}**
Do you have anything ...?	**Nu aveţi nimic ... ?**	noo a**vets^{y}** nee**meec**
cheaper/better	**ieftin/bun**	**yef**teen/boon
larger/smaller	**mare/mic**	**ma**reh/meec
Can I try it on?	**Pot să-l probez?**	pot serl pro**bez**
How much is this?	**Cît costă aceasta?**	cit **cos**ter a**chas**ta
Please write it down.	**Vă rog scrieţi aceasta.**	ver rog **scree**-ets^{y} a**chas**ta
No, I don't like it.	**Nu-mi place.**	noom^{y} **pla**cheh
I'll take it.	**Il cumpăr.**	il **coom**perr
Do you accept credit cards?	**Acceptaţi cărţi de credit?**	ac-chep**tats^{y}** certs^{y} deh **cre**deet

NUMBERS, see page 158

black	**negru**	**ne**groo^{oo}	orange	**portocaliu**	portoca**lee**^{oo}
blue	**albastru**	al**bas**troo	red	**roşu**	**ro**shoo
brown	**maro**	ma**ro**	white	**alb**	alb
green	**verde**	**ver**deh	yellow	**galben**	**gal**ben

I want to buy …	**Vreau să cumpăr …**	vra^{oo} ser **coom**perr
aspirin	**nişte aspirină**	**neesh**teh aspee**ree**ner
batteries	**nişte baterii**	**neesh**teh bate**ree**
bottle opener	**un deschizător de sticle**	oon deskeezer**tor** deh **stee**cleh
bread	**nişte pîine**	**neesh**teh **pîy**neh
newspaper American/English	**un ziar american/englezesc**	oon zyar a**me**reecan/**eng**lezesc
postcard	**o vedere**	o ve**de**reh
shampoo/soap	**un şampon/săpun**	oon sham**pon**/ser**poon**
sun-tan cream	**o cremă de bronzat**	o **cre**mer deh bron**zat**
toothpaste	**o pastă de dinţi**	o **pas**ter deh deents^{y}
a half-kilo of apples	**o jumătate kilogram de mere**	o zhoomer**ta**teh keelo**gram** deh **me**reh
a litre of milk	**un litru de lapte**	oon **lee**troo deh **lap**teh
I'd like … film for this camera.	**Aş vrea un film pentru aparatul acesta.**	ash vreh-**a** oon feelm **pen**troo apa**ra**tool a**ches**ta
black and white/colour	**alb-negru/color**	alb-**ne**groo/co**lor**

Souvenirs *Suveniruri*

album de artă	**al**boom deh **ar**ter	art book
carpetă/covor	car**pe**ter/**co**vor	carpet
fatăde masă	**fa**tser der **ma**ser	tablecloth
maramă	ma**ra**mer	embroidered headscarf
muzică populară	**moo**ziker popoo**la**rer	folk music
olărit	oler**reet**	pottery
tablou/pictură	ta**blo**^{oo}/pic**too**rer	painting

At the bank *La bancă*

Where's the bank/currency exchange office?	**Unde se află o bancă/un birou de schimb?**	**oon**deh seh **a**fler o **ban**cer/oon bee**ro**^{oo} deh skeemb

I want to change some dollars/ pounds into lei.	**Vreau să schimb nişte dolari/ lire sterline in lei.**	vra^{oo} ser skeemb **neesh**teh do**lar**^{y}/ **lee**reh ster**lee**neh in lay
What's the exchange rate?	**Care este cursul?**	**ca**reh **yes**teh **coor**sool

At the post office *Poşta*

I want to send this by …	**Aş vrea să expediez acesta (prin) …**	ash vreh-**a** ser expe**dyez** a**ches**ta (preen)
airmail/express	**avion/expres**	avee**on**/ex**pres**
A … lei stamp, please.	**Un timbru de … lei, vă rog.**	oon **teem**broo deh … lay ver rog
What's the postage for a postcard to the United States?	**Cît costă un timbru pentru o vedere la Statele Unite?**	cit **cos**ter oon **teem**broo **pen**troo o ve**de**reh la **sta**teleh oo**nee**teh
Is there any mail for me? My name is …	**Am vreo scrisoare? Numele meu este …**	am vro scree**swa**reh. **noo**meleh me^{oo} **yes**teh

Telephoning *La telefon*

Where's the nearest public phone?	**Unde este un telefon prin apropiere?**	**oon**deh **yes**teh oon tele**fon** preen apro**pye**reh
May I use your phone?	**Îmi permiteţi să folosesc telefonul dumneavoastra?**	ɨm^{y} per**mee**tets^{y} ser folo**sesc** tele**fo**nool doomna**vwas**trer
Hello. This is …	**Alo, … la telefon.**	**alo** … la tele**fon**
I want to speak to …	**Aş vrea să vorbesc cu …**	ash vreh-**a** ser vor**besc** coo
When will he/ she be back?	**Cînd se va întoarce?**	cɨnd seh va ɨn**twar**cheh
Will you tell him/her that I called?	**Vreţi să-i spuneţi că am sunat?**	vrets^{y} ser-y **spoo**nets^{y} cer am soo**nat**

Time and date *Anul şi data*

It's …	**Este …**	**yes**teh
five past one	**ora unu şi cinci minute**	ora **oo**noo shee cheench^{y} mee**noo**teh

EMERGENCIES, see page 158/NUMBERS, see page 159

quarter past three	**trei şi un sfert**	tray shee oon sfert
twenty past four	**patru şi douăzeci**	**pa**troo shee **do**-wer**zech**^{y}
half-past six	**şase şi jumătate**	**sha**seh shee zhoomer**ta**teh
twenty-five to seven	**şapte fără douăzeci şi cinci**	**shap**teh **fer**rer **do**-wer**zech**^{y} shee cheench^{y}
ten to ten	**zece fară zece**	**ze**cheh **fer**rer **ze**cheh
twelve o'clock	**ora douăsprezece**	ora **do**-wersprezecheh
in the morning	**dimineaţa**	deemee**na**tsa
during the day	**după-amiazăș**	**doo**per-a**mya**zer
at night	**seara**	**sa**ra
yesterday	**ieri**	yer^{y}
today	**azi**	az^{y}
tomorrow	**mîine**	**miy**neh
spring/summer	**primăvară/vară**	**pree**mervarer/**va**rer
autumn/winter	**toamnă/iarnă**	**twam**ner/**yar**ner

Sunday	**duminică**	doo**mee**neecer
Monday	**luni**	loon^{y}
Tuesday	**marţi**	marts^{y}
Wednesday	**miercuri**	**myer**coor^{y}
Thursday	**joi**	zhoy
Friday	**vineri**	**vee**ner^{y}
Saturday	**sîmbătă**	**sim**berter
January	**ianuarie**	yan**war**yeh
February	**februarie**	fe**brwa**ryeh
March	**martie**	**mar**tyeh
April	**aprilie**	a**preel**yeh
May	**mai**	migh
June	**iunie**	**yoo**nyeh
July	**iulie**	**yoo**lyeh
August	**august**	**a**^{oo}goost
September	**septembrie**	sep**tem**bryeh
October	**octombrie**	oc**tom**bryeh
November	**noiembrie**	no**yem**bryeh
December	**decembrie**	de**chem**bryeh

Numbers *Numere*

0	**zero**	zero	11	**unsprezece**	**oon**sprezecheh
1	**unu**	**oo**noo	12	**doisprezece**	**doy**sprezecheh
2	**doi**	doy	13	**treisprezece**	**tray**sprezecheh
3	**trei**	tray	14	**paisprezece**	**pigh**sprezecheh
4	**patru**	**pa**troo	15	**cincisprezece**	**cheench**ʸsprezecheh
5	**cinci**	cheenchʸ	16	**şaisprezece**	**shigh**sprezecheh
6	**şase**	**sha**seh	17	**şaptesprezece**	**shap**tesprezeceh
7	**şapte**	**shap**teh	18	**optsprezece**	**opt**sprezecheh
8	**opt**	opt	19	**nouăsprezeche**	**no**-wersprezecheh
9	**nouă**	**no**-wer	20	**douăzeci**	**do**-wer**zech**ʸ
10	**zece**	**ze**cheh	21	**douăzeci şi unu**	**do**-wer**zech**ʸ shee **oo**noo

30	**treizeci**	tray**zech**ʸ
40	**patruzeci**	**pa**troo**zech**ʸ
50	**cincizeci**	cheenchʸ**zech**ʸ
60	**şaizeci**	shigh**zech**ʸ
70	**şaptezeci**	**shap**teh**zech**ʸ
80	**optzeci**	opt**zech**ʸ
90	**nouăzeci**	**no**-wer**zech**ʸ
100/1,000	**o sută/o mie**	o **soo**ter/o **mee**-eh
first/second	**primul/al doilea**	**pree**mool/al **doy**leh-a
once/twice	**o dată/de două ori**	o **da**ter/deh **do**-wer orʸ
a half	**o jumătate**	o zhoomer**ta**teh

Emergency *Urgenţă*

Call the police	**Chemaţi poliţia**	ke**mats**ʸ po**leet**sya
Get a doctor	**Chemaţi un doctor**	ke**mats**ʸ oon **doc**tor
HELP	**AJUTOR**	azhoo**tor**
I'm ill	**Sînt bolnav(ă)**	sint bol**nav**(er)
I'm lost	**M-am rătăcit**	mam rerter**cheet**
Leave me alone	**Lasă-mă în pace**	**la**sermer in **pa**cheh
STOP THIEF	**HOŢUL**	**ho**tsool
My … are stolen.	**Mi s-a furat …**	mee sa foo**rat**
I've lost my …	**Am pierdut …**	am pyer**doot**
handbag	**poşeta/geanta**	po**she**ta/**jan**ta
passport/luggage	**paşaportul/bagajul**	pasha**por**tool/ba**gazh**ool
Where can I find	**Unde pot găsi**	**oon**deh pot ger**see**
a doctor who	**un doctor care**	oon **doc**tor **ca**reh
speaks English?	**vorbeşte englezeşte?**	vor**besh**teh engle**zesh**teh

TELEPHONING,see page 156

Guide to Romanian pronunciation

Romanian is understood and spoken in Moldova as well as Romania.

Consonants

Letter	Approximate pronunciation	Symbol	Example	
c	1) like **c in** cake	c	**cartofi**	kartof[y]
	2) followed by **e** or **i** like **ch** in **ch**eese	ch	**ceas**	**che**as
			cineva	**chee**neva
ch	like **k in k**ettle	k	**chibrit**	ki**breet**
g	1) like **g in g**irl	g	**rog**	rog
	2) when followed by **e or i**, like **g** in **g**ender	j	**ginere**	**jee**nereh
gh	like **g** in **g**irl	gh	**ghete**	**ge**teh
h	like **h** in **h**and	h	**hartă**	**har**ter
j	like **s** in plea**s**ure	zh	**juc&arie**	zhu**ce**ree-eh
r	rolled consonant similar to the Scottish **r**	r	**roată**	**rwa**ter
s	like **s in s**un	s	**student**	stoo**dent**
ş	like **sh** in **sh**ort	sh	**şiret**	**shee**ret
ţ	like **ts** in bi**ts**	ts	**ţară**	**tsa**rer

b, d, f, l, m, n, p, t, v, w, x, z are pronounced as in English

Vowels

a	like the vowel sound in c**u**t	a	**alfabet**	**al**fabet
ă	like **er** at the end of teach**er**; but the **r** should not be pronounced	er	**masă**	**ma**ser
â	pronounced exactly like î below; it only occurs in a few words	ɨ	**românește**	rom**ɨ**neshteh
e	1) like the **e** in **te**n; this is also pronounced at the end of the word, but to avoid confusion	e	**elev**	e**lev**
	is represented **eh**	eh	**carte**	**car**teh
	2) at the beginning of a word, like **ye** in **ye**s	ye	**este**	**ye**steh

i	1) like **ee** in b**ee**	ee	**intrare**	een**tra**reh
	2) if unstressed at the end of a word, **i** may be scarcely audible, softening the preceding consonant	^{y}	**bani**	ban^{y}
î	there's no exact equivalent in English; it resembles the **o** in less**o**n, kingd**o**m	ɨ	**înţeleg**	**ɨn**tseleg
o	like vowel sound in sp**or**t, without pronouncing the **r**	o	**copil**	**ko**peel
u	like **oo** in b**oo**k	oo	**munte**	**moon**teh

Diphthongs

The following diphthongs are the most frequent:

ai	like **igh** in h**igh**	igh	**mai**	migh
au	like **ow** in c**ow**	a^{oo}	**stau**	sta^{oo}
ău	like **o** in **go**	oh	**rău**	roh
ea	1) no exact equivalent in English; sounds almost like **a in ba**t	a	**dimineaţa**	deemee**na**tsa
	2) at the end of the word like **aye** in layer	eh-a	**prea**	preh-a
ei	like **ay** in b**ay**	ay	**lei**	lay
eu	no equivalent in English; start pronouncing the **e** of b**e**d then draw your lips together to make a brief **oo** sound	e^{oo}	**leu**	le^{oo}
ia	like **ya** in **ya**rd	ya	**iarbă**	**yar**ber
ie	like **ye** in **ye**llow	**ye**	**ieftin**	**ye**fteen
io	like **yo** in **yo**nder	**yo**	**dicţionar**	deectsyo**nar**
iu	like **ew** in f**ew**	yoo	**iubire**	yoo**beer**eh
oa	like **wha** in **wha**t	**wa**	**poate**	**pwa**teh
oi	like **oy** in b**oy**	oy	**doi**	doy
ua	like **wa** in **wa**tch	wah	**luaţi**	lwahts^{y}
uă	similar to **ue** in infl**ue**nce	wer	**două**	do-wer

Russian

Basic expressions *Основные выражения*

Yes/No.	**Да/Нет.**	dah/n^{y}et
Please.	**Пожалуйста.**	pah**zhahl**stah
Thank you.	**Спасибо.**	spah**see**bah
I beg your pardon.	**Извините.**	eezvee**neet**^{y}eh

Introductions *Знакомство*

Good morning.	**Доброе утро.**	**do**brah^{y}eh **oo**trah
Good afternoon.	**Добрый день.**	**do**briy d^{y}ehn^{y}
Good night.	**Спокойной ночи.**	spah**koy**nigh **no**ch^{y}ee
Good-bye.	**До свидания.**	dah svee**dah**nee^{y}ah
My name is …	**Меня зовут ...**	meen^{y}**ah** zah**voot**
What's your name?	**Как вас зовут?**	kahk vahss zah**voot**
How are you?	**Как вы поживаете?**	kahk vi pazhi**va**^{y}et^{y}eh
Fine thanks. And you?	**Хорошо, спасибо. А вы?**	**khah**rahsho spah**see**bah. ah vi
Where do you come from?	**Вы откуда?**	vi ahtkoo**dah**
I'm from …	**Я из ...**	^{y}ah iz
Australia	**Австралии**	ahf**strahl**ee^{y}ee
Britain	**Великобритании**	vee**lee**kahbreetahnee^{y}ee
Canada	**Канады**	kah**nah**di
USA	**США**	s-shah
I'm with my …	**Я с ...**	^{y}ah s
wife/husband	**женой/мужем**	zheh**noy**/**moo**zhehm
family	**семьёй**	se**m**^{y}**oy**
children	**детьми**	det^{y}**mi**
boyfriend	**другом**	**droo**gahm
girlfriend	**подругой**	pah**droo**gigh
I'm on my own.	**Я здесь один (одна).**	^{y}ah zd^{y}ehs^{y} ah**deen** (ahd**nah**)
I'm on holiday (vacation/ on business.	**Я здесь в отпуске/ командировке.**	^{y}ah zd^{y}ehs^{y} **fot**poosk^{y}eh/ kahmahndi**rof**k^{y}eh

GUIDE TO PRONUNCIATION, see page 175/EMERGENCIES, see page 174

Questions *Вопросы*

When?/How?	**Когда?/Как?**	kahg**dah**/kahk
What?/Why?	**Что?/Почему?**	shto/pahch^{y}ee**moo**
Who?/Which?	**Кто?/Какой?**	kto/kah**koy**
Where is/are …?	**Где ...?**	gd^{y}eh
Where can I get/find …?	**Где мне найти/достать ...?**	gd^{y}eh mn^{y}eh nigh**tee**/dah**staht**^{y}
How far?	**Как далеко?**	kahk dahlee**ko**
How long?	**Как долго?**	kahk **dol**gah
How much?	**Сколько?**	**skol**^{y}kah
May I?	**Можно?**	**mozh**nah
Can I have …?	**Можно мне ...?**	**mozh**nah mn^{y}eh
Can you help me?	**Помогите мне, пожалуйста.**	pahmah**geet**^{y}eh mn^{y}eh pah**zhahl**stah
What does this mean?	**Что это значит?**	shto **eh**tah **znah**ch^{y}eet
I (don't) understand.	**Я (не) понимаю.**	^{y}ah (n^{y}eh) pahnee**mah**^{y}oo
Can you translate this for me?	**Переведите мне это, пожалуйста.**	peereevee**deet**^{y}eh mn^{y}eh **eh**tah pah**zhahl**stah
Do you speak English?	**Вы говорите по-английски?**	vi gahvah**reet**^{y}eh pah ahn**gleey**skee
I don't speak Russian.	**Я не говорю по-русски.**	^{y}ah n^{y}eh gahvah**r^{y}oo** pah **roo**skee

It's *Это ...*

better/worse	**лучше/хуже**	**loo**ch^{y}sheh/**khoo**zheh
big/ small	**большой/ маленький**	bahl^{y}**shoy**/ **mah**leen^{y}keey
cheap/expensive	**дешевый/дорогой**	dee**shov**viy/dahrah**goy**
early/late	**ранний/поздний**	**rah**nniy/**poz**niy
good/bad	**хороший/плохой**	khah**ro**shiy/plah**khoy**
near/far	**близко/далеко**	**blee**skah/dah**lee**ko
open/ shut	**открытый/ закрытый**	aht**krit**tiy/ zah**krit**tiy
right/ wrong	**правильный/ неправильный**	**prah**veel^{y}niy/ nee**prah**veel^{y}niy
vacant/occupied	**свободный/занятый**	svah**bod**niy/**zah**neetiy

Hotel–Accommodation *Гостиница*

I've a reservation.	**Я заказал(а) заранее.**	^{y}ah zahkah**zahl**(ah) zah**rah**n^{y}eh
Do you have any vacancies?	**У вас есть свободный номер?**	oo vahss ^{y}ehst svah**bod**niy **no**mmeer
I'd like a … room.	**Я бы хотел(а) номер ...**	^{y}ah khat^{y}**ehl**(ah) bi **no**mmeer
single/double	**на одного/двоих**	nah **ahd**nahvo/dvah**eekh**
with twin beds	**с двумя кроватями**	s **dvoo**m^{y}ah krah**vaht**^{y}ahmee
with a double bed	**с двуспальной кроватью**	s **dvoo**spahl^{y}nigh krah**vaht**^{y}oo
We'll be staying …	**Мы пробудем здесь ...**	mi prah**boo**deem zd^{y}ehs^{y}
overnight only	**только сутки**	**tohl**^{y}kah **soot**kee
a few days	**несколько дней**	**n^{y}eh**skahl^{y}skah dn^{y}ay
a week	**неделю**	nee**d^{y}ehl**^{y}oo

Decision *Решение*

May I see the room?	**Можно посмотреть номер?**	**mozh**nah pahsmah**tr^{y}eht^{y}** **no**mmeer
That's fine. I'll take it.	**Хорошо. Это подойдет.**	kharah**sho**. **eh**tah pahdigh**d^{y}ot**
No. I don't like it.	**Нет, мне не нравится.**	n^{y}eht mn^{y}eh nee **nrah**veetsah
It's too …	**Здесь слишком ...**	zd^{y}ehs^{y} **sleesh**kayhm
dark/small	**темно/тесно**	teem**no/t^{y}ehs**nah
noisy	**шумно**	**shoom**nah
Do you have anything …?	**Есть ли у вас что-нибудь ...?**	^{y}eshst^{y} lee oo vahss **shto**neebood^{y}
bigger	**побольше**	pah**bol^{y}**sheh
cheaper	**подешевле**	pahdee**shehv**l^{y}eh
quieter	**потише**	pah**tee**sheh
May I please have my bill?	**Счёт, пожалуйста.**	shch^{y}ot pah**zhahl**stah
It's been a very enjoyable stay.	**Всё было очень хорошо.**	fs^{y}o **bil**lah **och**^{y}een^{y} kharah**sho**

DATE, see page 173/NUMBERS, see page 174

Eating out *Ресторан*

I'd like to reserve a table for 4.	**Я хотел(а) бы заказать столик на четверых.**	ʸah khat**ʸehl**(ah) bi zahkah**zahtʸ sto**leek nah chʸeetvee**rikh**
We'll come at 8.	**Мы будем в восемь.**	mi **boo**deem v **vos**seemʸ
What do you recommend?	**Что вы посоветуете?**	shto vi pahsah**vʸeh**tooeetʸeh
Do you have vegetarian dishes?	**Есть ли у вас вегетарианские блюда?**	ʸehstʸ lee oo vahss veegeetahree**ahn**skeeʸeh **blʸoo**dah

Breakfast *Завтрак*

I'd like an/some …	**Принесите, пожалуйста ...**	preenee**see**tʸe pah**zhalʸ**stah
bread/butter	**хлеб/масло**	khlʸeb/**mah**slah
cheese	**сыру**	**see**roo
egg	**яйцо**	**ʸai**tso
ham	**ветчину**	**vʸet**cheenoo
jam	**варенье**	vah**rʸeh**nʸeh
rolls	**булочки**	**boo**lahchʸkoo

Starters *Закуски*

ассорти мясное	ahsahr**tee** mees**no**ʸeh	assorted meats
блины	**blee**ni	savoury pancakes
икра	ee**krah**	caviar
колбаса	kahlbah**ssah**	sausage
осетрина	ahssee**tree**nah	sturgeon

baked/boiled	**печёный/варёный**	pee**chʸo**niy/vah**rʸo**niy
fried/roast	**жареный**	**zhah**reeniy
stewed	**тушёный**	too**sho**niy
underdone (rare)	**слегка поджаренный**	slʸek**ka** pahd**zhah**reenniy
medium	**средней прожаренности**	**sred**nʸey prah**zhah**reennahsti
well-done	**хорошо прожаренный**	khahrah**sho** prah**zhah**reeniy

Meat *Мясо*

I'd like some …	**Я хотел(а) бы ...**	^{y}ah khaht**^{y}el**(ah) bi
beef	**говядину**	gah**v^{y}ah**deenoo
lamb	**баранину**	bah**rah**neenoo
pork	**свинину**	svee**nee**noo
veal	**телятину**	tee**l^{y}ah**teenoo
chicken/duck	**курицу/утку**	**koo**reetsoo/**oot**koo
ветчина	**veet**ch^{y}eenah	ham
бефстроганов	beef**stro**gahnahf	beef Stroganoff
бифштекс	**beef**shtehks	beefsteak
голубцы	gah**loop**tsi	stuffed cabbage
котлеты по-киевски	kaht**l^{y}eh**ti pah**kee**^{y}ehfskee	chicken Kiev
плов	plov	rice with mutton
шашлык	shah**shlik**	grilled lamb pieces

Fish and seafood *Рыба и дары моря*

herring/perch	**сельдь/окунь**	s^{y}ehl^{y}d^y/**o**koon^y
prawns	**креветки**	kree**v^{y}eht**kee
salmon	**сёмга**	**s^{y}om**gah
sprats (in oil)	**шпроты**	**shprot**ti
sturgeon	**осетрина**	ahssee**tree**nah

Vegetables *Овощи*

bean	**фасоль**	fah**sol^y**
beetroot	**свёкла**	**sv^{y}ok**lah
cabbage	**капуста**	kah**poo**stah
carrot	**морковь**	mahr**kof^y**
cucumber	**огурец**	ahgoo**r^{y}ehts**
mushroom	**грибы**	gree**bi**
onion	**лук**	look
peas	**горох**	gah**rokh**
potatoes	**картофель**	kahr**to**feel^y
tomato	**помидоры**	pahmee**do**ri
каша	**kah**shah	buckwheat gruel
пельмени	peel^y**m^{y}eh**nee	stuffed dumplings
зелёный салат	zee**l^{y}on**niy sah**laht**	lettuce salad
щи	shchee	cabbage soup

Fruit & dessert *Фрукты и десерт*

apple	**яблоко**	^{y}**ah**blahkah
cherries	**черешня**	ch^{y}ee**r^{y}esh**n^{y}ah
orange	**апельсин**	ahpeel^{y}**seen**
plum	**сливы**	**slee**vi
lemon	**лимон**	lee**mon**
raspberries	**малина**	mah**lee**nah
strawberries	**клубника**	kloob**nee**kah
кефир	keh**feer**	sour milk yoghurt
компот	kahm**pot**	fruit compote
мороженое	mah**rozh**ehnah^{y}eh	ice-cream
пирожное	pee**rozh**nah^{y}eh	cake, small pie
сливки	**sleef**kee	cream
торт	tort	gateau

Drinks *Напитки*

beer	**пиво**	**pee**vah
(hot) chocolate	**какао**	kah**ka**o
coffee	**кофе**	**ko**fee
black	**чёрный**	**chor**niy
with milk	**с молоком**	s mahlah**kom**
fruit juice	**фруктовый сок**	frook**to**viy sok
mineral water	**минеральная вода**	meenee**rahl^{y}**nayah vod**dah**
tea	**чай**	ch^{y}igh
vodka	**водка**	**vot**kah
wine	**вино**	vee**no**
red/white	**красное/белое**	**krahs**no^{y}eh/**b^{y}e**lo^{y}e

Complaints and paying *Жалобы*

That's not what I ordered.	**Этого я не заказывал(а).**	**eh**tahvah ^{y}ah nee zah**kah**zivvahl(ah)
I'd like to pay.	**Пожалуйста, счёт.**	pah**zhahl**stah shch^{y}ot
I think you made a mistake in the bill.	**Вы не ошиблись?**	vi nee ah**shi**blees^{y}
We enjoyed it, thank you.	**Нам очень понравилось, спасибо.**	nahm **o**ch^{y}een^{y} pah**nrah**veelahs^{y} spahs**see**bah

Travelling around *Путешествия*

Plane *Самолет*

Is there a flight to	**Есть ли рейс на**	^{y}est^{y} lee rayss nah
St Petersburg?	**Санкт Петербург?**	sahnkt pehteer**boorg**
What time do	**Во сколько надо**	vah **skol**^{y}kah **nah**dah
I check in?	**регистрировать**	reegees**tree**rahvaht^{y}
	багаж?	bah**gahsh**
I'd like to …	**Я хотел(а) бы**	^{y}ah khah**t^{y}ehl**(ah) bi
my reservation.	**... заказ рейса.**	… zah**kahz** rayssa
cancel	**отменить**	atm^{y}e**neet^{y}**
change	**поменять**	pahmeen**^{y}aht^{y}**
confirm	**подтвердить**	pahttveer**deet^{y}**

Train *Поезд*

I want a ticket	**Один билет до**	ah**deen** beel**^{y}eht** dah
to Minsk.	**Минска,**	**meen**skah
	пожалуйста.	pah**zhahl^{y}**stah
single (one-way)	**в один конец**	v ah**deen** kah**n^{y}ehts**
return (roundtrip)	**туда и обратно**	too**dah** ee ah**braht**nah
first/	**мягкий вагон/**	**m^{y}ahkh**keeyvah**gon/**
second class	**жесткий вагон**	**zhost**kee vah**gon**
How long does the	**Долго ли надо**	**dol**gah lee **nah**dah
journey (trip) take?	**ехать?**	^{y}ekhaht^{y}
When is the …	**Когда ... поезд**	kahg**dah** … **po**eezd
train to Saratov?	**на Саратов?**	nah sah**rah**taf
first/last	**первый/последний**	**p^{y}er**viy/pahs**l^{y}ehd**neey
next	**следующий**	sl^{y}ehdoo^{y}ooshch^{y}eey
Is this the right train	**Это поезд**	**eh**tah poeezd
to Ivanovo?	**на Иваново?**	nah eevah**no**vah

Bus—Tam (streetcar) **Автобус–Трамвай**

What bus do I take to	**Какой автобус**	kah**koy** ahf**to**boos
the centre/downtown?	**идет в центр?**	ee**d^{y}ot** f tsehntr
How much is the	**Сколько стоит**	**skol**^{y}kah **sto**eet
fare to …?	**билет до ...?**	beel**^{y}eht** dah
Will you tell me	**Вы мне скажете,**	vi mn^{y}eh skah**zhi**t^{y}eh
when to get off?	**когда надо**	kahg**dah nah**dah
	выходить?	skho**dee**t^{y}eh

TELLING THE TIME, 173/NUMBERS, see page 174

Taxi *Такси*

How much is it to …?	**Сколько стоит доехать до...?**	**skol**ykah **sto**eet dah**yeh**khaty dah
Take me to this address.	**Мне нужно по этому адресу.**	mnyeh **noo**zhnah pah **eh**tahmoo ah**drees**soo
Please stop here.	**Остановите здесь, пожалуйста.**	ahstahnah**vee**teesy zdyehsy pah**zhahl**stah

Car hire (rental) *Прокат машин*

I'd like to hire (rent) a car.	**Я хотел(а) бы взять напрокат машину.**	yah khah**tyehl**(ah) bi vzyahty nahprah**kaht** mah**shin**noo
I'd like it for a day/week.	**Она мне нужна на день/неделю.**	ahnah mnyeh noozh**nah nah** dyehn/nee**dyeh**lyoo
Where's the nearest filling station?	**Где ближайшая заправочная станция?**	gdyeh blee**zhigh**shahyah zah**prah**vahchynahyah **stahn**tsiyah
Full tank, please.	**Заправьте, пожалуйста.**	za**prah**vytyeh pah**zhaly**stah
Give me … litres of petrol (gasoline).	**Налейте мне ... литров бензина.**	nah**lay**tyeh mnyeh … **lee**trahf been**zee**nah
How do I get to …?	**Как доехать до ...?**	kahk dah**yeh**khahty dah
I've had a breakdown at …	**У меня сломалась машина в ...**	oo mee**nyah** slah**mah**lahsy mah**shi**nah f
Can you send a mechanic?	**Можете прислать механика?**	**mo**zhityeh pree**slahty** meh**khah**neekah
Can you mend this puncture (fix this flat)?	**Можно заделать этот прокол?**	**mozh**no zah**dyeh**lahty **eh**taht prah**kol**

You're on the wrong road.	**Это не та дорога.**
Go straight ahead.	**Поезжайте прямо.**
It's down there on the left/right	**Это там налево/направо**
opposite/behind …	**напротив/сзади…**
next to/after …	**около/после…**
north/south/east/west	**север/юг/восток/запад**

NUMBERS, see page 174

Sightseeing *Достопримечательности*

Where's the tourist office?	**Где здесь бюро по туризму?**	gd^{y}eh zd^{y}ehs b^{y}oo**ro** pah too**reez**moo
Is there an English-speaking guide?	**Есть ли гид, говорящий по-английски?**	^{y}eshst lee geet gahvah**r^{y}ah**shch^{y}eey pah ahn**gleey**skee
Where is/ are the …?	**Где находится/ находятся...?**	gd^{y}eh nah**khod**deetsah/ nahkho**d^{y}aht**sah
beach	**пляж**	pl^{y}azh
castle	**замок**	**zah**mahk
cathedral	**собор**	sah**bor**
city centre/downtown	**центр города**	tsehntr **gor**rahdah
kremlin	**кремль**	kr^{y}ehml
market	**рынок**	**rin**nahk
museum	**музей**	moo**z^{y}ay**
Red Square	**Красная площадь**	**krahs**nah^{y}ah **plo**shch^{y}eed
shops	**магазины**	mahgah**zee**ni
university	**университет**	ooneev^{y}ehrsee**t^{y}eht**
When does it open/close?	**Когда открывается/ закрывается?**	kahg**dah** ahtkriv**vay**eetsah/ zahkriv**vay**eetsah
How much is the entrance fee?	**Сколько стоит билет?**	**skol^{y}**kah **sto**eet bee**l^{y}eht**

Entertainment *Отдых*

What's playing at the … Theatre?	**Что идет в театре ...?**	shto ee**d^{y}ot** f tee**ah**tr^{y}eh
How much are the seats?	**Сколько стоят билеты?**	**skol^{y}**kah **sto**eet bee**l^{y}eh**ti
Is there a discotheque in town?	**Есть ли в городе дискотека?**	^{y}ehst lee f **go**rahd^{y}e deeskah**t^{y}eh**kah
Would you like to dance?	**Хотите потанцевать?**	kha**tee**t^{y}ah pa**tahn**tsehvaht^{y}
Thank you. It's been a wonderful evening.	**Спасибо за чудесный вечер.**	spahs**see**bah zah ch^{y}oo**d^{y}ehs**niy **v^{y}eh**ch^{y}eer

DATE, see page 173

Shops, stores and services *Магазины*

Where's the nearest …?	**Где есть поблизости ...?**	gd^{y}eh ^{y}est^{y} pah**blee**zayhstee
baker's	**булочная**	**boo**lahch^{y}nah^{y}ah
bank	**банк**	bahnk
bookshop/store	**книжный магазин**	**kneezh**niy mahgah**zeen**
chemist's	**аптека**	ahp**t^{y}eh**ka
dentist	**зубной врач**	zoob**noy** vrahch^{y}
department store	**универмаг**	ooneev^{y}ehr**mahk**
grocery	**продукты**	prah**dook**ti
hairdresser	**парикмахерская**	pahreek**mah**-kheerskah^{y}ah
liquor store	**винный магазин**	**veen**niy mahgah**zeen**
news kiosk	**газетный киоск**	gah**z^{y}eht**niy **kee**osk
post office	**почта**	**poch^{y}**tah
souvenir shop	**магазин сувениров**	mahgah**zeen** sooveen**ee**rahf
supermarket	**универсам**	ooneev^{y}ehr**sahm**

General expressions *Общие выражения*

Where's the main shopping area?	**Где большие магазины?**	gd^{y}eh bahl^{y}**shi**^{y}eh mahgah**zee**ni
Do you have any …?	**У вас есть ...?**	oo vahss ^{y}ehst^{y}
Can you show me this/that?	**Покажите мне, пожалуйста это/то.**	pahkah**zhi**t^{y}eh mn^{y}eh pah**zhahl**stah **eh**tah/toh
Do you have anything …?	**Нет ли у вас чего-нибудь ...?**	n^{y}eht lee oo vahss ch^{y}ee**vo**-neebood^{y}
better	**получше**	pah**looch**^{y}sheh
cheaper	**подешевле**	pahdee**shehv**l^{y}eh
larger	**побольше**	pah**bol^{y}**sheh
smaller	**поменьше**	pah**m^{y}eh**n^{y}sheh
Can I try it on?	**Можно примерить?**	**mozh**nah pah**m^{y}eh**reet^{y}
How much is this?	**Сколько это стоит?**	**skol^{y}**kah **eh**tah **sto**eet
Please write it down.	**Напишите, пожалуйста.**	nahpee**shi**t^{y}eh pah**zhahl**stah
No, I don't like it.	**Нет, мне это не нравится.**	n^{y}eht mn^{y}eh **eh**tah nee **nrah**veetsah

NUMBERS, see page 174

I'll take it.	**Я возьму это.**	^{y}ah vahz^{y}**moo eh**tah
Do you accept credit cards?	**Вы принимаете кредитные карточки?**	vi preenee**might**^{y}eh kree**deet**nigh **kahr**tahch^{y}kigh

black	**чёрный**	**ch^{y}or**niy	grey	**серий**	s^{y}ehriy
blue	**синий**	**see**neey	red	**красный**	**krahs**niy
brown	**коричневый**	kah**reech^{y}**neeviy	white	**белый**	**b^{y}e**liy
			yellow	**жёлтый**	**zhol**tiy
green	**зелёный**	zee**l^{y}on**niy	light …	**светло-...**	**sv^{y}eht**lah
orange	**оранжевый**	ah**rahn**zhiviy	dark …	**тёмно-...**	**t^{y}om**nah

I want to buy …	**Я хотел(а) бы купить ...**	^{y}ah khah**t^{y}ehl**(ah) bi koo**peet^{y}**
aspirin	**аспирин**	ahspee**reen**
batteries	**батарейки**	bahtah**r^{y}ay**ki
newspaper	**газету**	gah**z^{y}eh**too
American/ English	**американскую/ английскую**	ahm^{y}eree**kahn**skoo^{y}oo/ ahn**gleey**skoo^{y}oo
shampoo/soap	**шампунь/мыло**	shahm**poon^{y}/mil**lah
sun-tan cream	**крем для загара**	kr^{y}ehm dl^{y}ah zah**gah**rah
toothpaste	**зубную пасту**	**zoob**nah^{y}ah **pah**stah
a half-kilo of apples	**полкило яблок**	pahl**kee**lo ^{y}**ah**blahk
a litre of milk	**литр молока**	**lee**ter mahlah**kah**
I'd like … film for this camera.	**Дайте мне, ... плёнку для этого аппарата.**	**dight**^{y}eh mn^{y}eh **pl^{y}on**koo dl^{y}ah **eh**tahvah ahpah**rah**tah
black and white	**чёрно-белую**	**ch^{y}or**nah-**b^{y}eh**loo^{y}oo
colour	**цветную**	**tsveet**noo^{y}oo

Souvenirs *Сувениры*

balalaika	**балалайка**	bahlah**ligh**kah
caviar	**икра**	**ee**krah
chess set	**шахматы**	**shahkh**mahti
icon	**икона**	ee**kon**nah
samovar	**самовар**	sahmah**vahr**
vodka	**водка**	**vot**kah
wooden doll	**матрёшка**	mah**tr^{y}osh**kah

At the bank *На банке*

Where's the nearest currency exchange office?	**Где ближайшее бюро по обмену валюты?**	gd^{y}eh blee**zhigh**shee b^{y}oo**ro** pah ob**m^{y}eh**noo vah**l^{y}oo**ti
I want to change some dollars/pounds into roubles.	**Я хочу поменять доллары/фунты в рубли.**	^{y}ah kha**choo** pahmee**n^{y}aht^{y}** **dol**lahri/**foon**ti v **roo**blee
What's the exchange rate?	**Какой валютный курс?**	kah**koy** vah**l^{y}oot**niy koors

At the post office *На почте*

I want to send this by …	**Я бы хотел(а) отправить это ...**	^{y}ah bi khah**t^{y}ehl**(ah) aht**prah**veet^{y} **eh**tah
airmail	**авиа**	**ah**veeah
express	**экспресс**	ehk**spr^{y}ess**
I want a …-rouble stamp.	**Пожалуйста, марку за ... рублей.**	pah**zhahl**shah **mahr**koo za … roo**bl^{y}ey**
What's the postage for a postcard to the United States?	**Сколько стоит открытка в США?**	**skol**^{y}kah **sto**eet aht**krit**ka f s-shah
Is there any mail for me? My name is …	**Нет ли для меня писем? Моя фамилия ...**	n^{y}eht lee dl^{y}ah mee**n^{y}ah pees**s^{y}ehm. mah^{y}ah fah**mee**lee^{y}ah

Telephoning *Телефон-автомат*

Where's the nearest public phone?	**Где ближайший телефон-автомат?**	gd^{y}eh blee**zhigh**shiy teelee**fon**-ahtah**maht**
Hello. This is … speaking.	**Алло. Это говорит ...**	ah**l^{y}o**. **eh**tah gahvah**reet**
I want to speak to …	**Позовите, пожалуйста ...**	pahzah**veet**^{y}eh pah**zhahl**stah
When will he/she be back?	**Когда он/она вернётся?**	kahg**dah** onn/ah**nah** veer**n^{y}ot**sah
Will you tell him/her that I called?	**Передайте ему/ей, пожалуйста, что я звонил(а).**	peeree**dight**^{y}eh ee**moo**/^{y}ay pah**zhahl**stah shto ^{y}ah zvah**neel**(ah)

NUMBERS, see page 174

Time and date *День и число*

It's …	**Сейчас …**	see**ch^{y}ass**
five past one	**пять минут второго**	p^{y}aht mee**noot** ftah**rov**vah
quarter past three	**четверть четвёртого**	ch^{y}eht**v^{y}ehrt^y** ch^{y}eet**v^{y}or**tahvah
twenty past five	**двадцать минут пятого**	**dvah**tsaht^y mee**noot** **p^{y}ah**tahvah
half-past seven	**пол восьмого**	pol vahs^y**mo**vah
twenty-five to nine	**без двадцати пяти девять**	b^{y}ehz **dvaht**sahtee p^{y}ah**ti d^{y}eh**veet^y
ten to ten	**без десяти десять**	b^{y}ehz deessee**tee** **d^{y}ehs**seet^y
noon/midnight	**полдень/полночь**	**pol**deen^y/**pol**nahch^y
yesterday/today	**вчера/сегодня**	fch^{y}ee**rah**/see**vo**dn^{y}ah
tomorrow	**завтра**	**zahf**trah
spring/summer	**весна/лето**	vees**nah/l^{y}eh**tah
autumn/winter	**осень/зима**	**os**seen^y/zee**mah**

Sunday	**воскресенье**	vahskreess**^{y}eh**n^{y}eh
Monday	**понедельник**	pahnee**d^{y}eh**l^{y}eek
Tuesday	**вторник**	**ftor**neek
Wednesday	**среда**	sree**dah**
Thursday	**четверг**	ch^{y}eet**v^{y}erk**
Friday	**пятница**	**p^{y}aht**neetsah
Saturday	**суббота**	soo**bot**tah
January	**январь**	een**vahr^y**
February	**февраль**	fee**vrahl^y**
March	**март**	mahrt
April	**апрель**	ah**pr^{y}ehl^y**
May	**май**	migh
June	**июнь**	ee**^{y}oon^y**
July	**июль**	ee**^{y}ool^y**
August	**август**	**ahv**goost
September	**сентябрь**	seen**t^{y}ahbr^y**
October	**октябрь**	ahk**t^{y}ahbr^y**
November	**ноябрь**	nah^y**yahbr^y**
December	**декабрь**	dee**kahbr^y**

Numbers *Числа*

0	**ноль**	nol^{y}	6	**шесть**	shehst^{y}
1	**один**	ah**deen**	7	**семь**	s^{y}ehm^{y}
2	**два**	dvah	8	**восемь**	**vos**seem^{y}
3	**три**	tree	9	**девять**	**d^{y}eh**veet^{y}
4	**четыре**	ch^{y}ee**tir**ree	10	**десять**	**d^{y}eh**sseet^{y}
5	**пять**	p^{y}aht^{y}	11	**одиннадцать**	ah**dee**nahtsaht^{y}

12	**двенадцать**	dvee**naht**saht^{y}
13	**тринадцать**	tree**naht**saht^{y}
14	**четырнадцать**	ch^{y}ee**tir**nahtsaht^{y}
15	**пятнадцать**	peet**naht**saht^{y}
16	**шестнадцать**	shis**naht**saht^{y}
17	**семнадцать**	seem**naht**saht^{y}
18	**восемнадцать**	vahsseem**naht**saht^{y}
19	**девятнадцать**	deeveet**naht**saht^{y}
20	**двадцать**	**dvaht**saht^{y}
21	**двадцать один**	**dvaht**saht^{y} ah**deen**
30	**тридцать**	**tree**tsaht^{y}
40	**сорок**	**so**rrahk
50	**пятьдесят**	peedees**s^{y}aht**
60	**шестьдесят**	shizdees**s^{y}aht**
70	**семьдесят**	s^{y}ehmdees**s^{y}aht**
80	**восемьдесят**	vosseemdees**s^{y}aht**
90	**девяносто**	deevee**no**stah

100/1,000	**сто/тысяча**	sto/**tis**seech^{y}ah
first/second	**первый/второй**	**p^{y}ehr**viy/frah**roy**

Emergency *Крайний случай*

Call the police.	**Позвоните в милицию.**	pahzvah**nee**tee v meelee**tsi**^{y}oo
Get a doctor.	**Позовите врача.**	pahzah**vee**tee vrah**ch^{y}ah**
Go away.	**Уходите.**	ookhah**dee**tee
HELP!	**НА ПОМОЩЬ!**	nah **pom**mahshch^{y}
I'm ill.	**Я болен (больна).**	^{y}ah **bo**leen^{y} (bahl^{y}**nah**)
I'm lost.	**Я заблудился (заблудилась).**	^{y}ah zabloo**deel**sah (zahbloodee**lahs^{y}**)
LOOK OUT!	**ОСТОРОЖНО**	ahstah**rozh**nah

TELEPHONING, see page 172

STOP THIEF!	**ДЕРЖИ ВОРА**	deer**zhi** vor**rah**
My … have been stolen.	**У меня украли ...**	oo mee**n^{y}ah** oo**krah**lee
I've lost my …	**Я потерял(а) ...**	^{y}ah pahteer**^{y}ahl**(ah)
handbag	**сумочку**	**soo**mahch^{y}koo
passport	**паспорт**	**pahs**pahrt
luggage	**багаж**	bah**gahzh**
Where can I find a doctor who speaks English?	**Где мне найти врача, говорящего по-английски?**	gd^{y}eh mn^{y}eh nigh**tee** vrah**ch^{y}ah** gahvah**r^{y}ah**shcheevo pah ahn**gleey**skee

Guide to Russian pronunciation

Russian is spoken and understood in Russia and most parts of the Ukraine and Belarus.

Letter	Approximate pronunciation	Symbol	Example	
б	like **b** in **b**it	b	**был**	bill
в	like **v** in **v**ine	v	**ваш**	vahsh
г	like **g** in **g**o	g	**город**	**go**rraht
д	like **d** in **d**og	d	**да**	dah
ж	like **s** in plea**s**ure	zh	**жаркий**	**zhahr**keey
з	like **z** in **z**oo	z	**за**	zah
к	like **k** in **k**itten	k	**карта**	**kahr**tah
л	like **l** in **l**amp	l	**лампа**	**lahm**pah
м	like **m** in **m**y	m	**масло**	**mah**shlah
н	like **n** in **n**ot	n	**нет**	n^{y}eht
п	like **p** in **p**ot	p	**парк**	pahrk
р	trilled (like a Scottish **r**)	r	**русский**	**roo**skeey
с	like **s** in **s**ee	s/ss	**слово**	**slov**vah
т	like **t** in **t**ip	t	**там**	tahm
ф	like **f** in **f**ace	f	**ферма**	**f^{y}ehr**mah
х	like **ch** in Scottish lo**ch**	kh	**хлеб**	khl^{y}ehp
ц	like **ts** in si**ts**	ts	**цена**	tsin**nah**
ч	like **ch** in **ch**ip	ch^y	**час**	ch^{y}ahss
ш	like **sh** in **sh**ut	sh	**шапка**	**shahp**kah
щ	like **sh** followed by **ch**	shch^y	**щетка**	**shch^{y}ot**kah

Voiced consonants are pronounced voiceless at the end of the word.

Vowels

а	between the **a** in c**a**t and the **u** in c**u**t	ah	**как**	kahk
е	like **ye** in **ye**t	^{y}eh	**где**	gd^{y}eh
ё	like **yo** in **yo**nder	^{y}o	**мёд**	m^{y}ot
и	like **ee** in s**ee**	ee	**синий**	**see**neey
й	like **y** in bo**y**	y	**бой**	boy
о	like **o** in h**o**t	o	**стол**	stoll
у	like **oo** in b**oo**t	oo	**улица**	**oo**leetsah
ы	like **i** in **i**ll	i	**вы**	vi
э	like **e** in m**e**t	eh	**эта**	**eh**tah
ю	like **u** in English d**u**ty	^{y}oo	**юг**	^{y}ook
я	like **ya** in **ya**rd	^{y}ah	**мясо**	**m^{y}ah**ssah

Other letters

ь makes the previous consonant soft. A similar effect can be produced by pronouncing **y** as in **yet** – but very short – after the consonant.

ъ is sometimes used to indicate the clear separation of sounds when pronouncing the syllables on either side.

Diphthongs

ай	like **igh** in s**igh**	igh	**май**	migh
яй	like the previous sound, but preceded by the **y** in **y**es	^{y}igh	**негодяй**	neegah-**d^{y}igh**
ой	like **oy** in b**oy**	oy	**вой**	voy
ей	like **ya** in **Ya**tes	^{y}ay	**соловей**	sahlah**v^{y}ay**
ый	like **i** in **i**ll followed by the **y** in **y**es	iy	**красивый**	krah**ssee**viy
уй	like **oo** in g**oo**d followed by the **y** in **y**es	ooy	**дуй**	dooy
юй	like the previous sound, but preceded by a short **y**-sound	^{y}ooy	**плюй**	pl^{y}ooy

Accentuation

If a vowel or diphthong is not stressed, it often changes its pronunciation.

о	unstressed, is pronounced like Russian **a**	ah	**отец**	aht^{y}**ehts**
е, я, ей, ий	unstressed, are pronounced like a short **ee** sound	ee	**теперь**	tee**p^{y}ehr^{y}**
			язык	ee**zik**

Slovenian

Basic expressions *Osnovni izrazi*

Yes/No.	**Ja/Ne.**	ya/ne
Please.	**Prosim.**	**proh**sim
Thank you.	**Hvala.**	**hvaa**la
I beg your pardon?	**Prosim?**	**proh**sim

Introductions *Predstavimo se*

Good morning.	**Dobro jutro.**	**do**bro **yoo**tro
Good afternoon.	**Dober dan.**	**doh**berr vec**hehr**
Good night.	**Lahko noč.**	**laa-**hko **nohch**
Good-bye.	**Na svidenje.**	na **svee**denye
My name is …	**Ime mi je ...**	**imeh** mi yeh …
What's your name?	**Kako vam je ime?**	ka**koh** vam ye i**meh**
How are you?	**Kako ste?**	ka**koh** ste
Fine thanks. And you?	**Dobro, hvala. Pa vi?**	**do**bro **hvaa**la. pa vi
Where do you come from?	**Od kod ste?**	ot koht ste
I'm from …	**Sem iz ...**	serm iz
Australia	**Avstralije**	aws**traa**liye
Britain	**Britanije**	bri**taa**niye
Canada	**Kanade**	**kaa**nade
USA	**Združenih držav**	zd**roo**zheni-h **derr**zhaw
I'm with my …	**Sem z …**	serm z
wife	**mojo ženo**	**mo**yo **zhe**no
husband	**mojim možem**	**mo**yeem **moh**zhem
family	**mojo družino**	**mo**yo droo**zhee**no
children	**mojimi otroki**	**mo**yimi ot**roh**ki
boyfriend	**mojim fantom**	**mo**yim **faan**tom
girlfriend	**mojo punco**	**mo**yo **poon**tso
I'm on my own.	**Sam sem.**	saam serm
I'm here on holiday (vacation)/on business.	**Tu sem na počitnicah/ poslovno.**	too serm na po**chee**tnetsa-h/ pos**low**no

GUIDE TO PRONUNCIATION/EMERGENCIES, see page 190

Questions *Postavljanje vprašanj*

When?/How?	**Kdaj?/Kako?**	kday/ka**koh**
What?/Why?	**Kaj?/Zakaj?**	kaay/za**kaay**
Who?/Which?	**Kdo?/Kateri?**	kdoh/ka**teh**ri
Where is/are …?	**Kje je/so…?**	kyeh ye/so
Where can I get/find …?	**Kje lahko dobim/najdem ...?**	kyeh la-h**koh** do**beem/naay**dem
How far?	**Kako daleč?**	ka**koh daa**lech
How long?	**Kako dolgo?**	ka**koh dow**go
How much?	**Koliko?**	**koh**liko
May I?	**Smem?**	smehm
Can I have …?	**Lahko dobim ...?**	la-h**koh** do**beem**
Can you help me?	**Mi lahko pomagate?**	mi la-h**koh** po**maa**gate
I understand.	**Razumem.**	ra**zoo**mem
I don't understand.	**Ne razumem.**	ne ra**zoo**mem
Can you translate this for me?	**Mi to lahko prevedete?**	mi toh lah**koh** pre**ve**dete
Do you speak English?	**Govorite angleško?**	govo**ree**te ang**leh**shko
I don't speak Slovenian.	**Govorim malo slovensko.**	govo**reem maa**lo slo**vehn**sko

A few useful words *Nekaj koristnih izrazov*

beautiful/ugly	**lepo/grdo**	**leh**po/**gerr**do
better/worse	**boljše/slabše**	**bohl^y**she/**slaap**she
big/small	**veliko/majhno**	ve**lee**ko/**maay**-hno
cheap/expensive	**poceni/drago**	po**tseh**ni/**draa**go
early/late	**zgodaj/pozno**	**zgoh**day/**poz**no
good/bad	**dobro/slabo**	**do**bro/**slaa**bo
hot/cold	**vroče/hladno**	**vroh**che/**hlaa**dno
near/far	**blizu/daleč**	b**lee**zoo/**daa**lech
old/young	**star/mlad**	star/mlat
right/wrong	**prav/narobe**	praw/na**roh**be
vacant/occupied	**prosto/zasedeno**	**pro**sto/za**seh**deno

Hotel–Accomodation *Namestitev v hotelu*

I've a reservation.	**Imam rezervacijo.**	i**maa**m rezer**vaa**tsiyo
We've reserved two rooms.	**Rezervirali smo dve sobi.**	rezer**vee**rali smo dveh **so**bi
Here's the confirmation.	**Tu je potrdilo.**	too ye poter**dee**lo
Do you have any vacancies?	**Ali imate proste sobe?**	**aa**li i**maa**te **pro**ste sobe
I'd like a … room.	**Rad (Rada) bi ... sobo.**	rat (**raa**da) bi ... sobo
single	**enoposteljno**	eno**pohs**tel^{y}no
double	**dvoposteljno**	dvo**pohs**tel^{y}no
with twin beds	**z dvema posteljama**	z **dveh**ma **pohs**telyama
with a double bed	**z zakonsko posteljo**	z **zaa**konsko **pohs**telyo
with a bath/shower	**s kopalnico/tušem**	s ko**paal**nitso/**too**shem
We'll be staying …	**Ostali bomo ...**	os**taa**li **boh**mo
overnight only	**samo eno noč**	sa**moh** eno nohch
a few days	**nekaj dni**	**neh**kay dni
a week (at least)	**(najmanj) en teden**	(**naay**man^{y}) en **teh**dern
Is there a campsite near here?	**Ali je v bližini kamp?**	**aa**li ye oo bli**zhee**ni kaamp

Decision *Odločitev*

May I see the room?	**Lahko vidim sobo?**	lah**koh** **vee**dim **so**bo
That's fine. I'll take it.	**V redu je, vzel (vzela) jo bom.**	oo **reh**du ye wzehl (**wzeh**la) yo bohm
No. I don't like it.	**Ne, ni mi všeč.**	neh ni mi wshehch
It's too …	**Je preveč ...**	ye pre**ve**ch
dark/small	**temna/majhna**	**ter**mna/**maay**hna
noisy	**hrupna**	**hroop**na
Do you have anything …?	**Ali imate kaj ...?**	**aa**li i**maa**te kaay
better/bigger	**boljšega/večjega**	**bohl^{y}**shega/**veh**chyega
cheaper/quieter	**cenejšega/tišjega**	tse**ney**shega/**teesh**yega
May I please have my bill?	**Lahko vidim račun?**	la-h**koh** **vee**dim ra**choon**
It's been a very enjoyable stay.	**Tu smo se imeli zelo lepo.**	too smo se i**meh**li ze**loh** le**poh**

Eating out *V restavraciji*

I'd like to reserve a table for 4.	**Rad(a) bi rezerviral(a) mizo za štiri osebe.**	rat (**raa**da) bi rezer**vee**ral(a) **mee**zo za **shtee**ri oseh**be**
We'll come at 8.	**Prišli bomo ob osmih.**	pri**shlee bo**h**mo** ob **os**mi-h
I'd like breakfast/ lunch/dinner.	**Rad(a) bi zajtrk/ kosilo/večerjo.**	rat (**raa**da) bi **zaay**terrk/ ko**see**lo/ve**chehr**yo
What do you recommend?	**Kaj priporočate?**	kaay pripo**roh**chate
Do you have vegetarian dishes?	**Ali imate vegetarijanske jedi?**	**aa**li **imaa**te vegetari**yaan**ske ye**dee**

Breakfast *Zajtrk*

I'd like …	**Rad(a) bi ...**	rat (**raa**da) bi
bread/butter	**kruh/maslo**	kru-h/**ma**slo
cheese	**sir**	seer
egg/ham	**jajce/šunko**	**yaay**tse/**shoon**ko
jam	**marmelado**	marme**laa**do
rolls	**žemlje**	**zheh**mlye

Starters *Predjedi*

goveja juha	go**ve**ya **yoo-**ha	clear beef broth
hladetina	hla**deh**tina	aspic
narezek	na**reh**zek	assorted cold cuts
pršut	perr**shoot**	dry-cured Italian ham
šunka	**shoon**ka	ham
vložene gobice	wlo**zh**ene **goh**bitse	pickled mushrooms

baked/boiled	**pečeno/kuhano**	pe**che**no/**koo-**hano
fried	**cvrto**	**cverr**to
grilled	**na žaru**	na **zhaa**roo
roast	**pečeno**	pe**che**no
underdone (rare)	**malo pečeno**	**maa**lo pe**che**no
medium	**srednje pečeno**	**srehd**nye pe**che**no
well-done	**dobro pečeno**	dobro pe**che**no

NUMBERS, see page 189

Meat *Meso*

I'd like some …	**Rad(a) bi ...**	rat (**raa**da) bi
beef/lamb	**govedino/ovčetino**	go**veh**dino/ow**cheh**tino
pork/veal	**svinjino/teletino**	svi**n^y**ino/tele**tee**no
čevapčiči	che**vaap**chichi	minced meat, grilled in rolled pieces
dunajski zrezek	**doo**nayski **zreh**zek	breaded veal escalope
golaž	**goh**lazh	gulash
meso na žaru	me**soh** na **zhaa**ru	assorted grilled meat
pečenka	pe**chehn**ka	beef, pork or veal roast
polnjene paprike	**pow**nyene **paa**prike	stuffed green peppers
svinjska	**sveen^y**ska	roasted pork
telečja krača	**teleh**chya **kraa**cha	veal shank
zelje s klobaso	**zeh**lye s klo**baa**so	sauerkraut with sausage

Fish and seafood *Ribe in morski sadeži*

jastog	**yaa**stok	lobster
jegulja	ye**goo**lya	eel
lignji	**leeg**n^{y}i	deep fried squid
morski list	**mor**ski leest	sole
postrvi	pos**terr**vi	trout
škampi	**shkaam**pi	scampi
školjke	**shkohl^y**ke	mussels
zobatec	zo**baa**tets	dentex

Vegetables *Zelenjava*

beans	**fižol**	fi**zhow**
cabbage	**zelje**	**zeh**lye
gherkin	**kisla kumarica**	**kee**sla **koo**maritsa
lentils	**leča**	**leh**cha
mushroom	**goba**	**goh**ba
onion	**čebula**	che**boo**la
potatoes	**krompir**	krom**peer**
tomato	**paradižnik**	para**deezh**nik
ocvrti jajčevci	ots**verr**ti **yaay**chewtsi	deep-fried eggplant
omleta s sirom	om**leh**ta s **see**rom	cheese omelet
omleta s šunko	om**leh**ta s **shoon**ko	ham omelet
pohan sir	**poh**han seer	breaded fried cheese

Fruit & dessert *Sadnje in deserti*

apple/banana	**jabolko/banana**	**yaa**bowko/ba**naa**na
gateau	**torta**	**tohr**ta
ice-cream	**sladoled**	sladol**eht**
lemon/orange	**limona/pomaranča**	li**moh**na/poma**raan**cha
plum/strawberries	**sliva/jagode**	**slee**va/**yaa**gode
jabolčni zavitek	**yaa**bowchni za**vee**tek	thin layers of pastry filled with apple slices and raisins
palačinke	pala**cheen**ke	crepes with jam or nut fillings
potica	po**tee**tsa	walnut roll

Drinks *Pijače*

beer	**pivo**	**pee**vo
(hot) chocolate	**kakav**	ka**kaa**w
coffee	**kava**	**kaa**va
black/with milk	**črna/z mlekom**	**cherr**na/z **mleh**kom
fruit juice	**sok**	sohk
orange	**pomarančni**	poma**raanch**ni
apple	**jabolčni**	**yaa**bowchni
mineral water	**mineralna voda**	mine**raal**na **vo**da
tea	**čaj**	chaay
vodka	**vodka**	**vot**ka
red/white wine	**črno/belo vino**	**cherr**no/**beh**lo **vee**no

Complaints and paying *Pritožbe in plačilo računa*

This is too bitter/salty/sweet.	**To je preveč grenko/slano/sladko.**	toh ye pre**vech** **gren**ko/**slaa**no/**slaat**ko
That's not what I ordered.	**Tega nisem naročil(a).**	**teh**ga **nee**serm na**ro**chiw (naro**chee**la)
I'd like to pay.	**Rad(a) bi plačal(a).**	rat (**raa**da) bi **plaa**chaw (**plaa**chala)
I think you made a mistake in the bill.	**Mislim, da ste v računu naredili napako.**	**mee**slem da ste oo ra**choo**nu nare**dee**li na**paa**ko
We enjoyed it, thank you.	**Všeč nam je bilo, hvala.**	wshehch nam ye bi**loh** **hvaa**la

NUMBERS, see page 189

Travelling around *Potovanja*

Plane *Avion*

Is there a flight to Vienna?	**Ali imate let za Dunaj?**	**aa**li i**maa**te let za **doo**nay
What time do I check in?	**Kdaj se moram javiti na letališču?**	kdaay se **moh**ram **yaa**viti na leta**leesh**chu
I'd like to … my reservation.	**Rad (Rada) bi ... rezervacijo.**	rat (**raa**da) bi rezer**vaa**tsiyo
cancel	**odpovedal(a)**	otpo**veh**daw (otpo**veh**dala)
change	**zamenjal(a)**	za**meh**nyaw (za**meh**nyala)
confirm	**potrdil(a)**	po**terr**diw (poterr**dee**la)

Train *Vlak*

I want a ticket to Koper.	**Rad(a) bi vozovnico za Koper.**	rat (**raa**da) bi vo**zow**nitso za **ko**perr
single (one-way)	**enosmerno**	**eno**smerno
return (roundtrip)	**povratno**	po**vraat**no
first class	**prvi razred**	**perr**vi **raaz**ret
second class	**drugi razred**	**droo**gee **raaz**ret
How long does the journey (trip) take?	**Koliko časa traja potovanje?**	**koh**liko **chaa**sa **traa**ya poto**vaa**nye
When is the … train to Jesenice?	**Kdaj pelje ... vlak na Jesenice?**	kdaay **peh**lye … wlaak na yese**nee**tse
first/next	**prvi/naslednji**	**perr**vi/nas**leh**dn^{y}i
last	**zadnji**	**zaa**dn^{y}i
Is this the right train to Maribor?	**Ali je ta pravi vlak za Maribor?**	**aa**li ye ta pr**aa**vi wlaak za **maa**ribor

Bus—Tram (streetcar) *Avtobus—Tramvaj*

What bus goes to the centre of town/ downtown?	**Kateri avtobus pelje v center mesta?**	kat**eh**ri **aw**tobus **peh**lye oo **tsen**terr **meh**sta

TELLING THE TIME, see page 188

How much is the fare to …?	**Koliko stane do ...?**	**koh**liko **staa**ne do
Will you tell me when to get off?	**Mi lahko prosim poveste, kdaj moram izstopiti?**	mi la-h**koh proh**sim po**veh**ste kdaay **moh**ram **ees**topiti

Taxi *Taxi*

How much is it to …?	**Koliko stane do ...?**	**koh**liko **staa**ne do
Take me to this adress.	**Peljite me na ta naslov.**	pel^{y}**ee**te me na ta **naa**slow
Please stop here.	**Prosim ustavite tukaj.**	**proh**sim oo**staa**vite **too**kay

Car hire (rental) *Najem avtomobila*

I'd like to hire (rent) a car.	**Rad(a) bi najel (najela) avto.**	rat (**raa**da) bi nay**ehw** (na**yeh**la) **aaw**to.
I'd like it for a day/week.	**Rad(a) bi ga za en dan/teden.**	rat (**raa**da) bi ga za en daan/**teh**dern
Where's the nearest filling station?	**Kje je najbližja bencinska postaja?**	kyeh ye nay**blee**zhya ben**tseen**ska po**staa**ya
Full tank, please.	**Napolnite, prosim.**	na**pow**nite **proh**sim
Give me … litres of petrol (gasoline).	**Dajte mi ... litrov bencina.**	**daay**te mi ... **lee**trow ben**tsee**na
How do I get to …?	**Kako pridem do ...?**	ka**koh pree**dem do
I've had a breakdown at …	**Avto se mi je pokvaril pri ...**	**aaw**to se mi ye po**kva**riw pri
Can you send a mechanic?	**Lahko pošljete mehanika?**	la-h**koh posh**lyete me-**ha**nika
Can you mend this puncture (fix this flat)?	**Lahko zakrpate to luknjo?**	la-h**koh** za**kerr**pate toh **look**nyo

☞ You're on the wrong road.	**Ste na napačni cesti.** ☜
Go straight ahead.	**Pojdite naravnost.**
It's down there on the …	**To je tam …**
left/right	**na levi/desni**
opposite/behind …	**nasprtoti/za**
next to/after …	**zraven/za**
north/south/east/west	**severno/južno/vzhodno/zahodno**

NUMBERS, see page 189

Sightseeing *Turistični ogled mesta*

Where's the tourist office?	**Kje je turistična agencija?**	kyeh ye too**reest**ichna agen**tsee**ya
Is there an English-speaking guide?	**Ali imate vodiča, ki govori angleško?**	**aa**li **imaa**te vo**dee**cha ki govo**ree** ang**leh**shko
Where is/are the …?	**Kje je/so … ?**	kyeh ye/so
botanical gardens	**botanični vrt**	bo**taa**nichni verrt
castle	**grad**	graat
cathedral	**katedrala**	kate**draa**la
city centre/downtown	**center mesta**	**cen**terr **meh**sta
exhibition	**razstava**	ras**taa**va
harbour	**pristanišče**	prista**neesh**che
market	**trg**	terrk
museum	**muzej**	moo**zey**
shops	**trgovine**	terrgo**vee**ne
ski slopes	**smučišča**	smu**cheesh**cha
zoo	**živalski vrt**	zhi**vaal**ski verrt
When does it open/close?	**Kdaj se odpre/zapre?**	kdaay se od**pre**/za**pre**
How much is the entrance fee?	**Koliko stane vstopnina?**	**koh**liko **staa**ne wstop**nee**na

Entertainment *Zabava*

What's playing at the … Theatre?	**Kaj igra v ... gledališču?**	kaay **igraa** oo ... glehda**leesh**choo
How much are the tickets?	**Po koliko so vstopnice?**	po **koh**liko so w**stohp**nitse
Would you like to go out with me tonight?	**Ali bi danes zvečer hoteli iti z mano ven?**	**aa**li bi **daa**nes zve**chehr** hoteh**lee** **eeti** z **maa**no vern
Is there a discotheque in town?	**Ali je diskoteka v mestu?**	**aa**li ye disko**teh**ka oo **meh**stoo
Would you like to dance?	**Bi radi plesali?**	bi **raa**di ples**aa**li
Thank you. It's been a wonderful evening.	**Hvala. Bil je čudovit večer.**	**hvaa**la. beel ye chudo**veet** ve**chehr**

TELLING THE TIME, see page 188

Shops, stores and services *Trgovina in usluge*

Where's the nearest …?	**Kje je najbližja ...?**	kyeh ye nay**bleezh**ya
bakery	**pekarna**	pe**kaar**na
bookshop/store	**knjigarna**	kn^{y}i**gaar**na
butcher's	**mesnica**	mes**nee**tsa
chemist's/drugstore	**lekarna**	le**kaar**na
dentist	**zobozdravnik**	zobozdraw**neek**
department store	**veleblagovnica**	veleblag**ow**nitsa
grocery	**špecerija**	shpetse**ree**ya
hairdresser/barber	**frizer**	fri**zer**
newsagent	**kiosk**	ki**oh**sk
post office	**pošta**	**poh**shta
supermarket	**supermarket**	**soo**perrmar**keht**

General expressions *Splošni izrazi*

Where's the main shopping area?	**Kje je glavni trgovski center?**	kyeh ye **glaaw**ni terr**gow**ski **tsen**terr
Do you have any …?	**Ali imate ...?**	**aa**li **imaa**te
Do you have anything …?	**Ali imate kaj ...?**	**aa**li **imaa**te kaay
cheaper	**cenejšega**	tse**ney**shega
better	**boljšega**	**bohl**^{y}shega
larger/smaller	**večjega/manjšega**	**veh**chyega/**maan**^{y}shega
Can I try it on?	**Ali lahko pomerim?**	**aa**li la-h**koh** po**meh**rim
How much is this?	**Koliko stane to?**	**koh**liko **staa**ne toh
Please write it down.	**Prosim napišite.**	**proh**sim na**pee**shiteh
No, I don't like it.	**Ne, ni mi všeč.**	ne ni mi **wshehch**
I'll take it.	**To bom vzel (vzela).**	toh bohm **wzehw** (**wzeh**la)
Do you accept credit cards?	**Ali vzamete kreditne kartice?**	**aa**li **wzaa**mete kre**deet**ne **kaar**titse

black	**črno**	**cherr**no	brown	**rjavo**	err**yaa**vo
orange	**oranžno**	or**aan**zhno	yellow	**rumeno**	**roo**meno
blue	**modro**	**moh**dro	green	**zeleno**	ze**le**no
red	**rdeče**	err**deh**che	white	**belo**	**beh**lo

NUMBERS, see page 189

I want to buy …	**Rad(a) bi kupil(a) ...**	rat (**raa**da) bi **koo**piw (kup**ee**la)
aspirin	**aspirin**	aspi**reen**
batteries	**baterije**	bate**ree**ye
newspaper	**časopis**	chaso**pees**
English/American	**angleški/ameriški**	angl**eh**shki/**a**merishki
shampoo	**šhampon**	sham**pohn**
soap	**milo**	**mee**lo
sun-tan cream	**kremo za sončenje**	**kreh**mo za **sohn**chenye
toothpaste	**zobno pasto**	**zohb**no **paa**sto
a half-kilo of apples	**pol kilograma jabolk**	pow kilo**graa**ma **yaa**bowk
a litre of milk	**liter mleka**	**lee**ter **mleh**ka
I'd like … film for this camera.	**Rad(a) bi ... film za ta fotoaparat.**	rat (**raa**da) bi ... **fee**lerm za **foh**to-apa**raat**
black and white	**črno-bel**	**cher**no**behw**
colour	**barvni**	**baar**vni
I'd like a hair-cut.	**Rad(a) bi se ostrigel (ostrigla).**	rat (**raa**da) bi se os**tree**gerw (os**tree**gla)

Souvenirs *Spominki*

idrijska čipka	**ee**dri^{y}ska **cheep**ka	lace-work from Idrija
kristalna posoda	kris**taal**na poso**h**da	crystal glassware
lectovo srce	**leht**stovo serr**tseh**	gingerbread heart
lončena posoda	lon**cheh**na poso**h**da	earthenware
tirolski klobuk	ti**rohl**ski klo**book**	Tyrolean hat
vezenine	veze**nee**ne	embroidery

At the bank *V banki*

Where's the nearest bank/currency exchange office?	**Kje je najbližja banka/ menjalnica?**	ky**eh** ye nay**bleezh**ya **baan**ka/ men**yaal**nitsa
I want to change some dollars/pounds into tolars.	**Rad(a) bi zamenjal(a) dolarje/funte v tolarje.**	rat (**raa**da) bi za**mehn**yaw (-yala) **doh**larye/**foon**te w **toh**larye
What's the exchange rate?	**Kakšen je tečaj?**	**kaak**shern ye te**chaay**

At the post office *Na pošti*

I want to send this by …	**To bi rad(a) poslal(a) ...**	toh bi rat (**raa**da) pos**laaw** (pos**laa**la)
airmail/express	**letalsko/ekssprays**	le**taal**sko/eks**prehs**
I want …-tolar stamps.	**Rad(a) be znamke za ... tolarjev.**	rat (**raa**da) bi **znaam**ke za ... **toh**laryew
What's the postage for a letter to the United States?	**Kolikšna je poštnina za pismo za Združene države?**	**koh**likshna ye posh**tnee**na za **pee**smo za **zdroo**zhene **derr**zhave
Is there any mail for me? My name is …	**Ali je kaj pošte zame? Ime mi je ...**	**aa**li ye kaay **pohsh**te **zaa**me. i**meh** mi ye
Can I send a telegram/facsimile?	**Ali lahko pošljem telegram/faksimile?**	**aa**li la-h**koh** **pohsh**lyem tele**graam**/fak**see**mile

Telephoning *Telefoniranje*

Where's the nearest telephone booth?	**Kje je najbližja telefonska go vorilnica?**	kyeh ye nay**bleezh**ya tele**fohn**ska govo**reel**nitsa
May I use your phone?	**Ali smem uporabiti vaš telefon?**	**aa**li smehm upo**raa**biti vash tele**fohn**
Hello. This is … speaking.	**Halo. ... pri telefonu.**	ha**loh** ... pri tele**foh**nu
I want to speak to …	**Rad(a) bi govoril(a) z ...**	rat (**raa**da) bi go**voh**riw (govo**ree**la) z
When will he/she be back?	**Kdaj se bo vrnil/vrnila?**	kdaay se boh **verr**niw/verr**nee**la
Will you tell him/her that I called?	**Bi mu/ji povedali, da sem klical(a)?**	bi mu/yee po**veh**dali da serm **klee**tsaw (-tsala)

Time and date *Ura in datumi*

It's …	**Je ...**	ye
five past one	**pet čez eno**	peht chez eno
quarter past three	**četrt čez tri**	che**terrt** chez tree
twenty past five	**dvajset čez pet**	d**vaay**set chez peht
half-past seven	**pol osmih**	pow **os**mee-h
twenty-five to nine	**pet čez pol devetih**	peht chez pow de**ve**ti-h

NUMBERS, see page 189

ten to ten	**deset do desetih**	de**seht** do de**se**ti-h
noon/midnight	**poldne/polnoč**	**pow**dne/**pow**nohch
in the morning/evening	**zjutraj/zvečer**	zy**oo**tray/zve**chehr**
at night	**ponoči**	po**no**chi
yesterday/today	**včeraj/danes**	w**cheh**ray/**daa**nes
tomorrow	**jutri**	**yoo**tri

Sunday	**nedelja**	ne**dehl**ya
Monday	**ponedeljek**	pone**dehl**yek
Tuesday	**torek**	**to**rek
Wednesday	**sreda**	**sreh**da
Thursday	**četrtek**	che**terr**tek
Friday	**petek**	**peh**tek
Saturday	**sobota**	so**boh**ta
January	**januar**	**yaa**nooar
February	**februar**	**feh**brooar
March	**marec**	**maa**rets
April	**april**	**apreew**
May	**maj**	maay
June	**junij**	**yoo**ni[y]
July	**julij**	**yoo**li[y]
August	**avgust**	aw**goost**
September	**september**	sep**tem**berr
October	**oktober**	ok**toh**berr
November	**november**	no**vem**berr
December	**december**	det**sem**berr

Numbers *Števila*

0	**nič**	neech	11	**enajst**	**enaayst**
1	**ena**	ena	12	**dvanajst**	dva**naayst**
2	**dva**	dva	13	**trinajst**	tri**naayst**
3	**tri**	tree	14	**štirinajst**	shtiri**naayst**
4	**štiri**	**shtee**ri	15	**petnajst**	pet**naayst**
5	**pet**	peht	16	**šestnajst**	shest**naayst**
6	**šest**	shehst	17	**sedemnajst**	sederm**naayst**
7	**sedem**	**seh**derm	18	**osemnajst**	ohserm**naayst**
8	**osem**	**oh**serm	19	**devetnajst**	devet**naayst**
9	**devet**	de**veht**	20	**dvajset**	**dvaay**set
10	**deset**	de**seht**	21	**dvajset ena**	**dvaay**set ena

SLOVENIAN

30 **trideset**	**tree**deset	
40 **štirideset**	**shteer**ideset	
50 **petdeset**	**peht**deset	
60 **šestdeset**	**shehst**deset	
70 **sedemdeset**	**seh**dermdeset	
80 **osemdeset**	**oh**sermdeset	
90 **devetdeset**	de**veht**deset	
100/1,000 **sto/tisoč**	stoh/**tee**soch	
first/second	**prvi/drugi**	**perr**vee/**droo**gee
once/twice	**enkrat/dvakrat**	**en**krat/**dvaa**krat
a half/quarter	**polovica/četrt**	polo**vee**tsa/che**terrt**

Emergency *V sili*

Call the police	**Pokličite policijo**	po**klee**chite polit**see**yo
Get a doctor	**Pokličite zdravnika**	po**klee**chite zdraw**nee**ka
HELP	**NA POMOČ**	na po**mohch**
I'm ill	**Bolan (bolna) sem**	bo**laan** (**bow**na) serm
I'm lost	**Zgubil(a) sem se**	zgu**beew** (zgu**bee**la) serm se
Leave me alone	**Pustite me pri miru**	pus**tee**te me pree **mee**ru
STOP THIEF	**PRIMITE TATU**	**pree**mite ta**too**
My … have been stolen.	**Ukradli so mi ...**	**ukraad**li so mi
I've lost my …	**Zgubil(a) sem ...**	**zgoo**bil (zgu**bee**la) serm
handbag/wallet	**torbico/denarnico**	**tohr**bitso/de**naar**nitso
passport/luggage	**potni list/prtljago**	**poht**ni list/perrt**lyaa**go
Where can I find a doctor who speaks English?	**Kje lahko dobim zdravnika, ki govori angleško?**	kyeh lah**koh** do**beem** zdrav**nee**ka ki govo**ree** an**glehsh**ko

Guide to Slovenian pronunciation

Consonants

Letter	Approximate pronunciation	Symbol	Example	
f, h, k, m, n, p, s, t, z	normally pronounced as in English			
b	1) like **p** in cup	p	**rob**	rohp
	2) elsewhere as in English	b	**barva**	**baar**va

TELEPHONING, see page 188

Slovensko

c	like **ts** in **ts**ar	ts	**cehsta**	**tseh**sta
č	like **ch** in **ch**air	ch	**čas**	chaas
d	1) like **t** in **t**ake	t	**grad**	graat
	2) elsewhere as in English	d	**dan**	daan
g	1) like **k** in **k**ey	k	**krog**	krohk
	2) elsewhere as in English	g	**gora**	**go**ra
j	1) as **y** in **y**es	y	**ja**	ya
	2) as above, but slightly pronounced	^{y}	**tretji**	treht^{y}i
l	1) as **w** in **w**ord	w	**bel**	behw
	2) as in English	l	**leto**	lehto
r	1) rolled (like a Scottish **r**)	r	**roka**	roka
š	like **sh** in **sh**ut	sh	**šola**	**shoh**la
v	1) like **w** in **w**ord	w	**avto**	**aaw**to
	2) when a preposition, as **oo** in m**oo**n	oo	**v vas**	oo **vaas**
	3) elsewhere as in English	v	**voda**	**vo**da
ž	1) like **s** in plea**s**ure	zh	**ženska**	**zhehn**ska
	2) at the end of a word as **sh** in **sh**ut	sh	**mož**	mohsh

Vowels

a	1) short as **u** in c**u**t	a	**brat**	brat
	2) long as **a** in c**a**r	aa	**vas**	vaas
e	1) short as **e** in m**e**t	e	**več**	vech
	2) similar to the **e** in bed but longer	eh	**mleko**	**mleh**ko
	3) as semivowel, as **ur** in f**ur** but without pronouncing the **r**	er	**pes**	pers
i	1) short as **i** in b**i**t	i	**miš**	mish
	2) long as **ee** in s**ee**n	ee	**sin**	seen
o	1) short as **o** in h**o**t	o	**proč**	proch
	2) long as **o** in sh**o**rt, but pronounced without moving tongue or lips	oh	**pot**	poht
u	1) short as **oo** in f**oo**t	u	**kruh**	kruh
	2) long as **oo** in m**oo**n	oo	**usta**	**oo**sta

OSLO
STOCKHOLM
HELSINKI
St Petersburg
TALLINN
ESTONIA
Novgorod
Pskov
RUSSIA
RIGA
LATVIA
MOSCOW
BALTIC SEA
LITHUANIA
Kaunas
VILNIUS
Kaliningrad
Gdansk
MINSK
POLAND
BERLIN
BELARUS
Kursk
WARSAW
Brest
Łódż
Kharkov
KIEV
CZECH REPUBLIC
Kraków
UKRAINE
Lvov
Dnepr
PRAGUE
Brno
SLOVAKIA
Dnepropetrovsk
BRATISLAVA
VIENNA
MOLDOVA
BUDAPEST
KISHINEV
ROMANIA
Odessa
SLOVENIA
HUNGARY
CROATIA
Timișoara
Brașov
Sevastopol
BUCHAREST
SARAJEVO
BELGRADE
Constanța
Danube
Varna
BLACK SEA
ADRIATIC SEA
SOFIA
BULGARIA
Dubrovnik
Plovdiv
Istanbul
ALBANIA
SKOPJE
TIRANË
ANKARA